The American Exploration and Travel Series

My Life in the Mountains
and on the Plains
The Newly Discovered
Autobiography

My Life in the Mountains and on the Plains

THE NEWLY DISCOVERED

Autobiography

BY DAVID MERIWETHER

•

EDITED AND WITH AN INTRODUCTION BY

Robert A. Griffen

UNIVERSITY OF OKLAHOMA PRESS

NORMAN

LIBRARY OF CONGRESS CATALOG CARD NUMBER: 65–11240

 Composed and printed at Norman, Oklahoma, U.S.A., by the University of Oklahoma Press. First edition, December, 1965; second printing, March, 1966.

To Belle Williams Morgan

who faithfully recorded the autobiography of her grandfather, and to John H. Graves, who for so many years preserved much of the Meriwether material.

Foreword

by John H. Graves

THE FOLLOWING SKETCH of the life of my grandfather, David Meriwether, was written in 1886 at his dictations by my cousin Miss Belle Williams (now Mrs. J. J. Morgan). My grandfather was then eighty-six years of age and his granddaughter, my cousin, Miss Williams, a girl of about fifteen years.

Knowing that this sketch of my grandfather's life had been written, I prevailed on my cousin, Mrs. Morgan, to lend me the manuscript, which I have caused to be typed off and some copies made for the benefit of my grandfather's descendants. I take advantage of this opportunity to say briefly that David Meriwether was truly a remarkable man, a most entertaining conversationalist, and from the vast stories of his experiences was wont to relate innumerable incidents of a most interesting nature. When an old man, he had the rare gift of being able to talk indefinitely about his past activities without the slightest trace of egotism. He was a man of rare abilities, a true American patriot, and would have achieved much higher distinction in political life but for the fact that during his most active years the Democratic party of which he was a faithful adherent was, in Kentucky, owing to the great influence of Henry Clay, a minority party.

It is to be regretted that my grandfather and his granddaughter, Miss Williams, did not complete this sketch. As will be seen, it ends abruptly in 1856 when he was governor of New Mexico. He could have written entertainingly of many other events in his life which are not here related and could have told from firsthand knowledge of the stirring events of the Civil War and the years immediately preceding that conflict.

HOW THIS SKETCH OF DAVID MERIWETHER CAME TO BE WRITTEN

My cousin Mrs. Morgan (nee Williams) gives me in the following lines an account of how these pages came to be written:

> After Aunt Mattie's death, grandpa and uncle Raymond were left all alone on the old place with no one to look after them. This so distressed and worried mamma that we finally broke up our home in Louisville and went down to the farm to care for the two old gentlemen. The first winter there, when I was fifteen years old, I got grandpa, after much persuasion, to tell me these things which I have written down just as he dictated. I am sure everyone in the family will recall his habit of walking round and round in his rooms, and most of his dictation was given as he did this. Round and round he would go, talking all the while, and I writing as fast as I possibly could. Some days he would keep this up until both of us would be worn out, and then for a time afterwards he would refuse to dictate. Then when the weather would be bad and he could not get outside, we would begin again. I can see him now, as he tramped back and forth, pausing sometimes to look out on the river he so loved, and I with one of the little old-fashioned tables pulled up close to the big fireplace, writing until my arms fairly ached.
>
> In the early spring grandfather took a heavy cold and was not able to dictate for many days. When he got well the outdoors were so inviting that he was not willing to get at it, and I never did get him interested again, and so this manuscript is very incomplete. I have wished often that I had urged him more than I did to complete this sketch, but then, as you all know, when grandfather said he would, he would; and when he wouldn't that was the end of it.
>
> I am sure all the relatives who read these unusual and sometimes thrilling experiences will realize now that grandpa was no

ordinary man. And too we have missed some rare reminiscences in my not having finished the account of his life.

John H. Graves

June, 1920
San Jose, California

Acknowledgments

DURING THE COURSE OF EDITING THIS MANUSCRIPT, many persons and institutions have been of material aid. First I would like to thank Mrs. Betsy Graves O'Neill and her husband, Dr. A. E. O'Neill, for the typescript of her great grandfather's autobiography, the loan of numerous Meriwether papers, and interviews. I would like especially to express my appreciation to a number of people in the area where David Meriwether served as territorial governor: to Hestor Jones, recording secretary of the Historical Society of New Mexico, with whom I have been acquainted since my first visit to Santa Fe in 1932; to Ruth E. Rambo, staff librarian, Museum of New Mexico, Santa Fe; to Morris K. Maxwell, Special Collections, Zimmerman Library, University of New Mexico, Albuquerque. I appreciate also the help given by the late Miguel Antonio Otero, territorial governor of New Mexico, 1897–1906; the late Mr. Tom Gable, first warden of the New Mexico Penitentiary, collector of customs, El Paso, Texas, and prominent in early New Mexico politics; Mr. William A. Keleher, Albuquerque, for his kind interest and suggestions; Mr. George Fitzpatrick, editor, *New Mexico Magazine*, Santa Fe, for the loan of early photographs. Futher assistance was gratefully received from a former New Mexico resident and friend, George P. Hammond, director of Bancroft Library.

I wish to express my gratitude to David Herron, director of the University of Nevada Library, Reno, and his staff, particularly Miss Helen Poulton, Mrs. Ruth Donavan, and Mr.

LaMar Smith, for their assistance, patience, and kindness in making information available to me and for providing a pleasant working environment; and to Richard H. Dillon, director, Sutro Library, San Francisco, goes my thanks for supplying additional information for the "Meriwether Story"; and to the Louisville Public Library, Louisville, Kentucky, also goes my thanks.

Those especially remembered for their contributions to the preparation of this manuscript for publication, either directly or indirectly, are Mr. J. J. Hill, director of the University of Nevada Library, retired; Professor Paul Eldredge, Department of English, University of Nevada; Professor Andrew F. Rolle, Department of History, Occidental College; Dr. Fred M. Anderson; my daughter, Professor Gloria Griffen Cline, Department of History, Sacramento State College; and most of all my wife, Grace Gillespie Griffen.

Robert A. Griffen

Introduction

DAVID MERIWETHER, born in Virginia, reared in frontier Kentucky, Indian trader in the unexplored American West, plainsman, and territorial governor of New Mexico from 1853 to 1857, enjoyed a career matched by few of his time in the first sixty years of the nineteenth century.

Meriwether's accomplishments as governor are a matter of fairly extensive record and have frequently been cited by historians. The Southwestern region he came to administer was then a vaster one than its present name implies, embracing as it did the present Arizona and southern Colorado as well as New Mexico. It had been organized as a territory only two years before he became governor. Extending out from the Río Grande was a series of settled communities of Pueblo Indians, with their age-old institutions and farming practices, and Spanish-speaking people newly received into United States citizenship. Surrounding them was a wild land of deserts and plains and mountains inhabited by wilder Indians. Superimposed over all were the recently arrived Anglo-American frontiersmen. The one link with the rest of the United States was the Santa Fe Trail from Independence, Missouri, with its infrequent traders' caravans and its monthly mail service. All of this may be read in the histories; how Meriwether coped with the problems of administration is his own story, however, and the story had to wait for his telling.

But the David Meriwether who went up the Missouri in 1819 under contract to Colonel John O'Fallon, who saw Santa Fe as a prisoner of the Spaniards in 1820, lived with his faithful Negro boy and three Indian companions on the Great Plains in a makeshift shelter through the bitter winter of 1820–21, and ultimately returned to New Mexico as chief of state—this man is little known to historians. The reason is simple: practically no data have been available concerning these years. Now, however, we are able to read his own account, never before published—a rare privilege, for the fur traders and the plainsmen of the Old West rarely kept records of themselves, much less prepared full-fledged autobiographies.

At the age of eighty-five, David Meriwether began dictating the story of his life to his granddaughter, Miss Belle Williams, at his old home eight miles below Louisville, Kentucky, in the year 1886. Miss Williams took it down in longhand. He was a meticulous man, with a deep interest in people and events and a penchant for preserving letters, papers, and news clippings. As the dictation progressed, he drew on this material as an aid to his naturally retentive memory. As a result there is a pleasing continuity and an astounding accuracy throughout the narrative.

A copy of the manuscript descended in the family to Mrs. Betsy Graves O'Neill, of Redwood City, California, a great-granddaughter. In 1930, Mrs. O'Neill permitted me to make my own complete typescript of this work. This and the large number of family papers in my possession, together with the data gathered in personal interviews and through other research have made this book possible.

I had one published account. Young W. W. H. Davis, who came out from Massachusetts to serve as United States attorney for New Mexico, became the governor's volunteer secretary, accompanying him to Indian councils far beyond the settlements. He was a fascinated listener to the stories of the older man, and when he returned to the East he wrote a book about his observations in New Mexico, including some of Meriwether's early experiences. I found this helpful in some instances as a parallel source. All this had to be supplemented by research in the phases of American history that formed the background of Meriwether's career. But mainly this book is the story told by a wise and reflective old man sitting in a white-columned house, looking out on the wide Ohio sweeping by toward the unexplored West of his early manhood, and recalling the events of his long life.

He remembered his meeting with Daniel Boone, Boone's life, his own life, the events of his childhood in Kentucky, and the long sweep of events in the Far West. He told how a survivor of the Pigeon Roost Massacre, perpetrated by followers of Tecumseh, roused the family at dead of night with the tragic story; and how he, a boy of ten or eleven, and a still younger brother were sent on horses to alarm the countryside. Later as a youth of fourteen he rode one hundred miles in forty-eight hours carrying dispatches that facilitated the movement of Kentucky troops to support Andrew Jackson at New Orleans. He recalled his association with William Clark of the Lewis and Clark Expedition, and with Clark's nephews, the O'Fallon brothers, one a fur trader, the other an Indian agent beyond the frontier. He gave his estimate, based on personal knowledge, of Toussaint Charbonneau, known in our day mainly as the husband of Sacajawea. He presented Kit Carson in a new and critical light, as he recalled that unlettered hero's ineptitude with government records and ledger-book accounting. He spoke of his contacts with Henry Clay, with Jefferson Davis, with Chief Justice Roger B. Taney of Dred Scott fame. To him all of these people were flesh and blood contemporaries, not characters in written history.

He came from hardy stock, long prominent in Virginia annals. The founder of the family was Nicholas Meriwether, who came from Wales in 1631 and acquired large landholdings in Westmorland County. Another Nicholas, David's uncle, was with young George Washington's Virginians in the Braddock

Expedition of the French and Indian War and was one of the four Americans who bore the wounded British general from the battlefield. In 1780 Nicholas and his son George, David's cousin, were authorized by the Virginia legislature to lay out a town at the Falls of the Ohio, where George Rogers Clark had already started the settlement that was the beginning of Louisville. Meriwether Avenue in the present city perpetuates the name.

William Meriwether, David's father, saw frontier service in the Revolution. At the age of eighteen he joined Captain John Rogers' company from Spotsylvania and Culpepper counties, the Virginia Light Dragoons, and became orderly sergeant. In 1781 he was listed as ensign, later succeeding his elder brother James as lieutenant. He was attached to the command of George Rogers Clark and participated in the capture of Kaskaskia and Cahokia and the surrender of the British garrison at Vincennes. One of his brothers who settled in Georgia was associated with Andrew Jackson in making treaties with the Southern Indians, and young David once accompanied his father on a visit to this uncle, making the long horseback ride through the Indian country on the way.

William Meriwether was carrying out a long family tradition of pioneering when he brought his family to Kentucky in 1805, bought land on the Ohio, and built a log cabin for his family there. There with the thriving little town of Louisville as the market, the river as the avenue of commerce, a few scattered neighbors in other cabins, and deer, wild turkeys, wolves, and bears in the surrounding timber, the boy David passed his formative years. From here on the story is his.

Robert A. Griffen

May 20, 1965
Reno, Nevada

Contents

Illustrations

My Life in the Mountains

and on the Plains

The Newly Discovered

Autobiography

I
The Kentucky Frontier

I WAS BORN IN LOUISA COUNTY, VIRGINIA, October 30, 1800, and was the third son of Captain William Meriwether,[1] a Revolutionary officer.

In 1805 my father removed to Kentucky with his family, where he purchased a farm on the banks of the Ohio River, about eight miles below Louisville, in Jefferson County. It [is] a part of the same farm I now reside on, and which has been my headquarters off and on for eighty-one years.

I was but a little over four years of age at the time of our removal to Kentucky, but I have a distinct recollection of the trip across the Allegheny Mountains[2] to the Monongahela River; at a place then called Redstone, we descended the Ohio River in two flatboats to Louisville, Kentucky.

My father carried our family to the residence of the widow of his brother James, about six miles above Louisville, near the Bardstown Road,[3] where the family remained until Father could purchase a farm and build log cabins for the reception of the family. In October, 1805, Father settled the family in a log

[1] For history of the Meriwether family see Malcolm H. Harris, *History of Louisa County, Virginia,* 62, 160, 387; Louisa H. A. Minor, *The Meriwethers and Their Connections: A Family Record,* 108–10, 118–19, 151–63; William Meriwether, "Petition to Circuit Court of the United States, Seventh Circuit, Kentucky District," 16 pp., Meriwether Papers; Richard H. Collins, *History of Kentucky,* II, 371; J. Stoddard Johnston, ed., *Memorial History of Louisville,* I, 44.

[2] The location of Louisa County in central Virginia makes clear why the Meriwethers took the course described, rather than the Wilderness Road, followed by many pioneers into the rich cane fields of Kentucky.

[3] Present Highway 31–E and 150.

house on a part of the farm where I have resided since, except for the years spent on the plains and in New Mexico. At that time this part of Jefferson County was very sparsely settled, there being but one house between our place and the city of Louisville and but one between us and the mouth of Salt River, a distance of twelve miles. The country then abounded in wild game, such as deer, turkeys, and occasionally a bear. Wolves were very abundant and frequently came up into the yard at night, making it necessary to house all the sheep, calves, and hogs to prevent their destruction by the wolves. At this time Louisville was a very small town, there being not more than one thousand inhabitants in it and but three small brick houses. The remainder [were] constructed of logs and frame houses. There were then but two or three houses on Jefferson Street and only three or four on Market, the remainder being on Main and Water streets. Where Green and Southern streets now are was covered with a forest of trees.

When I was but a few years older, it was made my business to protect the growing crops from the depredations of wild animals. In the early spring of the year I was awakened before daybreak in the morning to take the dogs and chase the deer out of the wheat patches; when the grain of the wheat had formed, I had to remain in the field all day to keep the wild turkeys from eating it. Then when the corn began to yield roasting ears, I had to go around the field repeatedly every day to keep the squirrels out; at night before going to bed, I had to take the dogs and go around the field to scare the raccoons out to keep them from damaging the corn. A few years later I was sent to school in a log cabin, near where the Mill Creek Church now stands, hence I had to walk to and from school, a distance of four miles each morning and evening. Therefore, between my duties on the farm and the long walk to school I didn't succeed very well in learning my books.

Up to about 1809 or 1810, the Indians were frequently seen on the opposite side of the Ohio River; indeed, one Indian and his squaw resided immediately opposite to where I now reside, on the farm now owned by Mr. Gunn. On one occasion the old Indian was taken sick, and Father went over every day and administered to him. But finally one morning his squaw came down to the river and hallooed over, saying that Almon was dead and she wanted somebody to come and help her plant him. Then, Father and Mr. Obidiah Newman together with us boys buried him, whereupon the old squaw packed all her effects on a little pony and went back to her tribe, which I think resided on the Blue River. The Indians in this vicinity at that time were all friendly to the whites but soon after became very hostile.

I think it was about 1809 that a family by the name of Collins removed from Kentucky to Indiana at a place called the "Pigeon Roost." The elder Collins together with his two sons-in-law formed this settlement. One morning about three o'clock the dogs made a tremendous noise barking, which together with a knocking at the door awoke me. I opened the door and found it to be old man Collins, who was an early friend of my father's. On the family's being aroused, Collins informed us that his settlement had been broken up by the Indians and most of his family killed.

This occurred shortly before the Battle of Tippecanoe. He informed my father that his sons and sons-in-law had volunteered and gone to Vincennes to assist General Harrison in the subjugation of the Indians of that vicinity.[4] . . . The Indians frequently, previous to that time, [had] visited his house in a friendly manner, and on the evening of the massacre, while he and

[4] The Battle of Tippecanoe was fought November 7, 1811. The great Shawnee, Tecumseh, had gone south to further his plan of building an Indian Confederacy when William Henry Harrison, territorial governor of Indiana, attacked his followers and destroyed his stronghold on the Wabash. Through the fame thus gained as a military hero, Harrison attained the presidency.

his daughter and daughters-in-law, together with a traveler who had called, were all sitting eating watermelon at the door of the elder Collins' house, he discovered a party of eight or ten Indians coming toward them. Apprehending no danger, he was not at all disturbed at seeing them. At this time the child of one of his daughters which had been left asleep in one of the cabins, which was but a few steps from the residence of the elder Collins, began to cry: its mother started to see what was the matter with it, when one of the Indians shot her down. Then Collins and the traveler who was with him ran into the house, together with three of the children, and barred the doors and prepared to defend themselves. Collins' daughters-in-law ran to their own houses, which were but a short distance away [and] barred their doors to protect themselves. The Indians soon broke into all the houses, save the one in which the elder Collins, the traveler, and the children had taken refuge, and slew all of the inmates. They then commenced an attack on the house of Collins, but he together with the traveler, being well armed, defended themselves manfully.

Collins stated that he was confident that he had killed three of the Indians when the Indians withdrew; and on the approach of night, Collins said that he took one of the small children on his back, and the traveler the other, the third child being able to run himself, and crept into the cornfield which was close by the house, thence into the woods, and after traveling all night, reached another white settlement, where the traveler and the children remained, while Collins proceeded to our place by procuring a canoe on the Indiana shore and crossing the river. Father then directed myself and my brother James to mount horses and alarm the country and request every man able to bear arms to meet in Louisville as soon as possible.

My older brother James was directed to go down the Ohio River and then cross to the Salt River road, thence up the road to about where Mill Creek Church now stands, then to return home and procure some provisions which Father would have ready for him, place them in a cart, and then carry them to Louisville. I was directed to proceed to the Salt River road at Shivelys Mills,[5] thence to proceed up the road, arousing the citizens as I went and requesting them all to meet at Louisville early that morning, while Father and Collins were to proceed to Louisville, arousing the people as they went; then to organize a party to go against the Indians by the way of Collins' settlement. By the middle of the day a large number had collected in Louisville. A party of about fifty men was organized and proceeded to Steppingsport, where they crossed the river.

The provisions that were brought by James, together with the food that had been cooked by the citizens of Louisville, were placed in bags on the pack horses, and I, though not over ten years old, was taken along to lead some of the pack horses. The party continued to travel until late at night. When the moon went down and we could no longer follow the trail, we camped.

I have very little recollection of what occurred in camp that night, for I had traveled from daybreak in the morning until sometime near midnight without eating a mouthful of food since leaving home and was completely exhausted. I recollect, however that sentinels were placed around camp, and that Father took some meat and bread out of one of the sacks, and we both ate a hearty meal, after which Father spread a saddle blanket beside a log, and then told me to lie down, then throwing a blanket over me told me to go to sleep, and, if I heard guns fired during the night not to get up but to lie still. But the latter charge was not necessary, for I do not believe a thunderstorm would have awakened me that night. Early the next morning we pro-

[5] The name Shively has been perpetuated by the naming of a district on Mill Creek, at the south city limits of Louisville. The present Dixie Highway, number 31–W, follows its east border.

ceeded, guided by Collins, and on arriving at the settlement, we found all the inmates, except those before mentioned, had been killed. All of their bedding and other light articles [were] taken away, being packed on two ponies which Collins had.

A party was then sent out to trace the Indians' trail, whilst the remainder busied themselves in burying the dead women and children. In the evening they returned and said that the Indians had scattered so they couldn't follow their trail [more than] a few miles beyond a large creek they had crossed. All hands then returned without seeing an Indian. This was known for many years as the massacre of Pigeon Roost settlement. And this was my first Indian expedition, but not the last by any means. Collins remained in Kentucky for some time after the destruction of his family and was frequently at our house.

Some time after the occurance of the foregoing incident, I do not recollect how long (for I am speaking of things that occurred over seventy-five years ago and when but a small boy), one evening just after dinner I was playing with a favorite dog in the front yard, when he began to bark vociferously, and, on looking down the river in the direction in which he barked I saw a party of eight or ten Indians walking toward the house. I immediately ran in and told my mother the Indians were coming; she commenced fastening the doors, and I ran out again to see what had become of them. This happened when my father was away from home, and I was the oldest white person on the place. On going out I discovered that the Indians had stopped some fifty or a hundred yards from the house, and a white man advanced alone towards me. On coming up, he shook hands with me and called me by name. He said, "David, don't you know me?" When I replied in the negative, he then said, "It is my different dress that prevents your knowing me." It was Mr. O'Fallon,[6] who had been

[6] "John O'Fallon was born near Louisville, Kentucky, November 17th, 1791. His mother was Frances Clark, youngest sister of George Rogers and William Clark.

at my father's house several times before this. He then asked if my father was at home, and I told him no. He asked where my mother was. I told him she was in the house half scared to death.

He then told me to ask her to come to the door, and, on doing so, he assured her the Indians were friendly and there was no danger. He was taking them to Washington City to visit the President. And on finding who he was, she became pacified. On seeing [this], we beckoned to the Indians, and they came into the yard and seated themselves on the grass. He informed my mother that they had descended the Mississippi in a keel-boat to the mouth of the Ohio and were going up the Ohio to Pittsburgh; and that when they had passed the mouth of the Salt River that morning he and the Indians had become tired of the confinement and slow progress of the boat and had gotten far ahead of the boat, and were very hungry and would like to have something to eat. My mother told him she had some cold victuals in the cupboard, but [not] enough to feed so many. He told her he saw some tame turkeys in the barn lot and asked for one of them, [and] she said he could have one if he could catch it. Mr. O'Fallon then called his interpreter to him and told him the Indians could have a turkey if they could catch it. The Indians were all unarmed, except a little boy about my own age, who had his bow and arrows with him. On the interpreter's explaining matters to the Indians, they directed the boy to take

His father was an educated Irishman, a surgeon in the Continental Army under George Washington." After the death of his father he was cared for by his uncles, William Clark and Major Croghan, later attending school at Danville. He entered the service of his Uncle William Clark, then superintendent of Indian Affairs. During the War of 1812 he was in turn ensign, 2d lieutenant, 1st lieutenant, and captain. He served as private secretary to General Harrison, as acting adjutant general at Fort Meigs, and aide-de-camp. He was a leading citizen of St. Louis, engaged in many business ventures, and was widely known for his integrity. Died in St. Louis on December 17, 1865.—See J. Thomas Scharf, *History of St. Louis, City and County*, I, 344.

his bow and arrow and kill one. Starting after the turkeys, he beckoned me to come with him, and he soon shot down one of the finest of the flock, which was cooked for the Indians; my mother having directed the Negro woman who cooked for the family to bake some bread, before long they were feasting on turkey and bread. My mother had a table set in the dining room for Mr. O'Fallon, and he dined there. I was much astonished to see with what skill the little Indian boy shot the turkey with his bow and arrow. After eating, we amused ourselves with shooting at birds in the barn lot, and, to my astonishment he rarely ever missed a shot.

In the evening my father returned home, and Collins, [who was] with him, immediately asked my father to loan him his gun for he intended to kill one or more of those Indians. My father and Mr. O'Fallon explained to him that they were friendly Indians and were not of the same tribe as those that had massacred his family, [to which] Collins replied that they had red skins, and he had sworn in his wrath to kill every one of that color that he could. Finally they got him upstairs and locked him up to prevent him from attempting to kill some of the Indians. Shortly after this, the keelboat having arrived, Mr. O'Fallon and the Indians proceeded on their journey. Mr. O'Fallon was very anxious for me to go with him to Washington City and told my father he would take me there and bring me back again without it costing him a cent. But my mother could not be induced to assent to this proposition, and hence I did not go.

It may be interesting to you to know how the people subsisted in this neighborhood, when we first settled here in 1805. We procured meat by hunting; the produce of our chase being salted away and smoked in the fall of the year, as we do our pork now. I recollect on one Christmas day, my mother said to father, "I have forty-five turkeys," and I forgot how many hams and saddles of venison, raccoons, and possums, which had been salted and were hanging in the meat house to be smoked for the next summer's use. People did not hunt for pleasure then as now, but to obtain meat to eat. In the spring, we subsisted on fish, which were much more abundant then in the rivers than now. Every Friday morning on going to school, we took our crawfish net with us and left it at some of the ponds we passed and used it on our return in the evening in catching crawfish, which were very abundant then, to be used as fish bait the next day. Early next morning we boys arose and went to the river to fish, which was our occupation during the entire day. We often caught enough fish during Saturday to supply the family nearly the whole of the next week. Many of these fish were salted and smoked as bacon is now, for provisions during the summer and fall. My father never allowed us boys to fish or hunt on the Sabbath day, but, as soon as the breakfast table was cleared away, every member of the family, both black and white, were assembled for prayers. Indeed, people were much more prompt in their attendance in religious services then than they are now. Although the country was sparsely settled, it was not unusual to see from one hundred to one hundred and fifty persons at the old stone meeting house, which then stood where the present Mill Creek Church now stands, whereas it is not unusual to see less than fifty now.

The Methodist preachers were then called circuit riders, and they preached nearly every day during the week. I recollect an amusing anecdote told by one of these circuit riders (I think his name was Light)[7] which occurred to himself on the first circuit to which he was appointed. He said his predecessor had given him a list of the appointments he would have to fill and the places where he could rest all night after preaching. One day after preaching, he went home with one of his congregation to

[7] The Reverend George C. Light was a prominent Methodist circuit rider and minister in Kentucky for many years. See Collins, *History of Kentucky*, I, 455.

spend the night. When he arose the next morning, he applied to a little son of his host for a basin and water to wash his face and hands. The boy replied, "We hain't got none." "Then," said the preacher, "how do you manage to wash your face and hands." The boy replied, "We go down to the spring and wash in the branch." "Well," said the preacher, "get me a towel and show me the way to the spring branch." The boy replied, "We hain't got no towel." "Then," said the preacher, "how do you wipe your face and hands?" The boy's reply was, "We just let it dry off." I then proceeded to the spring branch, and after washing, wiped my face on my handkerchief. I then asked for a comb to comb my hair, and the boy ran to the house and soon returned with an old horn comb which had lost about half its teeth. With this I managed to comb my hair, and, taking out my toothbrush, began to brush my teeth. At this point the old lady came to the door and called the boy and wanted to know if the circuit rider wasn't ready to come to breakfast, he answered her by saying. "He ain't quite ready yet, mammy. He has washed his face and hands and combed his haid, and is now sharpening his teeth, and you better kill another chicken, or they won't be any left for us."

As for clothing, it was all manufactured at home. Most farmers had a few sheep, the wool of which was spun and woven by the family, and which constituted our clothing for the winter. Each farmer raised enough cotton and flax out of which to make summer clothing. Indeed, I don't think I had a garment that was not made up and manufactured at home until I was over fifteen years of age. All the children, both male and female, went barefooted from early spring until late in the fall, when shoes and stockings were given them, all of home manufacture. You could not go to a store and buy ready-made shoes as now, but there were shoemakers in the country who went to each farmer's house and made the family shoes for the winter.

We often had great difficulty in getting our grain ground

into meal and flour, as mills were scarce. There was one mill on Mill Creek, near where the almshouse now stands, owned by Christian Shively, but this could only run in rainy seasons. In cold weather in the winter the water was frozen, and during drouths in the summer, it had no water to propel it. So my father procured a pair of small millstones and had erected a hand mill, which two men by hard work could grind about a bushel of grain an hour. On rainy days when the hands could not work out, they were employed at the hand mill. They often had to grind it at night after the labors of the day were over. This mill was free to all the neighbors who chose to use it, when not occupied by us, hence Mr. Obidiah Newman, David French, George Johnson, and others frequently used it.

In 1811 there occurred a series of shocks from earthquakes, which astonished and frightened the people of this vicinity very much. The shocks occurred at irregular intervals for several months, sometimes two or three in a week, and then probably none for a week or two. Some of the shocks were hard enough to cause the chairs to rock on the floor, the crockery to rattle in the cupboard, and the doors which were open to swing to and fro. Others were quite slight. My father's log house was built upon wooden blocks, two or three feet high, and, as the first shock occurred at night and was sufficiently severe to awaken the whole family, my father supposed that some of the blocks on which the house was built might have given way. He therefore lit a candle and went to examine, but, finding everything secure, returned to the room in which we were all assembled and told us it must have been an earthquake shock. The damage sustained in this vicinity was very slight, only a few brick walls in the city of Louisville being cracked and the tops of a few chimneys thrown off. But in the southwestern portion of Kentucky and the border state of Tennessee and about New Madrid, Missouri, the shocks were much more severe, [and] large portions of the earth sunk and filled with water, forming large ponds or lakes. The earth was cracked in many places.

I think it was about 1812 that the first steamboat[8] that ever appeared on the Ohio descended from Pittsburgh, where she was built, to Louisville. As there was no canal around the falls at that time, and the water was too low for her to pass over the falls, she was detained several weeks waiting for a rise of water, and, to make her expenses, made frequent trips up to Six Mile Island and back again, charging a small sum for each passenger. This boat was built by the celebrated Robert Fulton, and, as his brother, Abraham Fulton, was teaching school in the neighborhood and lived at my father's house, he gave us boys a ride from Louisville up to Six Mile Island and back on the steamboat. Shortly after this, the river having raised, she passed over the falls [and] down the Ohio, frightening the ignorant people on its banks very much.

My mother had a brother, Major William Winslow, who resided at the mouth of the Kentucky River. The town was then called [Port] William and was the county seat of Gallatin County, and my uncle was clerk of the Gallatin Circuit Court. He paid my father and mother a visit, I think about 1813. We had no school in our neighborhood at that time, and he prevailed on my parents to let me go and live with him, go to school in the old academy in that town, and assist him in his office. I remained there about a year, but, the close confinement not agreeing with me, I returned home again.

This was during the War of 1812, and, about the first of De-

[8] This was no doubt the *New Orleans*, the first steamboat to ply the western waters. She was built at Pittsburgh by Nicolas Roosevelt under Fulton Livingstone patents during 1810–11 and started down the Ohio on October 20, 1811. J. Roosevelt was the captain, with George Baker as engineer, Andrew Jack as pilot, and six hands to serve as firemen and roustabouts. After braving the Falls of the Ohio and the New Madrid earthquake, the boat reached New Orleans on January 12, 1812. Johnston, *History of Louisville*, I, 71–72.

cember, 1814, two regiments of soldiers rendezvoused at Louisville to descend the Ohio and Mississippi rivers to assist General Jackson in the defense of New Orleans. They were embarked in a large number of flatboats, from fifty to one hundred in number, and landed on the Kentucky shore, from my father's house up to Major John Hughes's,[9] a distance of two miles, where they were detained several days awaiting a supply of provisions.

[David Meriwether, then a lad of fourteen, was sent to Frankfort with a letter to the legislature urging them to send supplies.] I think the stage from Louisville made a trip every other day, hence I was given an order from the manager of the company in Louisville to the officers of the different stage stations on the road to furnish me a change of horses whenever necessary. I was directed to go to Frankfort without stopping to eat or sleep. I left Louisville about the middle of the day, riding my own horse to Middletown, where I procured a fresh horse, which carried me to Shelbyville, where I arrived in the night. There I secured a fresh horse which carried me to Frankfort, where I arrived shortly after breakfast. I recollect that I crossed the Kentucky River on a floating bridge composed of boats attached to each other, which extended across the stream.

On getting up into town, I inquired of a gentleman where the Jefferson County delegation boarded, and was informed that they, or at least part of them stopped at the Mansion House, and he kindly piloted me there. Whilst I sat on my horse in

[9] Major John Neville Hughes was of Welsh descent, born in Powhatan County, Virginia, August 11, 1763. At the age of fifteen he left Hampden Sydney College and enlisted in the Revolutionary Army and served to the close of the war. He became a member of the Meriwether clan when at the age of twenty he married Anne Meriwether, and they became the parents of twenty-six children. He came west about 1786 and later served in the War of 1812. He died at his farm on the Ohio River, six miles below Louisville, December 11, 1842. See Francis B. Heitman, *Historical Register of Officers of the Continental Army*, [hereafter referred to as *Historical Register*], I, 233; and Minor, *The Meriwethers and Their Connections*, 148–49.

front of the house, Colonel Samuel Churchill,[10] who I think was a member of the legislature from Jefferson County, appeared. Having seen him before, I made my business known to him by delivering to him the letter brought by me. He immediately told me to get down, ordered me a breakfast and had my horse taken care of. Then he took me to his room, where he read the letters and told me, after getting breakfast, to go to sleep in his bed and he would attend to my business for me.

Late in the evening I was awakened by Colonel Churchill, who told me to get up, mount my horse, and return to Louisville as soon as possible. I went to the door [and] found my horse all ready for me. I mounted him and rode to Shelbyville, where I arrived late at night. There I again mounted the horse left there the night before. I rode him to Middletown, arriving there after breakfast. I stopped long enough at the hotel to eat a little breakfast, when I mounted my own horse and proceeded to Louisville. It was a real relief to me to get on my own horse as he was a fine saddle horse, and the stage horses which I had ridden before were rough trotters. I was very tired and sore. I arrived in Louisville probably at ten or eleven o'clock, having made the trip from Louisville to Frankfort and back again, a distance of more than one hundred miles, in about forty-eight hours and had eaten but three meals in that time.

I found my father and the gentleman who had sent me at the hotel then kept by John Gwethney[11] at the corner of Fifth and Main streets, to whom I delivered the large package of papers,

[10] Colonel Samuel Churchill was a descendant of a distinguished colonial family who were residents of Virginia for more than a century prior to their emigrating to Kentucky by the famous "Wilderness Road" in 1787. He was a prominent planter and served in the Kentucky legislature from 1814 to 1819 and again in 1830. Collins, *History of Kentucky,* II, 357.

[11] John Gwethney (Collins spells the name Gwathney) was a resident of Louisville prior to 1800. He drew the plans for the first Jefferson County courthouse, built in 1811 and at that time considered the most handsome structure of its kind in the West.

and they seemed somewhat surprised at my early return. I was taken into a room where I went to bed and slept soundly for several hours. When I arose from my sleep, I felt so sore I could scarcely get my clothes on; after eating dinner I proceeded home, where I found the yard filled with soldiers.

I learned afterwards that the bank furnished the money, the provisions having been purchased beforehand. These were placed on two boats which were retained to receive them. The next morning the troops left for New Orleans. After the news of the Battle of New Orleans reached us, some months after, I was vain enough to claim some degree of credit for having contributed to the arrival of the Kentucky troops in time to take part in this celebrated battle.

It may not be known to many of the present generation that this great victory of the American troops was achieved after peace was made between Great Britain and the United States. The treaty of peace was signed, I think, on the twenty-fourth of December, 1814, and the battle fought on the eighth of January, 1815, but neither party had any information that peace was made.

[Meriwether makes casual mention of a trip he made to New Orleans at the age of seventeen.] On my starting to New Orleans in the fall of 1817, my father gave me a letter of introduction to Beverly Chew, a nephew of my mother, who was then employed in the custom house there. I do not recollect in what capacity, but he either was then, or afterwards became, collector of customs there. This cousin of mine received me very courteously and introduced me to a number of Kentuckians who resided in New Orleans. Among the rest was a Mr. John Clay, a brother of the celebrated Henry Clay, who was a merchant there; Mr. Weathers, and others. On my expressing a wish to view the celebrated battleground, he gave me a note of introduction to the gentleman who owned the field on which the battle was fought. I think his name was Dr. Flood. He very kindly piloted me over the field, pointing out where the different branches of the army were posted and the place where General Pakenham, the British commander-in-chief, fell mortally wounded; also where Colonel Rennie of the British army was killed. The latter approached nearer the Americans than any other British officer. On this battleground I picked up a musket ball, which I now have. The field was then cultivated in sugar cane. The slaves of the owner were cutting the cane, hauling it to the house, and grinding it. He informed me that in ploughing the land, he frequently ploughed up relics of the battle. I did not remain long in New Orleans, as the yellow fever had made its appearance, and I had no desire to make its acquaintance, but returned home to my father's as soon as I had finished my business.

I think it was about 1810 or 1811, I am not certain as to the date, as these occurrences happened over seventy-five years ago, and I am now eighty-six years of age. . . . my father decided to visit an elder brother of his, Colonel David Meriwether,[12] who resided in Georgia, and, as I was named after him, he decided to take me with him. This trip had to be made on horseback, he riding the fine saddle horse and I an Indian pony. We had to pass through several Indian tribes who were partially civilized; I think they were the Cherokees, Choctaws, and Chickasaws. This uncle of mine was a prominent citizen of Georgia, having previous to our visit been several times elected to Congress and in conjunction with General Jackson was appointed a commissioner to make treaties with some of these southern Indians.[13]

[12] David Meriwether was born near Charlottesville, Virginia, April 10, 1755. Here he served as brigadier of the state militia and as speaker of the House of Representatives. He was elected to Congress to fill an unexpired term in 1801 and reelected in 1802 and 1804. Then he retired to his plantation near Athens, where he died November 16, 1822.

[13] These treaties were for the purpose of obtaining land cessions. On April 20, 1817, David Meriwether wrote to his brother William: "I was from the first of August until October in the Cherokee and Chickasaw Nations with General Jack

Since that time, a new county being formed in Georgia, it was named Meriwether County.

One night whilst on this trip we stopped at a half-breed Indian's house. He was an elderly man and appeared to be intelligent, speaking English pretty well. I think his name was Pitchkin. He informed my father that his father was taken prisoner by the Indians and taken to the tribe [of] his captors, after which he was adopted as a member of the tribe. When he grew up he married a squaw. So his father was a white man, his mother an Indian. He further said that when but a little boy, his father returned with his mother and himself to the white settlements from whence he had been taken. There they remained quite a long time, how long he did not remember; his father having died there, his mother returned to the Indian tribe, carrying him and a younger sister with her. This accounted for his speaking English so well.

My father asked this man why they called Kentucky the "Dark and Bloody Ground," and he replied that this was a mistake, that Kentucky abounded in cane and wild turkeys, and, hearing the whites speak of the cane and turkeys, the Indians united the two words and called the country Kentucky, or the land of cane and turkeys.

I happened to be at Memphis about the year 1837. These southern Indians had congregated there and were waiting for steamboats to take them down the Mississippi and up the Arkansas River to their present residence known as the Indian Territory. Whilst at Memphis, I inquired of one of those Indians, who

[Andrew Jackson] and Major Frankling [Jesse Franklin] holding treaties with those tribes[.]The result make no doubt you have long Since heard and the lands purchased I think Such a desirable country that I should be glad to remoove there if It was in my power, but I fear I shall not be able to accomplish my wishes."—Meriwether Papers, O'Neill Collection, courtesy Mrs. Betsy Graves O'Neill [hereafter referred to as Meriwether Papers]. For an account of these negotiations see R. S. Cotterill, *The Southern Indians: The Story of the Civilized Tribes Before Removal*, 198–201.

appeared to be quite intelligent, about the man we had stopped overnight with on our trip to Georgia. In reply, he informed me that he was a relative of that man. I then asked him if he had ever heard of the origin of the name Kentucky. He replied in the affirmative, and that he had often heard his relatives and others give the same explanation.

II

Up the Missouri

IN MARCH, 1819, I was in the city of Louisville and happened to meet Colonel John O'Fallon, the man who had charge of the Indians who stopped at my father's house a number of years before. This gentleman had served during the War of 1812 and acquired the rank of colonel. On meeting him, he informed me he was about to send to my father's house for me, as he was about to embark in the Indian fur trade up the Missouri River[1] and wanted to employ me. On asking me how I would like to embark in this business, I told him I would like it very

[1] O'Fallon had been appointed sutler of the Yellowstone Expedition of 1819–20, and David Meriwether was employed to assist him as a combination trader and sutler to the troops. Colonel Henry Atkinson commanded the venture, with Major Stephen H. Long in charge of the scientific branch. It was designed as a follow-up of the Lewis and Clark Expedition. The object as announced by Secretary of War Calhoun was to proceed to the mouth of the Yellowstone or the Mandan villages in present-day North Dakota to extend protection to the northern frontiers and to promote the expansion of the fur trade. One of its purposes was to nullify the British influence over the Upper Missouri tribes. The enterprise was a popular one, heralded in news items and editorials of the day. But the government, disregarding recommendations, made use of the new water vessel, the steamboat, instead of the proved keelboat. The entire summer was spent in breasting the current of the Missouri, encountering breakdowns and groundings, necessitating the transfer of troops and cargo to keelboats. The expedition accordingly proceeded no farther than Council Bluffs (not the present Council Bluffs, Iowa) in the vicinity of the present Fort Calhoun, Nebraska, about twenty-five miles above the present Omaha, and constructed winter quarters known as Camp Missouri. There the troops suffered a severe epidemic of scurvy during the severe winter of 1819–20. The same bad planning plagued the scientific branch of the enterprise. However the *Western Engineer* with Major Long's party did reach Fort Lisa on September 17 and established "Engineer Cantonment," one-half mile above Fort Lisa and about five miles below Council Bluffs. See Hiram Martin Chittenden, *The American Fur Trade of the Far West*, II, 570; and Edwin James, *Account of an Expedition from Pittsburgh to the Rocky Mountains.*

much. Before I could make any engagement, however, I would go home and consult my parents. I was to let him know the next day. On returning home that evening I mentioned the subject to my father and mother, and it was finally concluded that my father would accompany me to Louisville the next morning and talk the matter over with Colonel O'Fallon. Colonel O'Fallon said he would employ me for not less than two years, and he would pay me $200 for the first year and $300 for the second. He would bear all expenses except my clothing, which I was to furnish myself. This proposition was acceded to by my father. Colonel O'Fallon at once drew up a written contract to that effect, which was signed by him, myself, and my father.

The Colonel then said that I must be supplied with clothing sufficient for two years, the winter clothing to consist of heavy warm woolen cloth, for such would be necessary in that northern climate. He then accompanied us to a dry-goods store and made a selection of these materials for us. He then informed us that he had been to Philadelphia and had purchased a large amount of goods suitable for the Indian trade and had them wagoned across the mountains to Pittsburgh, where a keelboat[2] was purchased and the goods loaded aboard. This boat was to descend the Ohio, then go up the Mississippi to St. Louis, and I was to be aboard as supercargo. He said that he himself had descended the Ohio from Pittsburgh to Louisville and expected the boat to arrive in five or six days, that she would be detained a day or two to take in additional cargo, and he would direct the captain of the boat to land at my father's house and take me aboard.

[2] The historic keelboat used before the advent of steam on the Western rivers derived its name from a keel running from bow to stern. It averaged from sixty to seventy-five feet in length, with a fifteen- to eighteen-foot beam and a hold three or four feet in depth. A deck house was built fore and aft, usually reaching within five or six feet of either end, to accommodate freight and passengers. The common means of propulsion was the cordelle, a long line to shore drawn by twenty or more men strung out along the bank. Poling, oars, and sail were often used also.

Then the difficulty was to get my clothing made before the boat should come. My mother and sister went immediately to work, [also] sending out for several of the neighboring ladies to assist. The task was accomplished in time and my clothing packed ready for departure. The boat did not arrive as soon as expected, so I went to Louisville to ascertain the cause of detention, when Colonel O'Fallon informed me that she had arrived the evening before and would call for me during the next day. When I then hastened home to be ready when the boat arrived, my mother handed me a purse containing ten dollars in cut silver money, which was the only currency in vogue at that time. This was also placed in my trunk. We sat up late that night, expecting the arrival of the boat, but she did not come. By daybreak the next morning she arrived and did not stop but sent a skiff ashore for me. I soon embarked and by diligent application of the oars soon overtook the boat a little below the mouth of Salt River.

On boarding the boat I found an old acquaintance, Captain Strothers Grey of the United States Army, who had been raised in Louisville, and who had been home on furlough and was then on his way to join his regiment stationed at Bellefontaine then a post on the Missouri River, four miles above its mouth. At the time of my embarkation, the Ohio River was very high, being full to the top of its banks, and there were many wild ducks to be seen in the overflowed bottoms. There was another passenger on board with his wife and son, who was near my age. Hence we two boys had fine times shooting ducks by going near the shore in our skiff.

On the first Sunday after my departure, this young boy proposed that we should go duck hunting, but, as my parents had always taught me to observe the Sabbath day, I for a long time declined but at length was prevailed upon to accompany my young friend in the skiff after ducks. He had the gun, and I managed the oars, but, on the first shot he fired, the gun burst and lacerated one of his hands very badly. I then hastened on after the boat as fast as possible, determining never to hunt on Sunday again. Captain Grey, having some knowledge of gun-shot wounds, dressed the poor boys' hand, and thus ended our duck hunting for that day.

The weather was very stormy and the boat heavily laden, hence some times we had difficulty in keeping her afloat. One stormy evening we reached the mouth of the Cumberland River, where we determined to land and spend the night. The boat was run a short distance up the Cumberland River to the then little town of Smith Island, where we landed. Soon it began to snow, and the wind increased in violence, hence there was great danger of the boat sinking. Immediately all the hands, excepting one and the captain, went up in town, and left the captain, myself, and the other two passengers to bail the water out of the boat as fast as the waves threw it in. We soon tired of this as it was hard work and very cold. The captain determined to go out and try and get the hands aboard again; he found them all drunk and they refused to come aboard, hence the captain, myself, the other two passengers, and one boat hand had to throw out the water by turns during the whole night. The next morning, the wind having subsided, we determined to go on our way, but, the hands still being drunk, we could not get them aboard. But, finding three men in the town who wanted to go to the mouth of the Ohio about sixty miles below, we took them and started, leaving our hands in the little town. When we got to the mouth of the Ohio, we found that where the town of Cairo now stands was entirely submerged, but, as we were compelled to stop here to procure a Mississippi pilot and additional hands, we rounded to and made fast to a tree standing out in the river.

There was but one dwelling house and a small warehouse there at that time, and these were entirely submerged by water, and there were a few people living in a flatboat. But we found a good pilot and a number of men familiar with the navigation of the river. We soon employed the pilot and he procured a crew of hands, and we left that evening to ascend the Father of Waters to St. Louis.

On arriving at a town, I think it was called Ste. Genevieve, our progress became very slow against the strong current of the Mississippi. Captain Grey, being tired of the boat, procured a horse and made the rest of the trip by land. In due time we arrived at St. Louis, where Colonel O'Fallon [had] informed me at Louisville that I would find him at Governor Clark's[3] in St. Louis when I arrived there. Colonel O'Fallon had gone through from Louisville to St. Louis by land. Governor Clark was the uncle of Colonel O'Fallon and was then governor of the territory of Missouri. I had no difficulty in finding his residence, where I reported my arrival to Colonel O'Fallon. He appeared to be very much surprised and pleased at our safe arrival, as Captain Grey had reached St. Louis before us [and] had informed him that he did not believe the boat would ever reach St. Louis.

He directed me to discharge the cargo into a warehouse that stood on the bank, as we would have to procure a larger boat to ascend the Missouri River. In two or three days the cargo was discharged, and, a receipt having been taken from the owner of the warehouse, and I having made out a bill of the wages due the hands, I presented them to the Colonel, for which he gave me a check on the bank for that amount. I drew the money, went down to the boat and paid off the hands. This was done just as the

[3] Governor William Clark was a native of Virginia, moving with his parents to Louisville in 1784. He served in the Indian campaigns with Anthony Wayne, resigning in 1796. In 1803 he again entered the army and in the following year was placed in joint command with Meriwether Lewis, of the famous Louis and Clark Expedition. He served as governor of Missouri Territory in 1813–21. From 1821 until his death in 1838, he was superintendent of Indian Affairs, with headquarters in St. Louis. He was also a principal in various activities, including the Missouri Fur Company.

Colonel came down to the boat and told me to go with him to Governor Clark's to spend the night, as he supposed I was tired of the boat. To this I objected, and I informed him that all my baggage, consisting of my trunk of clothing and bedding was on the boat and I was afraid to leave them. To this he replied, "There [is] no danger; the hands will take care of them till morning, when you can get them up into town." This induced me to reluctantly accompany him. On returning to the boat the next morning, I found the hands had stolen the two skiffs which we had and every item of my baggage and departed down the river.

Thus I found myself in an unfortunate predicament in a strange city with not a dollar in my pocket (all that my mother had given me was gone with my trunk) without a stitch of clothing but what was on my back, or a blanket to sleep on. Hence I returned to Governor Clark's residence very low spirited and anything but comfortable in mood. The Colonel however at once relieved my embarrassment by saying that he was the cause of my loss, and that he would replace me in as good condition as when I arrived, by supplying all my losses. He then informed me that Governor Clark had received some guests into his house and that he would have a bed fixed in a house which the Governor owned and used as a museum,[4] and he would make arrangements for me at the hotel to eat. He accompanied me to the hotel and introduced me to the proprietor, whose name was Potter. He then introduced me to the afterwards celebrated Senator Thomas

[4] This museum is described in the *Journal* of Captain John Bell, ". . . Thursday, April 27th, 1820. . . . In the Afternoon the Dr. [James] and myself accompanied Major Long and called on Governor Clark, the Govr. resides in the main street, in a new and elegant brick house, erected I am told at the expense of twenty two hundred dollars, adjoining it, is an old fashioned Spanish building called the Govr. council room, in which is a large collection of Indian curiosities, and specimens of mineral and fossil substances collected from different parts of the Western Country, the whole tastefully arranged for examination."—Harlin M. Fuller and LeRoy R. Hafen, eds., *The Journal of Captain John R. Bell*, 58.

Hart Benton, who had taken up his residence in St. Louis some time before, and I spent many pleasant hours with him.

Colonel O'Fallon informed me that he had been appointed sutler for the troops which were to proceed up the Missouri River and that Captain Bissell,[5] who was then sutler for the troops at Bellefontaine, was connected with him in the business. He therefore directed me to proceed to Bellefontaine and assist Captain Bissell in his business until the troops got ready to move up the Missouri. Before this time Colonel O'Fallon had procured for me a better outfit than the one I started with, and in the place of my loss of $10.00 he gave me $25.00. I therefore procured a conveyance to Bellefontaine, put all my effects on board, and took a boy with me to bring the conveyance back. Bellefontaine is about twenty miles by land from St. Louis and situated on the first high land on the Missouri above its mouth.

He described to me the situation of Captain Bissell's house, which was outside the fort, and a hundred or two yards distant from it. I therefore drove up to the door but found it closed with no person about the house. Then I found myself in a fix. I directed the boy to drive up to the gate of the fort, where I alighted, and directed him to remain there until I came back again. The gate was open, and I walked in, but, just as I got in a sentinel presented his gun and cried out, "Halt." This order I promptly obeyed. The sentinel then asked me what I wanted. I told him I wanted to see Captain Grey. He then called the sergeant of the guard and told him that a young man was there

[5] Captain Lewis Bissell was one of the prominent figures in the early history of St. Louis. He was born at Hartford, Connecticut, on October 12, 1789, and arrived at St. Louis on May 10, 1809. He served in the army from 1808 to 1816, then resigned and engaged in the sutler's business with Colonel O'Fallon at Bellefontaine. In 1823 he purchased a farm, which was subsequently included within the chartered limits of the city and was known as Bissell Point. See Scharf, *History of St. Louis*, I, 355–56; and Francis B. Heitman, *Historical Register of the United States Army, From its Organization, September 29, 1789, to March 2, 1903* [hereafter referred to as *Historical Register, U.S.A.*], I, 221.

who wanted to see Captain Grey. The sergeant directed him to let me in and was good enough to send a soldier with me to Captain Grey's quarters. I found he was absent. On telling the captain's servant that I was an old friend of the Captain and wanted to see him, the servant soon hunted him up.

He appeared very glad to see me, and, on explaining my situation to him, and telling him that I was to assist Captain Bissell in his business, he informed me that Captain Bissell could not be seen until dinnertime, as the troops were being paid off, preparatory to proceeding up the Missouri River, and, Captain Bissell having credited many of them, he was attending the paymaster's table to collect his accounts. He therefore told me to remain in his room until I could see Captain Bissell. He then when to the gate of the fort and directed that my baggage be brought to his room, where I remained until the bugle sounded for dinner. At this signal, the payment ceased, and Captain Grey sent his servant to request Captain Bissell to come to his room. On his arrival I was introduced to him, and I presented the letter from Colonel O'Fallon, and informed him of the object of my coming. He greeted me very cordially. I was then taken around by the two captains to the officers mess-room and introduced to them. Captain Bissell having no family, he messed with these officers, and I messed with them also. And here I desire to say that both Colonel O'Fallon and Captain Bissell were two of the most courteous gentlemen I have ever met in my long life. I remained in their employ three years and never had any cause of complaint with either, or a single word of dissatisfaction on either side.

The First Rifle Regiment under the command of Colonel [Talbot] Chambers was quartered at Bellefontaine when I arrived there, and it was understood that they were to remain until the 6th Infantry arrived to take their place. Then the rifle regiment was to proceed up the Missouri River to the mouth of the

Yellowstone, where it was to establish a permanent post. This was in consequence of the detention of the 6th Regiment at Pittsburgh, where they were to procure keelboats, then descend the Ohio to its mouth and ascend the Mississippi and Missouri to Bellefontaine. This plan was abandoned, and it was determined that the rifle regiment should take the keelboats occupied by the 6th Infantry and ascend the Missouri to Council Bluffs[6] and there erect a cantonment for winter quarters, and the 6th Infantry was to follow as soon as steamboats were procured.

I think it was about the middle of June[7] [1819] that the 6th Regiment, under Colonel Atkinson arrived and disembarked at Bellefontaine. Then the rifle regiment marched aboard the keelboats and proceeded up the river. I accompanied them in a keelboat owned by the company to act as sutler for them.

I will tell you at this point that before my departure up the Missouri River, I had been informed that the celebrated Colonel Daniel Boone,[8] whom I had once seen at my father's house when

[6] The name "Council Bluffs" was given this location by Lewis and Clark on the occasion of a council held there with the Otoe and Missouri Indians on August 3, 1804.

[7] Accounts from the *Missouri Gazette* seem to confirm this date.

June 9. "On Sunday and Monday last passed this place on their way to Belle Fontaine nine barges with the 6th Regiment U.S. infantry, commanded by Colonel Atkinson."

July 14. "The Military Expedition composed of the 6th Regiment U.S. infantry, left Bellefontaine of the 4th and 5th instant, in three steamboats and four keel boats, propelled by wheels and sail."

July 23. "Colonel Chambers with part of the Rifle Corps, left Belle Fontaine on the 14th inst., to proceed to Martin Cantonment."

Missouri Gazette, as quoted in *Publications* of the Nebraska State Historical Society, Xol. XX (1922), 21–24.

[8] Daniel Boone settled fifty miles above St. Louis in 1798 when it was still Spanish territory and served for some years as syndic of the Femme Osage District, where his sons and several friends from Kentucky had settled. In his later life he made his home with his son-in-law, Flanders Callaway, at La Charette. He died at Charette Village, at ninety years of age, one year after Meriwether's visit on September 26, 1820. He was buried at Charette, but both his and his wife's bodies were removed in 1845 to the cemetery near Frankfort, a few miles from the old fort of Boonesborough, by action of the citizens of Frankfort and the Kentucky legislature.

but a little boy, resided on the bank of the river, near a place then called Arrow Rock.[9] I asked my pilot if he knew the place, and he replied in the affirmative. I told him that I wanted to land at Boone's house and see him. So, being in advance of the troops a short distance, we hastened on and arrived at the Colonel's residence in the evening, when I proceeded to the house. Seeing a tall slender old gentleman sitting in the shade of the house, I inquired if that was Colonel Boone. He answered "Yes, what is left of him." Then telling him who I was, he greeted me very cordially. I remained at the house in conversation with the old Colonel until suppertime, and, at bedtime, I returned on board the boat. I never saw him afterwards.

The riflemen were very much adverse to leaving their comfortable quarters at Bellefontaine and ascending a long way above all white settlements to erect a cantonment for themselves. Hence desertions among them were frequent. Colonel Chambers determined if possible to stop this practice, and having arrested four deserters, he ordered them to be tied up and receive twenty-five lashes on the bare back each day for four days, and then have their ears cut off. As the troops had to stop each day to cook and eat their dinner, the Colonel ordered every man to attend this punishment. I did not suppose this order applied to me, as I was not in the military service. When we stopped that night, Lieutenant [Charles] Pentland, who was adjutant of the regiment, came to my boat and said that Colonel Chambers wanted to know the reason I did not obey his order to attend punishment that day. I said to him, "I did not suppose that this order applied to me and

---

See *St. Louis Enquirer*, October 14, 1820, as quoted in *Publications* of the Nebraska State Historical Society, Vol. XX (1922), 356.

[9] Arrow Rock was the Pierre a Fleche of early French explorers. The earliest ferry west of Franklin crossed the river at this point. The rock gives its name to a town founded in 1829, which for a time was the county seat and an important shipping point. See John Bradbury, *Travels in the Interior of America in the Years 1809, 1810, and 1811* . . . (Vol. V. in R. G. Thwaites, *Early Western Travels*), 162.

therefore absented myself and [will] continue to do so each day." The Lieutenant said, "If you know Colonel Chambers as well as I do, I think you would obey the order, for, if you fail to do so, you will be dealt with harshly." I still declined doing so when the Lieutenant said. "My young friend, take my advice and obey the order of the Colonel. If you do not wish to witness, you can shut your eyes, for your presence is all that the order requires." I therefore reconsidered my determination and consented to attend. Each day the whipping was repeated until the fourth, when Doctor Malone, the assistant surgeon of the regiment, was ordered to cut off each of their ears, and he did so.

One of the men who received this punishment was an Irishman, named Pat McCormack. The ears were all taken off on the Fourth of July. When poor Pat was standing on the bank of the river, brushing the blood with his fingers from his neck, as it trickled from his lacerated ears, the Colonel passed by. Pat exclaimed to him, "This is a hell of a way, Colonel, of celebrating the Fourth of July in this country." This so enraged the Colonel that he ordered a ball and chain to be attached to his ankles as an additional punishment. But poor Pat escaped all further punishment in this world by jumping off the boat that evening and drowning himself.

Captain Bissell did not accompany the rifle regiment, but remained to come up with the infantry. In due time we arrived at Martin Cantonment[10] situated on Corn Island in the Missouri

[10] Martin Cantonment or Camp Martin was situated a few miles above the present site of Leavenworth at Isle à La Vache (Meriwether calls this location "Corn Island"; actually it was Cow Island). Captain Martin with three companies of troops preceded the Yellowstone Expedition in the fall of 1818 and wintered at this point, expecting to proceed up the river in the spring. According to Chittenden, Major Long and his party spent a week at Martin Cantonment treating with the Kansas Indians, before proceeding up the Missouri, giving their date of leaving as August 25, 1819. However, the *Missouri Gazette*, dated September 22, says ". . . the Expedition and the keel boats arrived at Martin's Cantonment on the 28th, ult. All arrived on the same day. The keel boats left on the 4th, inst. The Johnson was expected daily." The *Missouri Intelligencer*, September 29th, said:

River, where two companies of the rifle regiment under command of Captain Martin had established themselves the summer before [1818]. Here Colonel Chambers determined to disembark and have some of his boats recaulked, as they leaked badly.

My boatmen, who were hired by the trip, had already complained loudly of our slow progress and had indeed become mutinous. One night, hearing a noise in the front of the boat, I proceeded to see what was the matter. There I found most of the men drunk and playing cards. Each man sat on the head of a keg of powder, and they were playing upon the head of another and had the candle stuck on still another keg, so there was imminent danger of our being blown up. I retired to my cabin again to reflect on what was best to be done. I awakened the pilot of the boat, who was called a patron, and also my interpreter and the steersman, and we armed ourselves and proceeded forward. On arriving where the card playing was going on, I remarked to the players, "Boys, I see you are amusing yourselves, won't you let me take a hand with you?" They exclaimed, "Oh yes, Captain, come on and join us." So seating myself on another keg of powder near the candle, I soon grasped it in my hand and threw it in the river. This action so enraged the drunken men that two or three fell afoul of me. But having a good heavy shillelagh [club] in my hand, and being assisted by my patron and the interpreter, we soon laid them on the bottom of the boat; then we retired to the cabin.

Early next morning the patron informed me that most of the men intended to leave the boat and return home. The patron, myself, and the interpreter soon armed ourselves and got ashore before them. I had a rifle and a pair of pistols; the patron had a gun also, and the interpreter had a shotgun. We seated our-

"Franklin, Sept 19th, 1819, Western Engineer left Martin Cantonment (Cow Island) on the 20th, ult." as quoted in *Publications* of the Nebraska State Historical Society, Vol. XX (1922), 29. See also Chittenden, *Fur Trade*, II, 569–924.

selves on a log near the bow of the boat, and pretty soon about half of the crew appeared with their effects packed up, ready to leave. I at once told them, "I will kill the first man that steps on shore and as many more as continue to follow him." This caused them to hesitate, and I then asked them, "Why have you behaved yourself in this way?" The leader of the party stated, "We hired ourselves by the trip, not expecting to be detained so much by the soldiers." I told him, "I will pay you extra for all detention; go back to the boat, consult among yourselves, and reply upon my word that you shall have justice done you." As they had become pretty well sobered by this time, they said, "If there is no further detention we will again go on duty. If we are detained again, we will all leave." This would place me in a sad predicament, as we were then several hundred miles above any settlement where I could procure men to supply their places.

I therefore called on Colonel Chambers to ascertain how long he would be detained at Martin Cantonment, when he informed me that it would be at least a week before he could start, and probably longer. I then informed him of the mutinous condition of my boat's crew. I had a large amount of public property on board belonging to the Indian Department, and I was afraid to proceed alone without an escort to protect me from the Indians. He then told me that he would furnish me with a company of soldiers to proceed next day, provided I would make arrangements by which a sutlering establishment could remain and accompany him. I then went to the sutler's store at Martin Cantonment and told the man in charge that I would be forced to leave and, as Martin Cantonment was to be abandoned, wished him to accompany the soldiers with his sutler's store.

To understand this sutlering business, I must inform you that no part of a soldier's ration of that day consisted of sugar, coffee, tobacco, or other articles of delicacy, as now, but each soldier had to purchase them with his own money. Therefore a man called a sutler was attached to each command, and his duty was to sell such articles to the soldiers. The gentleman having charge of the establishment at Martin Cantonment at once assented to this proposition. On reporting this to Colonel Chambers, he told me that he would order Lieutenant Field,[11] who commanded a company, to draw rations and be ready to accompany me the next day. I was very glad that Lieutenant Field had been selected, as he was born and raised in Jefferson County, Kentucky, and I had been acquainted with him in my early boyhood. In the evening of the next day—he being ready—we once more started up the river.

On arriving at the mouth of the River Platte, where we stopped for the night, my interpreter informed me that we were at least forty miles from Fort Lisa,[12] a trading establishment owned by Mr. Manuel Lisa; about ten miles below Council Bluffs were situated. But it was only about twenty miles across the bend of the river by land. [Because of this] Lieutenant [Samuel] Shannon, who was 2nd lieutenant in the company commanded by Field, proposed to leave the boats and proceed by land. So, next morning he packed up his lunch, together with a bottle of whisky and with his Negro servant started to make the trip by land. Next day, however Lieutenant Shannon was found on the bank of the river with his Negro, and they were in a most pitiable plight. He stated that he had fallen in with a party of Indians who had robbed him of everything he had, together with

[11] Gabriel Field of Missouri. See Heitman, *Historical Register U.S.A.*, I, 419.

[12] Fort Lisa was located about a mile above Cabanne's Post and five or six miles below old Council Bluffs. It was founded by Manuel Lisa as early as 1812, and it continued to be occupied as late as 1823. During this period it was the most important post on the Missouri River. It commanded the trade of the Omahas, Pawnees, Otoes, and other tribes. This location of Fort Lisa is verified by a letter from Father De Smet to N. Raney, December 9, 1867. See Chittenden, *Fur Trade*, II, 926; Letter, Father De Smet to N. Raney, as quoted in *Life, Letters and Travels of Father De Smet, S.J.;* and Hiram Martin Chittenden and Alfred Talbot Richardson, *Life, Letters and Travels of Father De Smet, S.J.*, IV, 1533.

a greater part of their clothing and the bottle of whisky. The Indians soon got drunk and made the Lieutenant and his servant dance for them. But one of them suggested that they didn't look alike—that one was white and the other black—and, as they could not make the Negro white, they wet some powder and blackened the white man. After night, the drunken Indians fell asleep, and the Lieutenant and his servant made their escape and were waiting the arrival of the boats.

On arriving at the place called Fort Lisa, which was no fort at all but a mere trading house, I presented an order to the man having it in charge, Mr. Michael Immell,[13] from Manuel Lisa,[14]

[13] Immell's name has been variously spelled, but this form is the one given in Heitman's *Historical Register*. Immell was an important figure in the fur trade of the Upper Missouri. He was in that area as early as 1809, and Armells Creek, which flows into the Yellowstone below the Bighorn, carries a corrupted form of his name. In 1822 he and other members of his party were killed in a Blackfoot ambush. O'Fallon said of him in a letter to General Clark, dated June 1, 1823: "He was brave, uncommonly large, and of great muscular strength. When timely apprised of danger, he was a host in himself."

See Richard Edward Oglesby, *Manuel Lisa and the Opening of the Missouri Fur Trade*, 141, 170ff., 175, 181–82, 186–87; Heitman, *Historical Register, U.S.A.*, I, 562; Letter, Benjamin O'Fallon to General Clark, as quoted in Chittenden, *Fur Trade*, I, 154; Dale L. Moran, *Jedediah Smith and the Opening of the West*, 63–64; and *Contributions* to the Historical Society of Montana, Vol. X (Helena, 1940), 286.

[14] Manuel Lisa was one of the outstanding figures of the American fur trade. He was born of Spanish parentage in New Orleans, September 8, 1772, carried on trading ventures in New Madrid, Ste. Genevieve, and Vincennes, and established his home in St. Louis in 1799. In 1802 he secured the rights to trade with the Osage Indians. In 1807, accompanied by George Druillard and forty-two men with trade goods worth about $16,000, he ascended the Yellowstone to the mouth of the Big Horn, where he established a post. He was the moving spirit in the organization of the St. Louis Missouri Fur Company in 1808–1809 and its most active member. In 1814 he was appointed sub-agent for the all Missouri tribes above the the Kansas River. From Fort Lisa near Council Bluffs he carried on trade with the Pawnees to the West and the Missouri tribes. He spent considerable time there, particularly during the winter months. He died on August 12, 1820, at the sulphur springs, south of St. Louis. See Oglesby, *Manuel Lisa;* Douglas, Missouri Historical Society *Collection*, III, 4, 380; Chittenden, *Fur Trade*, I, 126–37; Paul Chrisler Phillips, *The Fur Trade*, II, 505; and Bolton, Herbert Eugene, "New Light on Manual Lisa and the Spanish Fur Trade," *Texas Historical Quarterly*, Vol. XVIII (January, 1927).

who was in St. Louis when I left, directing him to let me discharge my cargo into their warehouse. On doing this as directed, I started the boat back to St. Louis, reserving only four men to remain with me. A few days after this, a small party of Indians came into the trading post, one of whom Lieutenant Shannon recognized as one of the party which had mistreated him and his Negro. On informing Lieutenant Field of this fact, the latter sent my interpreter for this Indian, and when coming on Lieutenant Field's boat, Shannon was asked if he was certain this was one of the Indians he encountered a few days before. Lieutenant Shannon and the Negro assured him in the affirmative, whereupon Lieutenant Field told the interpreter to tell the Indian that his lieutenant and Negro were deserters and he was entitled to a reward for having caused them to return to the boat, and, if any other of the party who encountered Lieutenant Shannon were present, to bring them on board to receive their reward also. He soon returned with three others, who were recognized by Lieutenant Shannon. Lieutenant Field then directed his soldiers to seize and tie them, whereupon he had a sound thrashing administered to each as their reward. Our interpreter soon after this informed us that there was a large party of Indians consisting of several hundred encamped a few hours march from us, and in all probability we would be attacked before next morning. The soldiers were set to work to build a barricade for the purpose of defense, should we be attacked. We traders also barricaded the houses and kept watch all night, but no Indians appeared. Shortly after this, Lieutenant Field's stock of provisions was reduced to a low ebb, and he was forced to embark his troops and proceed down the river to meet Colonel Chambers.

Before our arrival and for several years preceding, the employees of Manuel Lisa had been in the habit of sowing a turnip patch up on the bluff in the rear of their residences. Finding that they had not sown all his turnip seed, I determined to clear a little piece of ground adjoining their turnip patch and sow some seed also. As many of the employees of Mr. Lisa had married Indian squaws, I hired them and some of their husbands to assist me in preparing the ground for the reception of the turnip seed. We always proceeded to the top of the bluff immediately after breakfast, worked until dinnertime, came down for our dinner, and returned to work in the afternoon. One day on returning to our turnip patch and going to work, some Pawnee Indians had secreted themselves in the tall grass and bushes and soon opened fire upon the Indian squaws, who, together with our men, scattered in every direction and concealed themselves in the bushes. As there was but one place where the bluff could be ascended or descended, which was down a little ravine, and I being seated on top of the bluff at the head of the ravine, I immediately placed myself behind a tree with my gun in order to keep the way for our people to retreat open.

After firing, the hostile Indians would conceal themselves again in the grass and bushes. Whenever a squaw would attempt to make her escape down the bluff where I stood, she was fired at, but when a man attempted to do so, they let him escape without firing on him. I retained my position a long time to keep the route or retreat open until nearly all had escaped. The last squaw had taken a little boy two or three years old up with her. She took him upon her back and ran as fast as possible to the head of the ravine where I stood, but, on coming within twenty or thirty steps of where I stood, she was shot through and fell dead very near the tree behind which I was secreted. The little boy immediately extricated himself from his dead mother, ran around the tree, and squatted like a partridge between my legs. I retained my position for some time after this, not knowing whether all our party had escaped or not, as some of the squaws had been killed; I did not know how many.

When I was about to leave my position, I saw an Indian, some seventy-five or a hundred yards off, behind a tree watching me. This caused me to be fearful of leaving my covert, and I suppose he was equally fearful of leaving his. I therefore pulled off my hat and poked it around the tree to extract his fire. His ball struck my hat. He failed to run up and try to scalp me and commenced reloading his gun. In doing this, he exposed a part of his person, and I took a shot at him, whereupon I caught up the little boy in my arms and hastened down the rocky ravine as quickly as possible.

On reaching the house, Mr. Immell informed me that the squaws about the premises were of the Omaha tribe,[15] and there was a hostile feeling existing between this tribe and the Pawnees but no hostile feeling on the part of the Pawnees towards the whites. After some consultation between us, I proposed that if Mr. Immell would furnish me and my interpreter with horses and a guide, I would start after night and go to the Omaha village situated on the Elkhorn River, a tributary of the Platte, and get a party of Omahas, ascend the Elkhorn River, and intercept the Pawnees. This proposition being agreed to, we started after supper on our journey. On reaching the Omaha village, I told

[15] The Omahas (Siouan)—the name was sometimes spelled "Maha" in the first half of the nineteenth century—were once a powerful tribe, but Sioux oppressions and smallpox reduced their numbers to about four hundred. Their principal habitat was about one hundred miles above the present Omaha on the west bank of the Missouri. The Omahas were to an extent agriculturists as well as industrious trappers. Council Bluffs was the center of their trading activities, and they dwelt in permanent villages near that point. See Hodge, *Handbook of American Indians,* II, 119–21.

The Pawnee (Caddoan) proper consisted at one time of three bands or tribes under a single chief. These bands, in the order of their importance, were: the Chau-i, Kitkehahk-i, and Pita-hau-erat. After the northern migration of the tribes and their settlement in Kansas and Nebraska, the large allied tribe known as the Skidi or Pawnee Loups were added. These tribes have always been known in the writings of explorers and travelers in the West as the Grand, Republican, Tapage, and Wolf Pawnees, constituting the Pawnee Nation. Grinnell, *Pawnee Hero Stories and Folk Tales,* 215–16, 218; Hodge, *Handbook of American Indians,* II, 213–14.

these Indians what had happened and proposed that they should take a strong party, ascend the Elkhorn River, and intercept the Pawnees. The Omahas had to hold a council on this subject, which occupied the whole day, and we did not get off until late that night. On ascending the valley of the Elkhorn, to where the trail leading from the trading house to the Pawnee villages crossed the Elkhorn, we found the Pawnees had escaped us. The Pawnee villages were situated on the Platte River, at the junction of the North and South forks,[16] between fifty and one hundred miles west of the Elkhorn crossing. We therefore returned without accomplishing anything.

On my return to Fort Lisa I made no further efforts to sow turnips but employed my hands in making preparations for building winter quarters. Not knowing the exact spot where the troops would build their cantonment, we commenced sawing planks with a whip saw, taken along for the purpose, until the troops should arrive and select the sight for their cantonment.

16 The Pawnee villages during this period were principally along the Loup Fork of the Platte River, approximately the distance from Council Bluffs that Meriwether gives. Their villages were more or less permanent, with imposing lodges, some as large as sixty feet in diameter, built in a conical form with beams and poles and covered with sod and clay.

III
Council Bluffs

I THINK IT WAS THE LATTER PART OF AUGUST or the first part of September that the rifle regiment arrived,[1] and Captain Bissell, who was to be the head of our trading establishment, with them. The troops did not select a site on top of the bluff but a mile or two above, where the river strikes the bluff, in a level piece of bottom land between the bluff and the river, which had timber suitable for building on it.[2] All hands went

1 The exact date of the arrival of the troops of the Yellowstone Expedition at Council Bluffs is not definite; however, it is certain that they arrived in late September. Colonel Chambers with a portion of the rifle regiment left Bellefontaine on June 14, and the Sixth Regiment left on July 4 and 5, principally in keelboats. Five keelboats with two hundred and sixty troops were reported arriving at Franklin on July 2 and departing three days later. The steamboat *Western Engineer* with Major Long and his scientific party arrived at this point on July 14 and departed on the nineteenth. Colonel Chambers' command was reported arriving at Fort Osage on July 20. The *Western Engineer* was reported as leaving Martin Cantonment (Cow Island) on August 20, and Colonel Chambers as leaving that point on September 5, with keelboats and troops. Because of mutinous conditions aboard his boat, Meriwether left Martin Cantonment with an escort of troops at least one week before Chambers' command. In the newspapers of that period reports were made from St. Charles, Chariton, Franklin, and Fort Osage of the continuous mechanical difficulties with the steamboats as well as of low water in the Missouri. The steamboat expedition under Captain Craig had difficulties at Fort Osage, necessitating the transfer of cargo and men to keelboats. *Missouri Intelligencer,* as quoted in *Publications* of the Nebraska State Historical Society. Vol. XX (1922), 28–30.

2 This post was known as Camp Missouri. Paul Wilhelm, Duke of Württemberg describes the location as "a low point, about three miles farther up stream than the Bluffs, not far from a swamp." This agrees with Meriwether's account. The post was moved to the high sloping ground of the bluff some two or three miles down the river in 1820 because the floods, a scurvy epidemic, and general unhealthful conditions. It was subsequently known as Fort Atkinson and Fort Calhoun. Father De Smet stated on December 9, 1867: "The question of locality which has arisen about old Fort Atkinson, or Council Bluffs, built in 1819, I think I can answer satisfactorily. During the years 1838–39 I resided opposite what is now called the City

to work to get cover for the winter. Each company had its timberland allotted to it, and orders were issued that one should not trespass on the other. We had our portion allotted to us on the lower end of a grove of all slender cottonwood trees. As I had been raised in the backwoods and understood the building of log houses, the duty of superintending the erection of ours was consigned to me. I had but four men to help me, but, as only a portion of the soldiers were assigned to extra duty each day, I was allowed to hire those remaining idle. I usually kept from ten to twelve men employed. One day while cutting down trees and cutting up logs, some of my men happened to cut a tree upon Lieutenant Shannon's lot, seeing which, I went to Lieutenant Shannon and informed him of it and told him that he could cut a tree on my side of the line, which was satisfactory to him. During the day Major Biddle,[3] who had been assigned the duty of laying off and superintending the barracks (I think he was brigade inspector for the district) observed that my men had cut a tree on Lieutenant Shannon's side. He became furiously angry when I informed him of seeing Lieutenant Shannon and that he was satisfied with it. He said, "This arrangement shall not be made." I remarked in a jocular manner, "As the moon shines tonight, I could have the logs removed to our side of the line." This made him still more furiously mad. When we returned to the boats for dinner, he had a tent brought up and had it pitched near the logs in dispute. When we quit work that night, I observed to an Irish soldier that I had hired, if he could see

of Omaha. In 1839 I stood on the bluff on which the old fort was built in 1819 [the correct date is 1820]; some rubbish and remains of the old fort were still visable. Fort Atkinson was located where now stands the town of Fort Calhoun. Nebraska Territory, about sixteen miles in a straight line above the City of Omaha." —Paul Wilhelm, South Dakota Historical *Collections*, Vol. XIX, 360. See also Letter, Father De Smet to N. Raney, secretary Historical Society, St. Louis. As quoted in Chittenden and Richardson, *Life, Letters and Travels of Father De Smet*, IV, 1533.

[3] Thomas Biddle, Jr., of Pennsylvania.

how a certain tree leaned. The Irishman said, "Yes, it leans directly over the Major's tent." "Now," said I, "Pat, if this tree falls whilst we are eating supper, you will get a bottle of whisky by coming to my tent afterwards." So, while we were eating supper, I heard the tree fall, and on going there, I found the Major's tent smashed down. This made the Major still more furious. That night, Pat got his bottle of whisky.

The next morning on resuming our labors, the Major came to where I was and asked which of my men cut the tree down, and I informed him that I understood Pat had cut it down. Then he fell afoul of Pat and abused him in an outrageous manner, threatening to have him punished for it. Pat was able to prove by several men, who I suppose had shared the whisky, that the tree leaned in a different direction from the tent, but, when it was about to fall, there came a puff of wind which threw it on his tent. While the Major was raving about the matter, Colonel Chambers came up, and, having had the matter explained to him by me, he took Major Biddle aside and had a private conversation with him, at the close of which both marched off towards the river, and nothing more was heard of the matter.

I understood that this Major Biddle was a brother of the celebrated Nicholas Biddle, president of the United States Bank, who figured so conspicuously during General Jackson's administration. Major Biddle resigned soon after Missouri became a state, married, and settled down in St. Louis, and became a candidate for Congress against a gentleman, whose name, I think, was Pettis, and who beat the Major badly. This contest for a seat in Congress produced a very bitter feeling between the two candidates, and a duel ensued in which both were killed.[4]

I omitted to mention in its proper chronological order an oc-

[4] The duel took place August 29, 1831. The other principal was Spencer Pettis. Because of Biddle's defective eyesight the normal dueling distance was shortened. Both men were mortally wounded at the first shot.

currence which struck me with some force.[5] Major Long had been ordered, as before stated, to construct a small steamboat to explore the upper waters of the Missouri River, and he caused this boat, which was very small, to be constructed in such a manner as to impress the Indians that he might meet. She was a very small stern-wheel boat, the bow-sprit of which projected several feet beyond the bow and was constructed of sheet iron in imitation of a snake's head, and when a puff of steam escaped, it passed through this imitation of a snake's head, the jaws of which were fixed upon hinges so as to let the steam escape through the mouth.[6] This boat arrived at Fort Lisa in advance of the troops, and when a party of Indians came in for the purpose of trade, we saw the little boat slowly approaching, several miles below this settlement, and the Indians' attention was called to it. Seeing no men at work on board, one of them asked what made it come up the river. I told him it was a big snake swimming up the river with the little boat on its back. This astonished the Indians very much, and many seemed to doubt it. But on the approach of the boat, they discovered the snake's head opening and shutting its mouth and the waves from the paddle wheel escaping from the stern, and one of the Indians declared that this was true as he could see the snake switching its tail behind.

When the boat was about to land and commenced letting off

[5] These recollections with the description of Long's steamboat and the account of Major O'Fallon's council with the Indians were not a part of Meriwether's original autobiography but were found among his papers. They were probably dictated to his granddaughter at a later time and never incorporated into his connected narrative.

[6] The *Missouri Gazette* of May 26, 1819, describes the vessel as follows: "She is well armed, but carries an elegant flag, painted by Mr. Peale, representing a white man and an Indian shaking hands, the calumet of peace, and a sword. The boat is seventy-five feet long, and thirteen feet beam, drawn nineteen inches of water, with her engine, which together with all the machinery, is placed below deck, entirely out of sight. The steam passes out through the mouth of the figure head (a large serpent). The wheels are placed in the stern, to avoid the snags and sawyers which are also common in those waters. She has a mast to ship or not as may be necessary."

steam, the Indians became alarmed and moved back farther from the bank of the river. After the landing of the boat Major Benjamin O'Fallon,[7] the Indian agent, who had been a passenger, came ashore. (He was a brother of Colonel John O'Fallon who had employed me.) He tried to persuade some of the Indians to go aboard, but they were at first too much alarmed to do so. Finally, however, they selected two old men to go aboard, who did so, and they witnessed the operation of the engine slowly working off steam and were taken into the cabin. On coming ashore again they told the other Indians that there was no danger in going aboard, and the great Spirit, not man, had built the boat. Others then went on board, and these visitors becoming too numerous, a sentry was placed on the wharf plank to prevent too many at one time from getting on.

[When] Major O'Fallon [arrived,] he was informed that hostilities were likely to break out between the different tribes in that vicinity; that the Omahas, Iowas, Otoes, and Missouris had formed a combination against the Pawnees, who were about as numerous as all the others combined, and that a war of extermination was about to ensue. This he determined if possible to prevent and through the agency of the different tribes, invited

[7] Benjamin O'Fallon was born in Kentucky on September 20, 1793. He was a nephew of George Rogers Clark and Governor William Clark and was reared in St. Louis under the guardianship of his uncle, William Clark.

He was Indian agent at Prairie du Chien, and in 1817 he concluded treaties between the United States and the Otoes and Poncas. In 1819 he was appointed Indian agent for the Upper Missouri, at this time acquiring the complimentary title of major. It has been said that he possessed a remarkable knowledge of Indian habits and customs and was well acquainted with all phases of Indian life. He resigned his position as Indian agent in 1827 and returned to St. Louis. He was one of the principals of the St. Louis Fur Company, although his name does not appear in the reorganization of 1819. His memory is perpetuated by O'Fallon's Creek in Montana, which was named in his honor by William Clark on the Lewis and Clark Expedition. O'Fallon's Bluff west of North Platte on the Overland Trail was also named for him. It appears that he did not leave Bellefontaine with the Yellowstone Expedition but joined it at St. Charles on June 27 with his interpreter, John Dougherty. He died in Jefferson County, Missouri, December 17, 1842. See James, *Account of an Expedition.*

all of the above tribes to send their principal men to meet him in council[8] near the mouth of the Platte River, and at the appointed time and place a deputation from each tribe appeared. The council was opened with a speech from the Indian agent, which required a long time to deliver, as it had to be interpreted in several different languages. Major O'Fallon would deliver to his French interpreter a sentence which would be interpreted in French to the Indian interpreters, all of whom were either French-Canadians or of French-Canadian descent and therefore used the French language. Then each of the Indian interpreters would change it into the language of his tribe, when another sentence was given in the same manner.

The Major urged them all to make peace and live in harmony with each other and concluded by telling them that if they did not do so, he would bring the white soldiers among them and compel obedience to his wishes, and he advised them to retire to their respective camps, hold consultations, and give their answers the next morning. That night Major O'Fallon was informed that one of the interpreters had not interpreted his speech correctly, and being convinced of this, the next morning he directed his Negro man, Peter, to seize this interpreter, tie him to a tree, and give him a good thrashing, and then had part of one of his ears cut off, telling him to leave immediately. This astonished the Indians greatly.

The next morning the council was reassembled, and the Pawnees were requested to deliver their answer to what had been said to them the evening before. They immediately assented to Major O'Fallon's advice to make peace, and the Omahas were requested to give their answer, which was to the same effect; but when the Iowas were called upon and White Cloud arose for the purpose of delivering the answer for his tribe, Major O'Fallon turned his back upon him. The Indian asked the interpreter why

[8] For this council see *ibid.*, 236–47.

his brother turned his back upon him when he was about to talk. The Major directed the interpreter to say that he had not come to hear boys talk but to listen to the chiefs of each tribe. White Cloud answered, "How am I to know that the Major has been appointed by his nation to hold this council with the Indians?" On this being interpreted into English, the Major replied the cockade he wore in his hat was his emblem of office, to which White Cloud replied, "I knew this and therefore did not question his right to council with us, and if he [the Major] had known as much, he would know that the red feather stuck in my head was my emblem of office, and no one has a right to doubt my appointment by my tribe to deliver their answer; and if my brother does not receive their answer through me, he will get no answer at all," whereupon the Major agreed to hear it.

White Cloud, who was a very young man and had a very youthful appearance, commenced his address by saying, "My brothers call me a boy. It is true I have not seen as many days as my brother, but the Indians do not count their age by the number of times they have seen the snow fall in the winter or the grass grow green in the spring. They measure their age by the number of scalps of the enemy they can show [at the same time pulling from his pouch two or three scalps which he displayed] and by the number of scars they can show on their bodies, the wounds which have been inflicted by their enemies [at the same time pulling aside his blanket and showing a large scar on his side]." "Now," said he, "measure my age in this way, and long before my brother was born I saw the sun rise and set in my native trees." "My brother said he would force us to make peace with the Pawnees. Now, this is a question between Redmen and in which the white man has no right to interfere, but I will say to you that my tribe will not consent to make peace with the Pawnees. The Great Spirit has placed this broad river [pointing to the Missouri] between us, and woe to the

Pawnees who cross it. I know that we are not able to cope with the whites. I have seen some of your soldiers and know that they have better guns than we have, and I am told they are numerous as the sands on the riverbank or the great herds of buffalo on the prairies, but if the whites compel us to make peace with the Pawnees, we will, if we can do no better, scratch you with our toe and finger nails and gnaw you with our teeth. Now my brother has our answer." At this he stalked off in a very majestic manner, followed by the remainder of his tribe.

The eloquence and frankness of White Cloud pleased the agent very much, and he was sent for and brought into the white man's tent, where they conversed for several hours.

I have listened to Mr. Clay at the height of his fame as an orator and to Tom Marshall and other eloquent speakers in Kentucky, but I think White Cloud was the greatest natural orator I ever listened to. His language was not nearly so copious as ours, but his attitude, his gestures, and his countenance were that of a true orator. This was the same Indian who later accompanied me on my trip to Martin Cantonment.

After we traders had gotten into a snug winter quarters, we heard that a large party of Indians were encamped a hundred or so miles above the cantonment and that they had a large number of buffalo robes for trade, but were afraid to bring them down to where the soldiers were. I was then directed to take a number of articles suitable for the Indian trade and proceed up the river to this Indian encampment. Having borrowed a canoe from Manuel Lisa's trading house, I proceeded with my interpreter and two of the hands to propel it, to visit the Indians for the purpose of trade. On arriving, I soon purchased about six hundred buffalo robes, together with some other furs and peltries, not all of which I could get in my canoe. Having anticipated a contingency of this kind, I had taken a couple of axes and a few other tools with me. We therefore selected a tree suitable to make a canoe. The tree stood near the bank of the river, and I had it cut down. Then it was cut off the same length as the canoe I already had, which was about thirty feet, and we dug out another canoe. Then placing them side by side, about two feet apart, and lashing some poles across to the sides of both canoes, we formed a platform five or six feet wide, covering both canoes, reserving a place in the bow of each for the hands to sit and wield their paddles and a place at the stern for the steersman to stand. I spread my buffalo robes on this platform and started down the river again. At this time some small cakes of ice began to run in the river, which caused us to hasten as much as possible, but, having to land every night, as the snags were too thick for us to run after dark, the ice increased upon us. But we landed one evening safe at the cantonment and determined to let the cargo remain in the canoes until morning, as it was protected from the ice by a point of land that jutted into the river.

Next morning when about to commence discharging the cargo, Lieutenant [Thomas W.] Kavanaugh came down with a guard of soldiers and told me that Colonel [Willoughby] Morgan, then in command of the post, had ordered him to seize my robes. I therefore strenuously objected, but the Lieutenant informed me that the military officers had a legal right to press any article necessary to their comfort; and, that much sickness prevailing, and the steamboat having their hospital supplies on board and having failed to arrive, these robes were necessary for the sick in the hospital, and that I would be liberally paid for them. About this time Captain Bennet Riley[9] came down the bank, accompa-

[9] Riley was born in Virginia in 1787. He entered the army as an ensign of rifles, January 19, 1813, attaining his captaincy on August 6, 1818. He campaigned for many years on the plains and commanded the first troops as escorts on the Santa Fé Trail. After ten years of service he was breveted a major in 1828. In the Mexican War he was a trusted lieutenant of General Winfield Scott, who attributed much of his success at Monterey and Cerro Gordo to him. He was promoted to brigadier general on April 18, 1847, for gallant conduct at the battle of Contreras. He was in command of the Division of the West in California, where he acted as

nied by two other officers, who informed me they had been appointed a board to appraise the value of my robes. They therefore counted and examined them as they were unloaded, and then retired. That evening this board of officers came to our trading house and said that a price had been fixed on the robes, and, as all were well dressed and handsome articles, they had assessed a value of six dollars a robe, and asked if that price was satisfactory to me. I answered in the affirmative. It was much more than I had expected, as they cost me about one dollar and a half apiece, or, in other words, I had given goods that cost that amount in exchange for each robe.

It may be interesting to you to know how a trade was carried on with the Indians in those days. On the arrival of a trader at an Indian village or camp, he was taken to the chief's lodge, which is a tent made of skins, and here he was invited to eat. As soon as he had done this, the next in rank to the chief came and invited him to eat with him. Hence the trader was often feasted four or five times in the course of an hour or so. These headmen of the tribe then assembled at the head chief's lodge, to which the trader had returned. The trader was then asked what kind of goods he had brought to trade with them, and what kind of furs and skins he desired to purchase from them. The terms of the barter were here fixed. The next day a crier was sent through the village or camp, who proclaimed in a loud voice what the trader had to sell and what he wanted in return. Then commenced the bringing forward of their articles of trade, principally by the squaws, and, throwing them down in a pile, each one received the amount agreed upon the night before, which usually consisted of steel traps, blankets, some tinware, butcher knives, and occasionally beads, small looking glasses, and other trinkets

the last territorial governor. He died at Buffalo, New York, on June 9, 1853. The well-known military post Fort Riley, Kansas, was named in his honor after his death in 1853. See Heitman, *Historical Register, U.S.A.*, I, 831; and Captain W. F. Pride, *The History of Fort Riley*, 61–63.

to please the women. Hence there was no parleying with each individual as to the price he or she was to receive, all this having been arranged the night before.

Shortly after this, the weather became very cold, and the scurvy[10] broke out among the soldiers, for the want of fresh provisions and vegetables (of which the soldiers had none) and close confinement in stuffy rooms, which were overcrowded. This induced Colonel Morgan to apply to me to know if the Omaha Indians had any vegetables which could be purchased. I informed him that the only vegetables I had discovered while at their village a few months before were some small patches of corn, and it would be very difficult to procure this from them. We then called my interpreter to council him on the subject, when he informed us that nothing could induce them to part with corn, except whisky—but that would induce them to sell anything they had, even their wives and children, whereupon he desired me to take some whisky, go to their village, and purchase their corn. To this I replied that all traders, on obtaining a license to trade with the Indians, had to give a heavy bond with security (providing heavy penalties by law) against any white person who either gave or sold whisky to the Indians, and I could not comply with his wishes unless the Indian agent stationed there would give me permission to do so. The agent was Major Benjamin O'Fallon, whose home I had often visited. The case being stated to him, he replied, "David, you know the law, and you ought to know that I cannot dispense with its provisions, but, as this appears to be a case of necessity, I, myself, will not enforce the law against you." I then consented to comply with the wishes of the Colonel.

That night I procured two ten gallon kegs, and filling each half full of whisky, and packing up several other articles of trade,

[10] See James, *Account of an Expedition*, 283.

I put them on my two pack mules, taking with me one man and my interpreter, and started for the Omaha village on the Elkhorn River. We struck the river several miles below the village, where we filled the empty space in each keg with water, and concealing them in some willows and bushes which grew under the riverbank, we proceeded to the Indian village. On my arrival, after feasting me as usual, they desired to know what I had brought to trade with them. When I informed them of the articles I had, omitting the whisky, I was asked what I wanted in exchange. When I told them corn was the article I wanted, they promptly informed me they would not sell their corn, as they might need it during the winter for themselves. Anticipating such a refusal, I had provided myself with a small flask of whisky, which I carried in my pocket and which I had diluted in the same manner as that in the kegs. This flask I pulled out of my pocket, and pouring a little out in a cup, which I had with me, I gave each of the men in the lodge a small dram, whereupon I asked if they liked it. They replied, "It is good." They informed me that if I had brought a sufficient quantity that I could purchase their corn. When I informed them that I had some not far off, which I would trade them for the corn, they asked me how much I had. I gave them with my two hands an idea of the size of each keg and indicated two kegs of that size, and they wanted to know if it was all as good as the taste out of the flask, and which I responded to in the affirmative. It was then agreed that on my producing the whisky, they would give their corn for it. This being arranged, I awakened my interpreter and the hand with me, before daybreak, and told them to bring the whisky to the village. This they did about sunrise. I then told my interpreter to notify the headmen of the village that the whisky had arrived, and I wanted them to come and see it, which they soon did. I had inserted two brass faucets, one in each keg, but had the keys in my pockets. I then drew a little from each keg into a tin cup and desired them to taste it, which they did, and pronounced it good.

They shook each keg to see that it was full, and, they being satisfied on that point, I desired them to produce the corn and let me see how much they had. They immediately directed their crier to go through the village and announce that I had arrived and had whisky to trade but that I would exchange it for nothing but corn. Very shortly after, the Indians, both men and squaws, began to bring sacks containing corn already shucked, each sack containing on the average of one bushel. They soon had twenty or twenty-five sacks piled up, when I told them it was not enough for the whisky I had. So they continued to bring more sacks, I think about thirty. Then they informed me that was all, except for seed for next spring.

I told them they might have both kegs for the pile of corn, provided they would furnish me with ponies to pack it into the bluff and to send some of their young men to bring the horses back. Upon this, some boys were sent to bring ponies up, and it was announced that the trade had been made and that the whisky would soon be distributed. At this announcement the women began to gather up the children to take them off to hiding places, also all the arms they could get hold of. When the ponies came, a sufficient number were selected, and each animal had a packsaddle placed on its back and strongly girted with a lariat rope. Then a sack of corn was placed on each side of the saddle, near the top of the animal's back, and a third sack was placed on top of the saddle between the other two. This was secured by passing another lariat around the sacks and the animal's body and securely fastened.

Three young Indians having been selected to bring the animals back, I directed my interpreter to proceed to a creek we had crossed about ten miles distant, and there to camp for the night.

I remained behind a little while. When I had given them the keys to the faucets, showing them how to use the keys, I mounted my horse and proceeded to the top of a hill about three or four hundred yards distant. Here I dismounted, and hiding my horse behind the hill, I walked to the crest of the hill which overlooked the village. Soon after this the whisky began to take effect among the Indians, and such a scene I never witnessed before or never want to witness again.

The drunken Indians howled like wolves, sang and danced like devils, and fought and scrambled for the whisky. After viewing this scene, I mounted my horse and overtook the men in camp. On arriving at the cantonment, I delivered the corn to the proper authorities and repaired to our trading house. This corn was boiled with the meat for the soldiers until it became soft and formed a thick soup, which was distributed among the sick.

IV
A Journey of Mercy

I NOW COME TO THE HARDEST TRIP I ever made in my life. On the first day of January, 1820, Colonel Morgan came to our trading house with Doctor [John] Gail, the surgeon of the rifle regiment. In the course of conversation he informed us that scurvy was still increasing among the solders, some of whom were dying every day, and that the medicine and hospital supplies suitable for that disease were nearly exhausted, and they did not know what was to become of them. He also said that their medicine and hospital stores were on a steamboat which had met the ice at Martin Cantonment, which was some three or four hundred miles below,[1] and they could get no higher as the river had closed with ice.

I remarked to the Colonel, "Why don't you send a detachment of soldiers with pack horses to bring up the necessary medicines and hospital store?" To this he replied, "I had started a party the week before, but they soon returned, some of them frostbitten, and said it was so cold they could not go farther." I replied, "If the party were properly clad the trip could be made." The Colonel asked me what I would charge to go and bring the necessary articles up, and I told him that he hadn't money enough to hire me to do so, as the thermometer was then below zero, with no probability of its getting higher before spring, and the snow was half a leg deep on the ground. On certain conditions I would undertake to make the trip, but not

[1] The distance from Council Bluffs to Martin Contonment by river was two hundred and seventy miles.

for money. He responded that he didn't understand this. I replied, "Colonel, if you were sick and unable to help yourself, I would wash and dress you, but I couldn't be hired to do so." He then asked what conditions I desired to make. I replied, "I want to select my own men from amongst the soldiers and have them clad in the proper manner." He then asked me how many men would be required. I told him four or five, with a noncommissioned officer at the head. He then said, "I will agree to your terms, provided you will take but one man from each company, as all the companies are much reduced from sickness and death." This being satisfactory, I told him to send for Corporal Roderick of the rifle regiment and I would see if he was willing to go, as I wanted no man to go only in obedience to orders and not of his own free will. He then asked, "Why do you prefer Corporal Roderick?" I replied that he was hired to build our trading house, and he (Roderick) informed me that he was born and raised in the Highlands of Scotland, where the weather was often cold, and I had always found him to be an energetic and reliable man. The Colonel departed, saying he would send the Corporal down. When he arrived, I described the trip to him and the necessity for making it and asked if he was willing to go. He said he thought he could stand as much as I could and was willing to go. I then directed him to return to the cantonment and select four or five men from the rifle regiment, taking but one man from each company, and selecting none but reliable men and also men who were willing to make the trip. In the evening he returned with four others, to whom we described the hardships of the trip, and they were asked if they were willing to go with me. All expressed their willingness to go.

At this time, each company had a man that understood something of the tailoring business, whose duty was to mend the soldiers' clothing when it was needed. I then directed the Corporal to return to the cantonment and inform each commander from whom he had selected a man that the tailor of each company was needed to prepare a suit of clothing for the men, and that he request each captain to order the tailor of his company to report to me. He soon returned with four tailors, and I showed them a suit of clothing that had been made for me, consisting of a buckskin hunting shirt reaching down to about my knees, a pair of pants made of the same material, which reached nearly to the arm pits, a vest made entirely of otterskins, and an otterskin cap which would cover the ears and every part of the face, except the mouth, nose, and eyes. In addition to this, I wanted each man to have a pair of drawers and undershirt and several pairs of socks of what was called "South Sea baize," a woolen cloth about as thick as a good mackinaw blanket but with a much longer nap. I also wanted them to have a pair of buckskin mittens, lined with the same kind of baize, and which should come well up on the wrist so as to cover the coat sleeve. I also directed them to make each man a pair of moccasins of otterskins with the fur turned inside, and lacing high above the ankles.

Then, from our storehouse the necessary articles to make these garments was furnished and charged to the government at the usual prices. The tailors were instructed to have everything ready as soon as possible, and, if necessary, to get the tailors of other companies to assist them. On the evening of January 4, the Corporal brought the men down to the trading house dressed in their new wardrobes. Seeing that the men were properly equipped, I furnished each with a butcher knife and a tin cup, directing the Corporal to draw two camp kettles and a large tin mess pan. Then I told him to select fifteen or twenty Indian ponies from a herd which had been purchased by the government from the Indians, and also to procure a packsaddle for each, and to procure the skin sacks which contained the corn purchased from the Indians the fall before, and to draw four or five days' rations and to report to me the next morning, to make a start.

I then furnished the soldiers with three buffalo robes, and each of them with two heavy mackinaw blankets and several extra pairs of moccasins. Thus equipped, we started the next day, I taking two Indian ponies with me for my own use. We traveled down the western side of the Missouri River and passed an encampment[2] formed by Major Long of the Engineer Corps, who had caused a small steamboat to be built at Pittsburgh to explore the upper waters of the Missouri. This encampment consisted of a small detachment of troops with several officers of the Engineer Corps, the commanding officer being Major Long,[3] with Lieutenant Graham, Lieutenant Swift, and another whose name has escaped me.

The first night we camped a little below Fort Lisa, and the second night, at the mouth of the Platte River, near which we found a trading house, which had been recently erected by Mr. Robidoux,[4] a fur trader from St. Louis. In the evening, several

[2] "The site for a camp for the scientific party was located half a mile above Fort Lisa, five miles below Council Bluffs, and three miles above the mouth of the Boyer River. The place was christened Engineer Cantonment."—Chittenden *Fur Trade*, II, 570.

[3] Stephen Harriman Long was born in New Hampshire on December 30, 1784, and joined the army on December 12, 1814. The scientific expedition which he headed contributed greatly to the knowledge of the Southwest. In the spring of 1820 his party left the camp on the Missouri and set out by land to explore the region between that stream and the headwaters of the Red River. They marched up the Platte River, crossed to Pike's Peak, and observed the land spread out like a map from its summit. Then Long divided his command. One party under Captain John R. Bell followed the Arkansas to Fort Smith, Arkansas. The other under Long cut across country to the south and reached a creek which they believed to be a tributary of the Red River. It proved to be the Canadian, and they followed that stream across the present Texas Panhandle and Oklahoma to the Arkansas River and then down to Fort Smith. See James, *Account of an Expedition;* and Harlin M. Fuller and Leroy R. Hafen, eds., *The Journal of Captain John R. Bell.*

[4] This was Joseph Robidoux, the founder of St. Joseph. He was born in 1783, the son of a well-known fur-trading family. His father, also named Joseph, came from Montreal to Kaskaskia and then removed to St. Louis, where he became an influential citizen. The first territorial legislature met in his house in 1812. See Maximilian, Prince of Wied-Neuwied, *Travels in the Interior of America,* 257.

Indians of the Iowa[5] tribe crossed the Missouri River on the ice and came to our camp. Among them, I soon recognized White Cloud, a young man I had often seen at Council Bluffs, whose intelligence and frank deportment I much admired. With the assistance of Mr. Robidoux' interpreter I soon employed him as a guide. His only objection was that he would have to pass through the Otoe country, which tribe was hostile to his people; but, on my assuring him that we would protect him from the Otoes, if we encountered any of that tribe, he at once agreed to accompany me. I then directed him to return to his encampment on the other side of the Missouri and prepare himself for the trip, and come over the next morning, bringing his horse and equipment, also a pair of snowshoes for me. These snowshoes consisted of a light wooden hoop, about two and a half feet long and eight or ten inches wide, across which narrow leather thongs were woven. The foot being placed in the middle of this loop, and being attached to it from the instep, the shoes would sustain a person on the surface of the snow; and by bearing one's weight on the middle, the hoop would slightly contract, and, on relieving the shoes weight, the hoop would spring apart again, which assisted very much in walking.

White Cloud became famous afterwards, as he traveled through the United States and even Europe.[6] On his coming over the next morning, we departed again from our camp and crossed the Platte River on the ice near its mouth. It may be interesting to you to learn of our mode of travel. The train was led by White Cloud, on his snowshoes (as it was too cold for us to ride) leading his horse. I followed on my snowshoes, also

[5] The Iowas, the Otoes, and the Missouris all sprang from a common stock which was related to the Winnebago division of the Siouan family. They traded principally at the Robidoux post and to an extent at Council Bluffs.

[6] Father De Smet wrote of meeting White Cloud at the village of the Iowas in 1838: "There I talked with our former disciple Francis, called White Cloud, who since his father was killed has become Chief of the Nation." As quoted in Chittenden and Richardson, *Life, Letters and Travels of Father De Smet*, I, 152.

Governor David Meriwether During His Administration as Governor of New Mexico Territory, 1853–57.

Courtesy Museum of New Mexico

San Francisco Street in Santa Fe, 1862 (looking eastward).
Note the covered wagons and cathedral in background.

U.S. Army Signal Corps

leading my horse, then followed the pack animals, following in our footsteps and driven by the soldiers. We did not follow the meanders of the Missouri River, but kept near the upland, thereby cutting off bends of the river. But we had to go to the river each night to procure water for both ourselves and the animals, as all the small streams were frozen to the bottom. We found it laborious work to cut the ice, which was from two to three feet thick on the river, and then pass up water in the camp kettles for the animals to drink.

We usually camped between two and three o'clock in the afternoon, when we had to use our shovels to scrape away the snow for a space of ten or fifteen feet square, wherein to build our fires. Immediately on selecting a place for our camp, two men were set to work to clear the snow away, and two others to procure fuel wherewith to build a fire. As soon as a space of a few feet square was cleared, White Cloud or myself would strike fire with a flint and steel and some punk we had taken with us for the purpose and soon had a fire started with dry pea-vine, which hung upon the bushes, and small dry twigs. Then he and I would start out hunting, one going up the valley of the river and the other down, the Corporal and his party being left to finish clearing away the snow, making a good fire, and watering the animals. White Cloud and myself rarely ever returned to camp without a deer, and it was astonishing how much meat we could eat when we had neither bread or vegetables. Indeed it required a large deer to supply our supper and our breakfast next morning; while others would broil some on the coals, usually by sunset or a little after we had a pot of soup and broiled meat for our supper.

The horses were turned out immediately after camp was formed to browse upon the wild pea vine, which hung on the bushes, and they also ate the rushes which grew in the river bottom. Then we cut down one or two green trees with an axe which we had with us to cut our fuel, and shaved the bark off the trees with a drawing knife brought for the purpose. This bark we fed to the horses, and they were very fond of it. As these horses had been accustomed to camping with their former owners, they never strayed far from camp. After supper was over, we employed ourselves in drying and rubbing our moccasins to keep them soft, until bedtime, when it was arranged that we take alternate watches during the night. One man would sit up a few hours, then waking the other; then the second man would sit up, and so on, we keeping this up during the entire night. Each man when on watch had to keep the camp kettle boiling so as to have our meat cooked for breakfast at daybreak. When the water became low in the kettle it was replenished by a supply from the mess pan, which had been brought from the river in the evening. After eating our breakfast, we commenced packing up, and started again by sunrise, never stopping our march until camping time the next evening; so we ate only morning and night. The night after we left the mouth of the Platte River, on returning from my hunt, I was informed by the Corporal that one of the soldiers, named Neishman, had refused to do duty. I asked him if he had tried to use persuasion. He said, "Yes, but to no purpose. The man obstinately refused to assist in any way." I then tried my eloquence upon him, but to no purpose. I then stepped into the bushes and cut a good cudgel. On coming back, I found the man seated before the fire, and, upon coming up behind him, I struck him on the side of the head and knocked him down, whereupon I applied my stick to his posterior vigorously until he begged for quarter. I then told him to start the next morning on his return to the cantonment, which he could easily do by following our trail, and to tell Captain Riley, to whose company he belonged, that if he couldn't supply me with a better man, I didn't want any. So he went to work cooking some provisions for his return trip. The next morning we departed, leaving this man sitting by the fire. When we had gotten a hundred yards distant, he hailed me, requesting me to stop; and, on coming up, he said he desired to go on with us, but he was told that he was not wanted. He then said that he knew if he went back with my message to Captain Riley, he would catch hell, but if I would let him go on with us, he would be one of the best men in the party. He was allowed to remain and was as good as his word, for we had no better man than he during our trip.

In about ten days, I think, we reached Martin Cantonment,[7] and we commenced forming an encampment a hundred yards or so from that post, whereupon an officer seeing us, came out to know who we were and what we wanted. Being told, he kindly offered me a room in the barracks for myself. I told him that we had become accustomed to sleeping in the open air, and that I thought that we had better continue to do so. He then invited me to come in and eat my meals with him and his men, which proposition was assented to.

That evening we visited the steamboat expedition which was moored to the bank of the river, a short distance below the cantonment.[8] Here I found Captain Silas Craig, a Kentuckian, whom I had known in Kentucky. He received me very cordially and invited me to live on board whilst I stayed there. For the reasons given, I declined his hospitality.

The next morning after arriving, I presented a requisition from the surgeon at Council Bluffs upon whoever might be in charge of the medicine and hospital stores at Martin Cantonment, for the different kinds of medicines desired. I found a hospital steward in charge of these medicines, which had been taken from the boat and placed in a storeroom in the cantonment for

[7] Martin Cantonment was approximately two hundred and seventy miles from Council Bluffs and eighty miles above Fort Osage.

[8] The steamboat expedition wintered at Martin Cantonment, having abandoned the idea of progressing farther. *Missouri Gazette,* October 27, 1819, quoted in *Publications* of the Nebraska State Historical Society, Vol. XX (1922), 30.

the fear the boat might be destroyed by ice. This hospital steward was set immediately to work selecting and packing up articles specified in the requisition brought by me. Captain Craig having informed me that he had a considerable amount of freight, consisting of sugar, coffee, tea, etc., consigned to our trading house at Council Bluffs, I desired him to let me have a barrel of sugar and a sack of coffee to take with me for our return consumption. To this he readily assented, upon my giving him a receipt for it. My men became dissatisfied because permission was not given them to take up their quarters in the cantonment after my requesting the officers in command not to let them remain in the cantonment after tattoo at night. During our encampment here, White Cloud was employed in seeing that our animals did not stray off, whilst the other men assisted in packing up the articles to be taken back, in sacks brought for that purpose. The barrel of sugar and the coffee were packed in sacks of suitable weight for transportation on the pack horses.

I found at Martin Cantonment a young officer of the Sixth Infantry named [Andrew O.] Waterhouse, whose company he had never joined, and, this company being at Council Bluffs, he was ordered to accompany me, which I had cause to regret during our whole trip. I found him to be a vain weak man, who had never camped out in his life before, he having been raised in Massachusetts, I think in Boston, and he attached great importance to his being an officer in the United States Army. Having procured a horse, saddle, and bridle, some blankets, etc., with a cloth sack in which his wardrobe was packed, he reported himself as ready for departure. I told him that we would leave the next morning and that he had better have some provisions cooked, which he could carry in a beaver sack, to which he would resort if we failed to kill game at any time.

That night White Cloud informed me that he thought we had better go up the eastern side of the river, as there was less danger of meeting with any Otoes, and that the traveling might be better. So, the next morning, Waterhouse having reported himself at our camp, we packed up our cargo, crossed the river, and proceeded on our return. When we camped that night, Lieutenant Waterhouse directed the Corporal to have his horse well fed, curried, and blanketed. The Corporal informed him he had no corn, or anything to feed him with, nor any curry comb or blanket. This made Waterhouse rather irritated. I then interfered and told him that on a trip of this kind, each man must provide for himself. As we had brought a little provisions with us from Martin Cantonment, none of us went hunting as usual; and, on Waterhouse producing the provisions he had brought, I found they consisted of three frozen biscuits and a small piece of cooked meat. I thought this a scant supply for a trip of at least two hundred and fifty miles by land. I divided my provisions with him that night and the next morning, when he said he expected to find provisions on the road. He frequently assumed command of the Corporal and his men. When I directed them to do one thing, he would countermand the order and direct something else, which induced me to beg of him not to interfere with my men. He responded, "I am an officer in the United States Army, and these men are soldiers, and I have a right to command them." I told him that these men were detailed for extra duty and he had no right to interfere with them.

A few evenings after this, before our usual hour of encampment, we came to a spring running from the bluff, and, looking across the frozen pond, I discovered a gang of elks standing under a bank, which protected them from the wind, and where the sun could shine on them. They were only a few hundred yards from us, and I determined to camp and try and kill one, and we could procure water from the spring which was not frozen. After starting a fire, White Cloud and I started in different directions to try our luck in killing elk. I made a detour in one direction and he in another. Before leaving, I directed the Corporal to continue preparing the camp, and, if I fired twice in quick succession, it would be a signal that I had killed one, and to send two men to help bring the meat into camp. I soon shot one down, and as the others ran in the direction of White Cloud, he followed after them. Then I immediately loaded my gun again and fired a signal shot. As the elk was not entirely dead, I cut its throat, by which operation I got my hands covered with blood, which soon froze, rendering my hands practically useless. I kept looking in the direction of camp, but could see no person coming to carry in the meat. I therefore hastened to the campfire, where I found it had burned down very low, and Waterhouse and each of the men were standing behind a tree.

On asking the Corporal why he had not sent for the meat, he said that the Lieutenant had said that White Cloud and myself had been attacked by the Indians, and he ordered each man to get his gun and get behind a tree to defend himself. On this I lost my temper and told the Lieutenant that if he interfered with my men again, I would shoot him down like a dog, and for very little I would have done so then. I then started two men to bring in two hams of the elk, and the others to get wood and replenish the fire. My hands and feet were so cold when I arrived at camp, that, on pulling off my moccasins, I found my feet so hard frozen that I could not indent them with my thumb. But White Cloud having arrived, he got a few shovels of snow, and throwing it down not far from the fire, he advised me to tramp in the snow with my bare feet and to rub my hands with snow. This I did for some time, and the process relieved me from the effects of the frost.

This was the coldest night of our trip, for on arriving at Council Bluffs, where a register of the weather was kept, I found that the thermometer had stood at 32 degrees below zero. . . .

When the men arrived with the meat, I directed them to

put some in the camp kettle and set it boiling, while I broiled some on the coals. Then Waterhouse directed one of the men to broil him some, which so irritated me that I drew my pistol and threatened to blow his brains out and told him that if he wanted any of the meat, to cook it himself. This alarmed him, and I afterwards heard him ask the Corporal if he thought I would kill him. The Corporal said, "Certainly, he is just the man to do it if you interfere with his arrangements again."

On arriving at the mouth of a small river emptying into the Missouri River, I found that Captain Martin had taken a portion of the sick soldiers in sleighs and with his company had transported the sick men and formed a camp, thinking this might relieve them, as they could get plenty of fresh meat there. We camped there that night and were invited to eat supper with him. In going into his hut for that purpose, we found a large raccoon roasting for our supper. Waterhouse protested that he couldn't eat raccoon, when Captain Martin told him he could go without it or eat it, just as he pleased, whereupon this delicate individual ate the coon. The next morning, Captain Martin advised me that by passing over the point of a hill some five or six miles distant we could save a distance of eight or ten miles, but that we must be very cautious as the hillside would be slippery and we might fall over a precipice of over fifty or one hundred feet. He sent a man with us to pilot us on our way. On leaving the Captain's camp, Waterhouse asked, if he should fall over this precipice and be killed, whether we would give his body a decent burial. The Captain responded in the negative. Waterhouse then asked what he would do with the body, in the event of losing his life. The Captain responded that he would have it cut up and bait his wolf traps with it, as that was the only purpose that such a damn fool's body was fit for.

A few days before we arrived at our journey's end, White Cloud started as usual on a hunt but did not return till after dark.

When asked what had detained him so long (by this time I had picked up a good deal of his language, and he some of mine) he told me that some Otoes were camped nearby. I asked him if he had seen any of them. He said that he had not but that he had seen their tracks in the snow; and, as every tribe of Indians made their moccasins in a different manner, he knew from their tracks that they were Otoes. He then asked me if I thought I could find my way home without guidance. I told him yes and asked why he proposed to leave us. I told him that I expected him to accompany me to Council Bluffs, and there to receive his pay. He said, "These Otoes have some horses, and I intend to find their camp tonight and steal some of them, and, if you find me gone in the morning, proceed without me, for you can know what I am about." I tried to dissuade him from this, but when I awoke in the morning, I found he was not in camp, so we packed up and started without him. About the time of our starting, it began to snow heavily. Shortly after getting out of the timberland on to the prairie, I heard a yelling and hallooing behind us, which caused us to halt. Then three Otoe Indians rode up and said a part of their horses were gone, and they had followed our trail, thinking it was the trail of their own horses. This I understood from their signs and a few words of their language which I had picked up, and I very well knew what had become of their horses. The three Indians then turned back, and we proceeded on our journey.

On reaching the bank of the Missouri River, I fired off my gun as a signal of my arrival. An old six-pounder was brought out of the cantonment, and I was given a salute—the first I ever received in my life.

We crossed the river on the ice opposite the cantonment, as the bank at that point had been graded for the purpose of permitting the garrison to haul water in barrels placed on sleds, for its use. On reaching the opposite bank, I was met by several officers. Delivering to them the hospital supplies which I had brought up, I proceeded with my pack horses, together with White Cloud's horse, which we had used as a pack horse also, down to our trading house, where all was well, except one of the clerks named Potts, who was infected with scurvy. We had several clerks, one named Rainey, one named Rodgers, and one Peter Carr, who was a whole-souled energetic man.

This trip [had] occupied us twenty-seven days, during which time the mercury was never above zero. That night I slept in a house for the first time in nearly a month, during which time I never changed my clothes, with the exception of the socks on my feet. Some time after midnight I awoke suffering with pains in my bones and a sense of suffocation in my lungs. I awakened a Negro boy named Alfred,[9] who slept in the room with me, and directed him to make a good fire and open the door to let fresh air in. When this was done, I got up and dressed myself and walked about a while, when my pains ceased, and, fresh air having come into the room, the sense of suffocation went away. I then went to bed again and slept soundly until morning.

[The following paragraphs were probably dictated after the narration of the hazardous trip to Martin Cantonment was written, for they were not included in the body of the original manuscript.]

On our trip to Martin Cantonment the aurora borealis often made a very brilliant appearance, and one evening I discovered a phenomenon which I have never seen before or since, and the cause of which has never been satisfactorily explained to me. When the sun was about an hour and a half in the west, and the moon about the same height above the horizon in the east, I observed two other suns, one on each side of the true sun; and on

[9] This colored boy followed Meriwether's fortunes during the Yellowstone Expedition, his adventures with the Pawnees, and his imprisonment at Santa Fe in 1820.

looking at the moon in the east, I discovered two other moons also, one placed on each side of the true moon, and these false suns and moons added so much to the brilliancy of the light that we had to shade our eyes with our hands to enable us to see what we were about.

On asking White Cloud if he had ever seen such a sight before, he said, "Yes, several times." I then asked him what it indicated. He said, "After a while the false suns and moons will fade away, and if the ones on the north side of the sun and moon should disappear first, we will have warmer weather." (He did not use the words "north" and "south," for he did not know the meaning of such terms, but indicated the direction by pointing with his hand.) He also said, "If the southern suns and moons disappear first, the weather will be still colder." This induced me to watch them closely. Just before the setting of the sun, the northern imitation beside the sun gradually faded away before the one on the southern side; and looking at the moon, I found that the northern imitation of the luminary was gone, and as White Cloud predicted, the next day we found the weather decidedly milder.

V
Indian Trader

After breakfast this morning, Captain Bissell proposed that, as a number of ladies and some children were in the cantonment (the wives and children of the officers of the Sixth Regiment, who had come up with their husbands and fathers the fall before), and they were destitute of both sugar and coffee and all such things which I had brought up from Martin Cantonment and which had been taken into the hospital for the use of the sick, we should send each lady a supply of both sugar and coffee from our stores, which was done that day. During the day, these ladies and the husbands of others came down to thank us for the presents received by them.

I found that Colonel Morgan had become deranged at seeing the distress of his men; shortly after I had left for Martin Cantonment, he was taken down to the Engineer Cantonment to see if that would not relieve the pressure on his mind, and Captain [Andrew J.] Magee of the rifle regiment was in command. Major [Daniel] Ketchum, another superior officer was also on the sick list.

The next morning a sergeant belonging to Captain Magee's company came to our house and told me that the Captain was in a great rage against me and that he, the sergeant, had been sent to order me up to the Captain's quarters. I told the sergeant to tell Captain Magee that I was very stiff and sore from my journey, and that if he desired to see me, to come to our house. Presently the sergeant returned with more men and orders to arrest me and bring me to the cantonment, and there being no alternative, I had to go. Captain Bissell appeared much irritated at this but advised me to submit quietly and said he would attend to my case for me. I then accompanied the sergeant to Captain Magee's quarters and found him in a furious rage. He cursed me and asked why we had disposed of sugar and coffee to the officers' wives and children. I told him that it was our private property and we had a right to dispose of it as we pleased. This appeared to irritate him still more, and he ordered the sergeant to take me to the guard house and place me under guard.

Here I was placed in a room without a fire, where I remained for some time. Becoming very cold, I asked the sergeant of the guard if he would send a man down to our house to procure some blankets for me to sleep on, for I expected to remain all night. This he refused to do. I told him I would go myself at the risk of my life, but I could not get out of the house without passing through the room occupied by the guard, where I could see was a good fire. I asked him to allow me to warm myself by his fire, whereupon a sentinel was placed at the door leading from my room into his, with orders to shoot me if I attempted to pass.

This created considerable hub-bub among the guards, and one of them slipped out and went into the room occupied by the officer of the guard and soon returned with orders from the officer to bring me into his room. On arriving at his room, I found that Lieutenant [William D.] McCray was officer of the guard. He received me kindly, invited me to take a seat by the fire and asked me how long I had been under guard, and said he did not know that I had been placed in the guard house or I should have been brought into his room sooner, and also invited me to eat supper with him, which was brought into the guard house. Soon after, Lieutenant Pentland, the adjutant of the regiment, came in and informed us that Colonel Morgan's mind having become rational, he had returned late that evening and again assumed command of the post. He also told the officer of the guard that he had orders to have me released and to conduct me to Colonel Morgan's quarters. On my arriving there, the Colonel asked me why I was placed in the guard house. I told him that I did not know, unless it was because we had given the ladies some sugar and coffee. He told me I was released, and to return to our trading house, which I did very quickly.

When I arrived at the house, Captain Bissell informed me that he had seen Colonel Morgan and a number of other officers in my behalf, and they all expressed great indignation against Magee for his tyrannical conduct, particularly the husbands of the ladies who had received the sugar and coffee. He then told me to go to bed and think no more of the indignity, for justice would be promptly done me.

On the next day, a number of officers in the cantonment came to the trading house and expressed much regret at the trouble and indignation against Magee for his conduct, which soothed my feelings. Through these officers I learned that Captain Magee intended to prefer charges and have me tried by court-martial. A few days after this, Lieutenant Pentland, adjutant of the regiment, informed me that charges had been filed with Colonel Morgan, who had appointed a board of officers to investigate the matter; and, handing me a copy of these charges, he asked when I would be ready for trial. I told him, "At any moment, and the court can meet whenever it suits them." That evening the Adjutant called again and said the court would convene the following day at ten o'clock in Major Ketchum's room. The next morning I went there accompanied by Captain Bissell and found the court was composed of Major Ketchum and Major [William Sewell] Foster, of the Sixth Regiment, and Captain Riley, of the Riflemen, with Lieutenant Shaler as judge advocate. I was then asked if I objected to any member of the court, and I replied in the negative but demurred to the jurisdiction of the court, as I did not belong to the military, and I denied the right of a military court to try me, but, as it might be inferred that from such a course I was afraid of an investigation of my conduct, I would waive this demurrer and consent to an investigation. The members of the court were then sworn and the charges against me read, the principal one of which was that I had converted public property to my own use. The judge advocate introduced Neishman (I had flogged him on our trip to Martin Cantonment) as the first evidence against me. He testified that I had taken a barrel of sugar and a sack of coffee out of the public storehouse at Martin Cantonment and brought them to our trading house on three pack mules. I was then asked if I desired to ask this man any questions, whereupon I inquired if he knew this sack of coffee and barrel of sugar were public property, to which he replied [that] they were taken from the public storehouse where other public property was stored. I then asked him if these articles were not marked with the name of the company that employed me. To this he replied that he saw the marks upon them but did not read them. The next question was, "Did you not see me give a receipt to Captain Craig who commanded the Steamboat Expedition?" His reply was, "Captain Craig was present, but I saw no receipt given." Here the judge advocate rested his case, and I was asked if I desired to introduce any witnesses. I said, "Yes, I desire Corporal Roderick and the other three soldiers who accompanied me to Martin Cantonment to be called," and an orderly was dispatched for them.

Corporal Roderick, having been sworn, stated that this barrel of sugar and sack of coffee was marked with the name of the firm who employed me, and that he saw Captain Craig deliver to me the same and take my receipt upon the back of the bill of lading, all of which was corroborated by the other three soldiers. He also stated that I had carried them in the sacks on my own two horses, and the horse owned by the guide, White Cloud, and had brought them up to Council Bluffs; also, that upon my arrival, I had turned the pack horses belonging to the government over to the proper officials, but the three bearing the sugar and coffee were taken to our trading house. I then had Captain Bissell sworn, who testified that he was the head manager of the firm at Council Bluffs and that this sugar and coffee was turned over to him. Here I stated that I was through. Then the courtroom was cleared of all persons except the members of the court, who remained for deliberation.

I was taken charge of by an orderly who was directed to take me to Captain Riley's room. In a short time, I was called back to the courtroom and informed that I had been honorably acquitted by a unanimous vote of the court and that the finding of the court would be presented to Colonel Morgan for his approval, and that I could return to my quarters.

This result gave me great gratification. During the evening of that day, Lieutenant Pentland came to see me and told me the Colonel had approved of the finding of the court and would issue a general order to that effect. That night our house was crowded with officers who had called to congratulate me on the result of the trial. Captain Bissell took several of the officers into his private room to hold consultation. After this was over, he came into my room and said it was the unanimous opinion of my friends that I should address a letter to Colonel Morgan, requesting him to have Captain Magee arrested and tried for ursurpation of power in having me arrested and placed in the guard house without authority of the law.

So, next morning, Captain Bissell and myself concocted the following letter:

Lieutenant Col. Willoughby Morgan:
1st Rifle Regiment.
Commanding Cantonment, Missouri
Sir:

I regret extremely to inform you that great injustice has

> been done me by Captain Magee, commanding company "B" of your regiment, and I regret also that I was compelled to apply to you for justice, but I am happy in having you to make my application to. As you are aware, Captain Magee had me placed in the guard house without any investigation, filed charges against me which have not been sustained, and having been honorably acquitted by a court of inquiry organized by yourself, and you having approved of the findings of that court, I therefore request of you to have the said Captain Magee arrested and brought before a court-martial for trial, I pledging myself to place before said court and sustain charges and specifications sufficient to convict him of usurpation in office.

This letter was handed to Colonel Morgan by Captain Bissell the next morning. After reading it, he told Captain Bissell that he was sorry he could not comply with my wishes as his command was so reduced by sickness that he could not spare the services of a single officer. Captain Magee was the only officer of his company fit for duty, and if [Colonel Morgan] caused him to be arrested, there would not be a sufficient number of officers of the proper grade at this post to compose a court for trial. Therefore, he desired me to withdraw my letter until spring, when other officers of a higher rank who were absent on furlough would report for duty and a court could be organized. This proposition Captain Bissell assented to on my behalf.

After this another conversation was held by my friends, which resulted in an opinion that I should immediately challenge the Captain to fight a duel, whereupon a challenge was written and presented to Captain Magee by Captain Bissell as my pledge. He said, "I will respond next morning," at which time Lieutenant Pentland informed me that as I was but a boy, and Captain Magee a man of middle age and accustomed to the smell of gunpowder, Captain Magee declined to meet me. At

Water Color, by Karl Bodmer, Showing the Ruins of the Army Post (Fort Atkinson) at Council Bluffs.

Courtesy Joslyn Art Museum, Omaha

Western Landscape, a Painting by Samuel Seymour, Artist
and Sketcher of the Stephen H. Long Expedition
of 1819–20, Which Meriwether Accompanied as Sutler.

Courtesy Joslyn Art Museum, Omaha

this Captain Bissell arose from his seat and told the Lieutenant that he himself was a man about the age of Captain Magee and was also accustomed to the smell of gunpowder, and he would stand in the boy's place, "And you tell 'Capy' Magee that he must fight me."

This gave me great pain, and when Lieutenant Pentland departed, I said to Captain Bissell, "I will never consent to your fighting my quarrel." He said it would not result that way, as he thought that message would bring the Captain to his milk. That night Lieutenant Pentland called again and asked if an apology from the Captain to Meriwether would be satisfactory, to which Captain Bissell replied, "If a sufficient apology is made and in a proper manner, it will be satisfactory." Lieutenant [Pentland] called next morning, bearing a note addressed to me by Captain Magee, saying that he had no doubt done me an injustice and was sorry for it. After reading it, I handed the note to Captain Bissell, who also read it and remarked to the Lieutenant, "The insult was of a public character, and nothing but a public apology will be satisfactory," whereupon the Lieutenant invited Captain Bissell to go with him to visit Captain Magee. On Bissell's return he told me he had brought Magee to his "milk," as he had predicted, and that it had been arranged for Captain Magee to give a little party that night at his quarters to which both of us had invitations, also that it was arranged for a number of officers to be present, and Captain Magee would there make a public apology in the presence of the whole company. This was truly gratifying to me, as I disapproved of dueling, and, having witnessed several duels while with the military, my abhorrence of it was not lessened.

So that night Captain Bissell and myself proceeded to Captain Magee's quarters. On knocking at the door, it was opened by Magee himself, and Captain Bissell stepped in, followed by me. The room was filled with officers of the army. Magee said in a loud voice that he had done me a great injustice, which he regretted extremely, and for which he desired to make most ample apology, and extending his hand to me, he said, "Here is my hand as an evidence of my extreme regret for what I have done and said to you." We shook hands, and the matter ended. After remaining awhile in conversation with the officers, Captain Bissell and myself returned to our quarters, I feeling a great relief and pleasure at the amicable result of this difficulty.

On my return from Martin Cantonment, I found the soldiers in a pitiable condition, scarcely enough well men to take care of the sick, and many had died. But on the disappearance of the snow in the spring, large quantities of wild onions were found and also a root, called by the French *pomme de terre*, or ground apple. These had been covered by leaves and grass, which being mashed down by the snow had protected them from the frost. This vegetable was a singular plant to me and was a species of sweet potato or yam. Each was about the size of a hen's egg or a little larger, and one was attached to the next one by a small ligament about an inch long, and some strings were two or three feet in length. They were not unpleasant to eat raw and when cooked resembled in taste the sweet potato. With the discovery of these vegetables, detachments of invalid soldiers were sent out to gather them, and great quantities were brought in to be eaten, both raw and cooked. This together with the weather becoming warmer, so that the soldiers could sleep with their doors and windows open, also walk about in the fresh air, soon caused comparative health to be restored. On entering the cantonment in the fall before, I think there were between six hundred and seven hundred soldiers. Between two and three hundred had died during the winter.

When Mr. Jefferson was inaugurated President of the United States he appointed Meriwether Lewis, a distant relative of ours,[1] his private secretary, and, having purchased Louisiana, of which Missouri was then a part, and having to appoint a commissioner to receive possession from the French government, his private secretary was chosen for the office, and Lieutenant Clark was appointed to command his military escort. They proceeded to St. Louis and, procuring two small keelboats,[2] went up the river with orders to cross the Rocky Mountains and take possession of the purchased territory on the Pacific Coast.

This trip required three years to make. On reaching Council Bluffs, Lewis and Clark assembled all the Indians in that vicinity and held a council with them, after which the place always bore the name of Council Bluffs. They then proceeded as high up the Missouri River as they could get before the ice commenced running and there formed a camp for the winter.

The next spring they proceeded to the foot of the Rocky Mountains, where they placed rocks in their boats and sunk them, then marched across the mountains to the headwaters of the Columbia River, descending which, they arrived on the Pacific Coast, where they spent the second winter. Retracing their steps the next spring, they raised their boats and descended to St. Louis. About this time, a territorial government having been established for Missouri, Meriwether Lewis was appointed to the office of governor, which he held until his death, when Clark succeeded him in the office of governor, which he held until Missouri was admitted into the Union as a state.

[1] Colonel Robert Lewis married Jane Meriwether. A son of this union was Colonel William Lewis, who married Lucy Meriwether; they were the parents of Meriwether Lewis, all being descendants of Nicholas Meriwether, of Wales, who died in Westmoreland County Virginia, on December 19, 1678. Minor, *The Meriwethers and Their Connections*, 108–39.

[2] Instead of the two keelboats that Meriwether mentions, there was one keelboat, fifty-five feet long, drawing three feet of water and propelled by oars, sail, and two open boats or "periogues" with six or seven oars to each. See Elliott Coues, ed., *The Journals of Lewis and Clark*.

I derived these facts from a very interesting account of their travels[3] published after their return, which I read in my boyhood; and also from my interpreter, who was the same employed by Lewis and Clark on their expedition. This interpreter was named Chavano [Charbonneau],[4] and though he was an old man when I first saw him, I derived much assistance from his council when I first embarked in the fur trade, as he spoke the language, I believe, of every Indian tribe on the Missouri from the Rocky Mountains to its mouth. He derived a knowledge of these languages from being engaged by the Indian traders, such as Chouteau, Manuel Lisa, and others, while Missouri was owned by Spain and France. In the spring of 1819 [actually 1820],[5] I was directed to place some Indian goods on a pack

[3] The Biddle edition, written by Nicholas Biddle and edited by Paul Allen, published in New York in 1814.

[4] Toussaint Charbonneau was a French-Canadian by birth whom Lewis and Clark found at Fort Mandan at the present Bismarck, North Dakota. He was living at Metaharta, the middle village of the grosventre or Minnetarees on Knife River. He was a well-known character of the Upper Missouri for many years and is mentioned by many travelers of that period, particularly Maximilian. From available sources it appears he was an employee of the North-West Fur Company as early as 1793, and later acted as interpreter for Sublette and Campbell.

His name has been spelled with a number of variations. Maximilian spells it "Charbonneau," others, "Tonsart Chadbono," while Meriwether calls him Chavono. F. F. Gerard, an old interpreter who resided at Fort Berthold, is inclined to believe he died in the smallpox epidemic of 1837. However, Larpenteur saw him in 1838: "To our surprise and joy we found that it was old Mr. Charbonneau, who had been 40 years among the Missouri Indians. He used to say that when he first came on the river it was so small that he could straddle it." Wheeler in his *The Trail of Lewis and Clark*, says, " 'Tonsart Chabono,' undoubtedly the Lewis-and-Clark Charboneau was made interpreter at the U.S. Mo. Sub-Agency, July 1st, 1837, at a salary of $300.00." To the present generation Charbonneau is better known as the husbands of Sacajawea, "The Bird Woman." See Olin D. Wheeler, *The Trail of Lewis and Clark, 1804–1809*, I, 133–34; and Charles Larpenteur, *Forty Years a Fur Trader*, I, 141.

[5] In the original manuscript written in longhand by Meriwether's granddaughter from his dictation the date is given as 1819. This is in error, probably in the writing; it hardly seems possible that Meriwether would confuse the year, as he is consistently most accurate throughout the narrative. It is easily ascertained that the correct year is 1820. He went up the Missouri with the Yellowstone Expedition in 1819; the scurvy epidemic was the winter of 1819–20; he made the trip to

horse and proceed to the Pawnee Villages, probably about one hundred miles west of Council Bluffs, for the purpose of opening a trade with them.

On my arrival there, I found that the Pawnees had occasionally made visits to the frontier settlements of New Mexico for the purpose of stealing horses from the Mexicans,[6] and I found that a party of Indians on such an errand the summer before had captured an old Mexican and his son, whom they found a long distance East of these settlements, prospecting for gold. The boy was probably about ten years of age and a bright sprightly little fellow, but the man was old and morose. The boy had acquired some knowledge of the Pawnee language, and from him I learned through my interpreter that his father and himself had belonged to a large party of Mexicans who had come eastward for the purpose of hunting and looking for gold.[7] One day the old man and his son had gone some distance from the camp of the main party and were captured by the Pawnees, and that night the Pawnees succeeded in stealing most of the Mexican horses and started home.

He said he had found a little gold dust on one stream, which his father had in his pocket. On my desiring to see it, the old man produced the quill of a large bird, in which the gold was concealed, and I induced him to give me a little of it. These Mexicans were not kept in close confinement, as it was thought impossible for them to escape. The old man was made to assist in

Martin Cantonment in January and February of 1820; and he speaks of the recovery of the troops in the spring. The troops were not at Missouri Cantonment in the spring of 1819; they did not arrive until the fall of that year.

[6] "The white settlers of New Mexico became familiar with the Pawnee early in the 17th century through the latters' raids for procuring horses, and for more than two centuries the Spanish authorities of that territory sought to bring about peaceful relations with them, with only partial success."—Frederick Webb Hodge, ed., *Handbook of American Indians North of Mexico*, II, 214.

[7] Natives of the present New Mexico for generations made their annual fall hunt for buffalo to the eastward into the Llano Estacado. Tascosa in Oldham County, Texas, was a favorite gathering place.

getting wood and tanning skins, and the boy in herding the horses with the Indian boys. The old man, however, did escape, leaving the boy, and I never heard of [the man] afterwards.

One day this boy came to me crying and said that one of the Indian boys had become angry with him and had told him that when the men of the tribe returned from a buffalo hunt they were on, they intended to burn him at a stake. I directed my interpreter to inquire and see if such was the case, and I assured the boy that it should not be done. A few days after this my interpreter told me that he could not learn much about the matter, but from the conduct of the Indians he thought it very possible that it was true, whereupon I consulted with the agents of other trading houses who were present and proposed that we should buy the boy. I was selected to negotiate the trade. So, assembling the party that had captured the Mexicans, I told them that I had become much attached to this boy and desired to buy him. At first they appeared reluctant, but finally stipulated a price, which was to be paid in goods (as the Indians did not know the value of money), and would amount to from four hundred to five hundred dollars, which I declined giving. A short time after this, they desired me to make them an offer for the boy, when I offered them a certain number of steel traps, plugs of tobacco, blankets, etc. The cost of [these goods] would be about one hundred and forty dollars. Then the man who was at the head of the party who had made the capture said that both he and his wife had become attached to the boy, but if I could add to my bid a looking glass for each of them, a certain number of strings of glass beads, a few strings of wampum, and a few papers of vermillion with which they could paint themselves, I might have the boy. This raised the price to about one hundred and fifty dollars, and I agreeing to their proposition, the next day was appointed for the exchange.

That night the agents for the other trading houses were sent for, and all agreed to the bargain I had made, and each brought forth his proportion of the purchase, which, as there were three of us, amounted to about fifty dollars each. It was then agreed, that as Manuel Lisa was the only Spaniard among the traders, the boy should be transferred to his custody, and he was hurried off to Lisa's trading post as soon as possible, for fear the Indians might want to take him back again.[8]

Shortly after making this trade and having exchanged all my goods for furs, I packed the furs on the horses and returned to Council Bluffs, where I found that Colonel O'Fallon had arrived on a steamboat while I was absent. I exhibited to him the few grains of gold which the old Mexican had given me and told him that I had learned from the Indians that there was a good country from the Missouri to the Mexican settlements for a road, for there were no high mountains to cross as we had supposed; and, the Mexican having given me very exaggerated accounts of the gold and silver found in his country, I suggested that an exploring party be sent over to ascertain the practicability of a route for wagons and the amount of gold and silver in New Mexico. This he said he would take under consideration.

[8] An item appeared in the *Missouri Gazette* pertaining to a Mexican boy ransomed from the Pawnees at about this time: "The Pawnee were also at war with Spaniards of Santa Fe, and lately defeated a hunting party of them within United States territory, killing seven. They found a Spanish boy of ten years concealed in Spanish baggage and kept him to offer as a sacrifice 'to the Great Star,' as they declared. The boy has been recently purchased by Mr. Lisa from the Pawnee priests and providentially saved from the fire."—*Missouri Gazette*, n.d., quoted in *Publications* of the Nebraska Historical Society, Vol. XX, 14. Edwin James also mentions the ritual of the sacrifice to the Great Star and the Spanish boy in question: "A fine Spanish boy, vowed to sacrifice him to the Great Star, and accordingly placed him under care of the magi, for that purpose."—James, *Account of an Expedition, XV*, 151. He states further that Mr. Pappan who was in the village contributed a quantity of goods for the release of the boy.

VI
Prisoner in Santa Fe

A FEW DAYS after [my suggestion about the New Mexico trip], Captain Bissell called me into his room and asked me if I would undertake such a trip. To this I replied that the Indians were talking of making another raid into Mexican settlements that summer, and if the company would furnish me with suitable outfit and let me have a Negro boy that some times acted as our cook, I would agree to make the trip with this party of Indians, and that arriving at the Mexican settlements would separate myself from the Indians and go to Santa Fe.[1] On consultation, Colonel O'Fallon and Captain Bissell agreed to my terms, and procuring two good horses, one for Alfred [the Negro boy] and one for myself, and a mule to pack our baggage, I again started for the Pawnee villages. I took with me a few trinkets, such as tobacco and little articles, to make presents to the Indians I might encounter. We also took a few cooking utensils, our guns, my pistols, and plenty of ammunition.

On our arrival at the Indian villages, I told the Indians what I proposed to do, which pleased them greatly, and they said they would make up a party and start before very long. I think it was about the latter part of June when a party of seventeen

[1] Meriwether's attempt to break the Spanish barrier against outside contact came one year too soon. Mexico was then in the process of achieving independence, and the new government welcomed American traders. In 1821 William Becknell on a trading expedition to the Indians wandered over the border. He encountered a troop of Mexican soldiers, who instead of arresting him invited him to take his goods to Sana Fe. When he returned to Missouri with the report of his profits, other trading expeditions followed. This was the beginning of the famous Santa Fé Trail. See Warren A. Beck, *New Mexico: A History of Four Centuries*, 109–19.

Indians, commanded by one of their chiefs, who had captured the Mexican before mentioned, and whose English name was Big Elk,[2] myself, and Alfred started on our perilous trip. We traveled in a southeasterly[3] direction over a country which the Indians appeared familiar with, until we reached the Arkansas River. During this time we saw immense herds of buffalo, antelope, some elk, a few deer, and often large droves of wild horses. We ascended the valley of the Arkansas River for about a week when we forded the stream, which was very wide but shallow, and very soon came into sandy, arid country, where game appeared less numerous.

Finally the Indians said, as game was getting scarce, we had better camp and kill some and jerk it for our supply on our return trip. We went up into a hollow between the hills where there was some timber and encamped and, with tomahawks, cut some forked sticks and drove them into the ground, forming two parallel rows about three feet apart and probably twenty or thirty feet long. In the forks of these sticks, we placed some small poles lengthwise of the rows; the Indians cut some straight, slender willow branches, and then descended into the plains and killed several buffalo which they cut in steaks and brought

[2] Big Elk was a sub-chief of the Pawnees. He is not to be confused with the Omaha chief also named Big Elk whose portrait appears in M'Kenny & Hall [folio] (Philadelphia, 1836).

[3] This was probably an error in transcription. Their direction was southwest, most likely striking the Arkansas in the vicinity of Chouteau Island, a well-known point on the river, deriving its name from the battle fought there in the spring of 1816 between the Chouteau–De Munn Expedition and a large war party of Pawnees. A crossing later established at this location and known as the "Upper Ford" of the Arkansas, was in general use until about 1820. Meriwether mentions their traveling up the valley about a week before entering the foothills where there was some timber. Indians traveling unencumbered with families and the usual equipage would average approximately thirty miles a day; thus it would appear that they struck the Arkansas about two hundred miles below the foothills.

Incidentally, the Chouteau–De Munn Expedition was a trapping enterprise that invaded Spanish territory. The party was captured and imprisoned and its furs and equipment confiscated.

into camp. Then thrusting the small sticks through the pieces of meat, we placed them across from one of the poles to the other, and by building a small fire under the meat, the smoke of which would keep off the flies, we cured it. When well cured this meat was as hard as sole leather but was brittle and could be easily broken, and by breaking it up and putting it into our camp kettles to stew it soon became a soft palatable article of food.

Having cured what we supposed would be sufficient for our return trip, we found a small cave in the rocks, where we concealed our meat, and, blocking up the entrance with large stones to prevent the depredations of wolves, which were very numerous, we resumed our journey. In all of our trips we encountered numerous prairie dog towns; and as it may be interesting to learn something of these little animals, I will give a brief account of them. They reside in communities, consisting often of many thousands. They burrow in the ground like rats, and at the mouth of each hole is a hillock made by the excavated dirt being brought out. They are of yellowish-brown color and about the size of a large rat and have very short legs and tail and heavily built bodies. I have seen towns of a half mile long and a quarter of a mile wide, and in a space of six or eight feet square there would be a hillock raised and a hole descending through the top of it. It is my opinion that they place sentinels on watch, for, on approaching a town, I invariably saw a few individuals sitting each on top of his mound; on our approach, they would commence barking, somewhat like a little dog, when all would disappear in their holes.

I invariably saw a small species of owl, about the size of a partridge, and also rattlesnakes in their towns. It is the opinion of some travelers that these owls and snakes live in harmony with the prairie dogs, but it is my opinion that they congregate at the prairie dog towns for the purpose of depredating on the young ones. It is a mystery to me where these little dogs get water, as I have often found these towns ten or twenty miles from that article. The Indians say that they burrow down in the ground until they arrive at water, the truth of which I am not prepared to dispute. But I think that they have subterranean passages from one hole to another, as on subsequent trips across the plains, where water was convenient, I employed two or three men with buckets to carry and pour water in one of their holes, but after working for several hours could not raise the water to the surface. It is also a mystery to me where they get their food for winter. I know that they live upon the grass during summer, for I invariably found the grass all eaten for some distance around a town, where there was nothing else for many miles for them to subsist on. The Indians eat them and say they make good meat.

We finally reached a stream, which on subsequent trips I found to be the Colorado River,[4] a tributary of the Red River, which we forded. The bed of this stream was probably twenty-five or thirty feet wide and about knee deep to our horses. On arriving on the opposite bank, we camped, and I started up the river to hunt. I hadn't gone far when I came to a bank of sand on which I discovered numerous tracks of horses and mules and some tracks of men. I immediately returned to camp and told

[4] The Colorado River or Río Colorado which Meriwether forded was doubtless the headwaters of the Canadian River. It flows through a reddish soil which imparts its color to the water, hence its name. "The Mexicans and Indians on the borders of Mexico are in the habit of calling any river, the waters of which have a red appearance, 'Río Colorado,' or Red river, and they have applied this name to the Canadian in common with several others; and as many of the prairie Indians often visit the Mexicans and some even speak the Spanish language, it is a natural consequence that they should adopt the same nomenclature for rivers, places, etc."—Randolph B. Marcy, *Exploration of the Red River of Louisiana*, 4–5. See also W. W. H. Davis, *El Gringo: or New Mexico and Her People*, 240–41.

the Indians that I thought it a dangerous place to spend the night, and Big Elk said he would go and examine the tracks. On his return, he said the tracks were old and had been made a long time since, and there was no danger in camping there. I, being of a different opinion, directed my Negro boy to saddle our horses and pack our mules, and we recrossed the river. Then we proceeded up a hollow between two high hills where there was a little wood, and camped.

The next morning a little before daybreak, I heard the sound of firearms, and on running to the point of one of the hills, I saw by the flashes of the guns that the Indians were being attacked. Just before the break of day, Big Elk and another Indian came galloping in, and he said he believed all his party excepting those two had been killed. But in a little time another came in badly wounded. On being asked who had attacked them, they said they were not certain, but thought [their attackers] were Mexicans.

After the sun had risen, I again proceeded to the top of the hill to see if I could discover who the attacking party were, when I soon came to the conclusion that they were Mexicans. We remained concealed in this hollow until ten or eleven o'clock, when I told Big Elk that I wanted to see for certain who they were, and would cross the river for that purpose. To this he strenuously objected, but, thinking this a good opportunity for me to separate myself from the Indians, I told them that if I didn't return before night, to retrace their steps to the place where we had cached our meat and remain there until I did return.

Having torn up one of my shirts and bound up the Indian's wound, which was a severe flesh wound, I tied the remainder of the shirt to a stick to be borne as a flag of truce. Alfred and myself departed. On reaching the river, I found that most of the Mexicans had left, but some remained, stripping the dead Indians and catching their horses. As soon as we reached their side of the river, about half a dozen Mexicans[5] seized our horses' bridles and led them up the river, where I found the remainder of the Mexicans at their camp in a thick wooded grove of timber, some four or five miles above where the battle had been fought, when by signs we were directed to dismount, and everything of value was taken from us except the clothes we had on. I saw a few of the Mexicans who had been wounded in the battle, but I think none were killed. When night came on, we were given something to eat, which was acceptable for we had eaten nothing since the night before. We were then tied with our hands behind us and our feet together and directed to lie down on a blanket which was spread for us, where I spent a miserable night.

The next morning we were given something to eat and started in a westerly direction. A few friendly Indians who were with the party went in advance, and Alfred and myself were directed by signs to follow. Then came twenty or thirty Mexicans behind us, all of the others riding, but we on foot. This was the most miserable day of my life, for I felt as though I would as soon die as live.

After marching a few hours, we came to a high rocky hill, and I determined that I would walk no farther. So, sitting down upon a rock, I waited the advance of the Mexicans who were but a short distance behind me. By signs they directed me to follow the Indians, but I shook my head and refused to do so. Then one of the Mexicans rode up near me with a lance and raised it as though he intended to thrust me through with it. Here Al-

[5] It is quite possible that the commander of this Mexican detachment was Colonel Vizcarra. He was prominent on the Spanish frontier controlling marauding Indians and discouraging white neighbors to the north from entering their territory. R. L. Duffus describes Meriwether's capture: "Out of the mountains rode the Spanish Colonel Vizcarra with a swarm of cavalry at his heels; the Pawnees were beaten and scattered and Meriwether was taken to Santa Fe."—*The Santa Fe Trail*, 65–66. See also Fred S. Perrine, "Military Escorts on the Santa Fe Trail," *New Mexico Historical Review*, Vol. II (April, 1927), 190.

fred began to cry and said, "Marse Davy, get up and come along or they will kill you." To this I responded, "Let them kill me; I will not walk another step farther." Then Alfred placed his hand upon my feet and indicated that they were sore; and placing his fingers astride the finger of the other hand and pointing to some extra horses and mules, the Mexicans understood, and and a mule was lassoed by a Mexican and brought up to me. Then signs were made for me to mount. Upon my doing so, without any saddle, a Mexican took hold of a lariat rope which was tied around the mule's neck, and we resumed our journey. In two or three days after this, we reached a Indian pueblo village,[6] situated on the Pecos River.

When the Spanish government conquered the Indians of New Mexico, this government agreed with each tribe of Indians that if they would settle in villages,[7] go to work, and cultivate the soil, build a church, and support a priest, they would have a grant of land. And this village was built by a tribe called the Pecos Indians. Here we spent the night, and the next evening reached the city of Santa Fe,[8] where I was taken before the governor. But he couldn't speak a word of English or I a word of

[6] The pueblo referred to was Cicúique or Cicye. It had been established long before the advent of Coronado. Captain Alvarado visited it in 1540. One of his men described it thus: "There is one called Cicúique that is larger than any of the others and very strong. Its houses are four and five stories high, some of them being very fine. It has eight large patios, each with its corridor. These people neither plant cotton nor raise turkeys, because it is fifteen leagues east of the river [Río Grande] and close to the plains where the cattle [buffalo] roam."—H. E. Bolton, *Coronado On the Turquoise Trail*, 187. The ruins of Cicúique are partially visible to this day a short distance from the present town of Pecos.

[7] It is an error to assume that the Pueblo Indians gave up a nomadic life upon the coming of the Spanish invaders. Prior to Coronado's coming many pueblos had existed along the fertile valley of the Río Grande for an untold period.

[8] Meriwether reached Santa Fe from Pecos Pueblo by the ancient highway through Glorieta Pass. This route had been used for centuries by the Indians as a gateway to the plains country for the people of the Río Grande Valley and farther west on their annual trek eastward for buffalo. The distance from Pecos Pueblo to Santa Fe through Glorieta Pass over our present highways is approximately thirty-four miles.

Spanish, so no communication could pass between us. That evening I was taken to jail,[9] at the door of which I was separated from my Negro. On the door's being locked upon me, I found myself in a small, close, dirty apartment, with only a small window about the size of a pane of eight by ten glass to admit a little fresh air and light.

About night my jailor came with a small earthen bowl with boiled frijoles or red beans. I found [the dish] so strongly seasoned with pepper that I could not eat it. But I soon devoured the tortillas as I was very hungry. Then, spreading my blanket on the dirty floor, I lay down and tried to get a little sleep. In this I was sadly disappointed, as I thought the bed bugs and fleas would eat me up before morning.

In a short time a fable which I had read in Webster's old school book when a boy, about good dog Tray, who got a miserable thrashing for being caught in bad company occurred to my mind; and I resolved, if I ever got out of this scrape, I would try and avoid bad company the balance of my life. After a breakfast of frijoles and tortillas next morning, I heard a knock at my little window, and, casting my eyes in that direction, I discovered a Mexican who said, "Parlez vous francais, Monsier?" This caused me to spring to my feet. I responded, "Oui, oui, Monsieur," and approached the window. Then he asked me who I was, and I told him I was an American. Then he told me that the governor wanted to see me, and, calling the jailor, the door opened and I walked out, when I at once discovered that the gentleman was a Catholic priest who told me in French to follow him.

[9] The historic old building known as the "Palace of the Governors" was constructed between 1609 and 1614. It served as a fortification against the Indians as well as a residence of the governor and his family during the Spanish, Mexican, and the early years of American control. At the west end was the prison where Meriwether was confined. See Historical Society of New Mexico, "Old Santa Fe and Vicinity," n.d., 9–12.

We proceeded to the Governor's office, [and the Governor] repeated the same question as to who I was, and I responded, "An American." Again he said through the interpreter, "Americans are bad people." On my asking him why he thought so, he said, "You have forcibly taken a province from Spain called Florida." It at once occurred to my mind that before leaving home I had read in the newspapers a statement to this effect, "After Florida had been purchased the Spaniards had refused to deliver possession, and General Jackson had proceeded with his army to St. Augustine and taken it by force."[10] I suppose the Governor alluded to this fact.

He then asked me what had brought me to New Mexico, and I informed him that we had heard that much gold and silver was in their country, while we had none in ours, and that I had been sent by a trading company to find out if it was practicable to make a road to New Mexico by which we could transport our articles of merchandise in wagons and exchange them for gold and silver which they had. At this he shook his head in a very incredulous manner, and I was ordered back to jail, where I spent another miserable night.

A few days after this the good priest again visited me and asked me in French how I had spent my time. I told him, "Most miserably." He asked me if I got enough to eat, I told him, "Yes." He asked me if good water was given me to drink, to which I responded in a like manner.

Then he asked me if I had anything to complain of, and I told him that I had to keep fighting the flies all day, and the bed bugs and fleas all night. To this he replied "Poor fellow, I'm very sorry for you, and I will try and do something for you." A few hours after this, he returned and asked me if I were released if

[10] This is not strictly accurate. Jackson invaded Florida while it was still a Spanish possession. The United States government then pressured Spain into ceding it. The treaty had been signed but not ratified at the time Meriwether was captured.

I would promise not to try to escape. To which I replied, that it was impossible, as I had no means of recrossing the plains.

He then took me to the Governor again, who told me that if I would promise not to try to escape, he would let me out in the day, but that I must report to the jail every night to be locked up. I was told that I might walk about the plaza, which is an open space in the middle of the city, about one hundred yards square, and built up all around except at each corner, where streets passed out. That evening I felt like a bird out of a cage and walked around the plaza about half a dozen times, but reported at the jail at night where I ate my supper and was locked up.

Some time after this I met the priest in the plaza and showed him how the bugs had bitten my face, hands, and neck and asked him if he could not give me a better place to sleep in than the jail. He said he had been talking to the Governor and that we would then go to the Governor and see what he had determined to do. On reaching the Governor's office, he showed him the condition of my face, hands, and arms. Then they had a long conversation in Spanish, which I did not understand, and at the end of which I was informed that the Governor had agreed that I should not be locked up anymore, upon the priest's becoming responsible that I would not escape, and that he [the priest] had agreed to do so. So I thanked the Governor, and we left the room. On getting out I asked the priest if he could not procure me some employment by which I could earn my board. To this he replied, "You can stay at my house tonight, and I will see what I can do tomorrow." So he took me to a little church or chapel in the suburbs of the town, behind which he had a little house with two or three rooms for his own accommodation. The next morning he told me that I might assist an old man who was working in the garden, and he gave this man some instructions. As this was in the fall of the year, I found nothing to do except to gather the pods of red peppers and beans. I remained in this employment for probably a week, he informing me he could get no other employment for me.

We had frequent conversations about my country. He asked me how I came to speak French, and I told him that I had studied it a little when at school, and that I had resided for several months with a French family. (By the way, this French home was at the corner of 6th and Main streets in Louisville, where Honorie and Colmesville had a large commission house. The family consisted of old Mr. Honorie and his daughter and his son Frank Honorie, also Mr. Colmesville, who had married Mr. Honorie's daughter. They all resided together in the back part of the house on 6th Street.) The priest asked me if there were many Catholics in my country. To this I replied that the French family with whom I had resided were all Catholics and that in St. Louis more than half of the citizens were French Catholics. He said, "I am very glad to hear it."

One evening this good priest came in and said he had good news for me; he had had a long conversation with the Governor that day, and he thought that I would be permitted to return to my friends very shortly; we were to see the Governor the next morning on this subject. The Governor repeated again that the Americans were bad people, that they had forcibly taken Florida from Spain, and that a number of years before that soldiers had been sent into Mexico to seize it, but all had been taken prisoners and sent down to El Paso.

I asked him who had commanded the troops that had been captured. Then he spoke a few words to an officer, who went into another room and soon returned with a paper which the Governor looked over and then said that the commanding officer of the Americans was named Don Zebulon. This brought to my mind a fact I had read in the papers before leaving home, that Lieutenant Pike had a number of years before been sent West on an exploring expedition, with a small detachment of soldiers who had been captured. This officer's name was Zebulon Montgomery Pike,[11] but I thought it prudent to say nothing of my knowledge of this subject.

The Governor then told me that if I would promise never to return he would set me at liberty, which promise I readily made him. He then asked what guarantee I had to give for my compliance with this promise. I replied that the only guarantee I could give was to repeat an old saying in my country, "A stray dog always lives longest where he was treated best," and that I had been much better treated in my own country than in his. This caused a laugh among the whole party, and the Governor then said, "You must leave tomorrow, and if ever you return, I'll have you shot." To this I replied, "I will take it as a favor if your Excellency will take me out on the plaza and have me shot today." He then asked me why I desired to be shot, and I told him that when his people had taken me prisoner, I was well mounted, armed, and equipped for the trip, and that everything had been taken from me, and, if I started across the plains without a proper outfit, I would perish in a week, and I would rather be shot at once than to die a lingering death from cold and starvation. He then asked me to give to the priest a memorandum of what had been taken from me. The priest proceeded to write down the

[11] The Zebulon Pike Expedition left Bellefontaine on July 15, 1806. The stated objective was the exploration of the sources of the Red and Arkansas rivers, a peace between the Kansas and Pawnee Indians and a better understanding with the tribes encountered. In November he came in sight of the great peak that bears his name, and calculated its altitude. Wandering through the mountains and canyons, encountering terrible hardships, and failing to find the Red River, the party was discovered on a branch of the Río Grande by a detachment of Spanish cavalry under Don Facundo Melgares. They were taken to Santa Fe and sent to Chihuahua before they were finally escorted to the border and released. Strangely enough, Melgares was afterwards appointed governor of New Mexico, and it was he who was questioning Meriwether. See Zebulon Pike, *Account of an Expedition . . .* ; and L. Bradford Prince, *Historical Sketches of New Mexico*, 228–29.

articles from my dictation, after which we returned to the priest's house, the Governor telling me to come again in the morning.

On doing so, the Governor said that he had recovered my gun and one of my pistols and that they were very fine ones; also that he could recover nothing else at that time, but if I would transfer to him the other property which I had lost, if he recovered it he would furnish me with three mules and supply the other articles as far as he could, and that I must be ready to leave the next morning. On coming up the next morning with the priest, I saw my Negro boy holding three mules at the door of the Governor's and making a fine display of his ivory, saying, "Marse Dave, I never expected to see you again." One small mule had some articles packed on its back, and the other two had Mexican saddles on them, and we were told to mount and never return. I then said to the Governor, " Your people had me once and they will do so again before night unless I am protected by some person whom you can send to travel with me until I get beyond the settlements." He then ordered the mules to be taken away and told me to come again the next morning and he would try to furnish me with the necessary protection. On coming again the next morning, I found Alfred with the mules and two Mexicans mounted on horses, one of the Mexicans, the priest informed me, was a corporal, and the other was also a soldier, and they would accompany me beyond the frontier settlements. The priest then talked vigorously to the corporal, but a few words of which I could understand. The Governor then handed me my rifle and my one pistol, and giving each of us a butcher knife, said the other things were packed upon the little mule, and told us to mount. I then bade him adieu, and going up to the priest, thanked him cordially for his kindness to me. He said, "I have prayed to the Virgin and a number of the Saints to give you their protection, and if you ever get into difficulties on your route, I advise you to do the same thing." Then handing me a bundle which the old gardener had brought, he told me it would serve for a pillow when I slept at night, and not to open it until after I had separated from the corporal.

Then, mounting our mules, Alfred leading the pack mule, we crossed the Santa Fe River[12] on our return trip,[13] as far as the Pecos Village, where we stayed all night. Then ascending the next morning a high hill or mountain on the opposite side of the Pecos River, we entered a very rough country which we continued to travel over for two or three days. Then the corporal (as well as I could understand him) said one morning that would be the last day he would travel with us. Soon after starting along the bridle path that morning, I told Alfred that I must have the corporal's horse, for the mule I was riding was a rough trotting animal, both obstinate and vicious, and I asked him if he had ever stolen a horse. He said, "No." I then told him that when we camped at night, he must lie awake and when the Mexicans were asleep, he must take the corporal's horse and lead it along the path several miles, and, hiding it well, return to camp. Alfred said he had a better plan: that we two could lie awake, and when the Mexicans were sleep, we could kill them both, and take the horses and all they had, I replied, "The corporal has not injured us in any way, but on the contrary had treated us kindly, and I would not consent to his being injured in any way. But, on getting up the next morning and finding the corporal's horse gone, I will give him my mule in place of the horse and I will

[12] The Santa Fe River or Río Santa Fe is located two blocks south of the Plaza in the center of town and empties into the Río Grande. The name "river" is a misnomer, for most of the year it carries only a small volume of water.

[13] According to W. W. H. Davis "They were not permitted to leave the country by the same route they had entered it, but were sent by the way of Don Fernandez de Taos in charge of a corporal and two men."—*El Gringo*, 242. It is more logical to assume that Meriwether followed the route he mentions in the narrative, by the way of Pecos Village. Traveling northeast from that point he would encounter a rough mountainous terrain to the west of Tecolote Peak; thence more open country would be found near the headwaters of the Gallinas River and the present town of Sapello.

walk until we come to where the horse is hidden." A few hours after this arrangement was made, Alfred and myself were in the path just ahead of the Mexicans, when hearing a halloo and looking back, we saw the corporal swinging his hat in the air and hallooing out, "Adios, Senor, Adios." and he started on the back track. So nothing was left to me but continue riding the abominable mule.

The night after this, we camped and consumed what little provisions we had remaining, and, on opening the bundle given me by the priest, I found it contained a woolen shirt, a pair of buckskin pants, and a pair of moccasins, which pleased me not a little, as the clothes I had on were nearly ready to fall off of me.

We proceeded on our journey without anything to eat for about three days, as we saw no game to kill. On the third day, I saw a wolf scratching at the side of a rock. Dismounting and giving Alfred the mule to hold, I crept up as near to the wolf as I could to shoot it. We found it to be very poor, and from the length of its tusks, very old. After cutting off its head and taking out its entrails to lessen the weight, I placed it before Alfred on the withers of his mule, and we proceeded on our journey, intending to camp at the first place where we could get wood and water. Late in the evening we found such a place and made camp. We had then been nearly three days without food, so, starting a fire, we commenced cooking some of the wolf. We placed part of it in a camp kettle that had been furnished me on leaving Santa Fe, and filling the kettle with water, boiled it as soon as we got a fire started. After it had boiled probably half an hour, I dipped out a cupful, and cooling it, began to drink. I drank about half of it and gave the remainder to Alfred, and then commenced picking up wood for our night's fire, as the nights were getting quite cold. After this was accomplished, we both took another draught of wolf soup, and then replacing the kettle on the fire and replenishing it with more water, we both became quite sleepy. Then after catching our mules and tieing them up as usual for fear of their straying off, we took some soup and tried to eat some of the meat but found it so tough that we soon abandoned it. Then we lay down and went to sleep, still leaving the kettle on the fire, which we replenished with wood whenever we awakened during the night.

The next morning we turned our mules out to graze, whilst we cooked and ate our breakfast. On examining the contents of our camp kettle we found that by continuous boiling, the fibers of the meat had separated, and hence we could eat it with less difficulty. On finishing breakfast, we saddled up and mounted again, taking some of the wolf with us. This was the route we had followed when prisoners, but was farther north. We had to continue in the trail or path, as it wound over the least elevated portion of the mountains.

One evening on approaching the top of a hill, I discovered a considerable stream of water a few miles off, and, on reaching the stream, I concluded that it was the stream on which we had been captured. We found fine grass and plenty of water there, so we camped for the night. The next day we proceeded downstream, and about night came to the place where the Mexicans were camped before attacking the Indians, where we struck camp ourselves. The next morning, we went down to the battleground, where we saw numerous bones of the Indians who had been killed. We were now on the trail which we followed before being attacked by the Mexicans, and we traveled on as fast as I could get my obstinate mule to go. I think it was nearly a week after this that we arrived at the place where we had cached our meat, and I found my three Indians still there. The wounded one was pretty well recovered. We remained here two or three days, repairing damages and preparing for our future trip across the plains. Here for the first time I donned the clothes furnished me by the priest. (The name of this good man, I am sorry to say, has escaped my memory. Indeed his name was rarely mentioned by the Mexicans, as they called him "Father," and the Governor's name also was seldom ever mentioned, as he was addressed as "His Excellency," but I think his name was Baca.[14] I gave my old clothes to Alfred, as he was needing them badly.

The night before our departure, I became very uneasy, as the Indians who sat on the opposite of the fire conversed in a low tone, not a word of which I could understand, although I had learned a good deal of the Pawnee language. The next morning I asked Big Elk what he and his companions were talking about the night before, when he replied, "We were discussing the route we should take back." He also said that the buffalo had all left the plains and gone away—pointing his hand to the south—except a few old ones who went to the mountains for the winter, and that the antelope always went to the timberland during the winter. "So," he said, "I think we had better not attempt to cross the open plains but keep near the spurs of the mountains, where we can procure wood for fire." I at once agreed to this. As two of the Indians' horses had strayed into camp the morning after the battle, I exchanged my abominable mule for an Indian pony, and here I resolved that if ever we had to kill one of our animals for food, this mule should be the first sacrificed.

I think we traveled about two weeks, when we came to the Arkansas River, which we crossed with difficulty, as the ice was running and the horses and mules were reluctant about entering the water. Here we found the weather extremely cold, as the North winds came sweeping down the valley of this river; so we

[14] Meriwether is mistaken here. Melgares was the last Spanish governor. Bartolome Baca was a Mexican governor, serving from 1823 until September 13, 1825. Probably when Meriwether returned to Santa Fe as territorial governor thirty-three years later, he heard mention of Baca and assumed this was the official before whom he had appeared as a prisoner. See L. Bradford Prince, *A Concise History of New Mexico*, 150.

mounted the hills on the east side thereof traveling in an easterly direction. After a while we came to a stream running in a northeasterly course, which we concluded was a tributary to the South Fork of the Platte River. Here the weather became so cold and snow so deep, that we concluded to seek a proper place and camp for the winter. So ascending a steep hollow where we saw there was wood, we found a shelving rock which projected six or eight feet from the wall beneath, and a little distance from it, a small trickling spring from under the rocks. Knowing that a spring never freezes, and there being sufficient wood for fuel, we determined to make this our winter camp. The next morning we commenced cutting down with our tomahawks some slender poles, eight or ten feet long, which we placed with the butts upon the ground and the tops leaning against the shelving rock.

We decided to kill our animals and stretch their skins over these poles to protect us from the cold. Having done this, we tied the skins to the poles with little strips taken from the legs of the animals. We soon formed a rude though comfortable house, fifteen or twenty feet long and eight or ten feet wide. We then packed up the horse and mule meat at the outside end of our dwelling and built a little pen around it to keep off the wolves. There was a small crevice in the rock, extending from the bottom to the top, which we intended to use for our chimney, so we built a little funnel of loose rocks on the top about two feet high, and [we] formed a door out of one of the animal skins, about four feet high and two feet wide.

A short time after we located our house, there came a tremendous snowstorm, during which the snow fell about a foot deep, which made our house still more close and comfortable. But, for fear it might be blown off by the wind, we carried water from the spring and with our cups sprinkled it over the snow, which soon froze hard. Every day we watched by turns, one sitting at the mouth of our chimney and looking down the hollow, which was destitute of timber, to look for the approach of hostile Indians. And thus we continued in this cave, eating horse and mule meat for I think over two months, which would bring us to about the first of February [1821].

One day Alfred, being on watch, sang out, "Indians are coming." This caused me to mount to where he was, when I discovered that a party of Indians were walking directly toward us and were almost a mile distant. Seeing that they had discovered the smoke of our camp, we commenced preparing our arms. Two of the Indians had very indifferent guns, and the others had bows and arrows. Alfred had an old Mexican musket that had been given him in Santa Fe, and I had a good rifle and pistol. I then sent Alfred to see how many Indians there were. He said he had counted nine. We then placed our arms in the farther end of the house from the door and awaited their arrival.

On reaching the door, one of them hallooed, and Big Elk opened it. I asked him what Indians they were, and he replied that he did not know, that they could not understand each others language, but that he thought they were either Cheyennes or Arapaho Indians. Our visitors soon made signs that they were hungry and wanted something to eat. Having some meat already cooked, we gave it to them, expecting they would soon leave, but on their remaining we became quite uneasy.

During the early days of our encampment here, we had made some candles from the tallow of our horses and mules. This was done by getting dry twigs of willow and working the tallow around them with our hands, Finding a boulder in the spring branch about the size of a man's head and somewhat resembling it in shape, I had for my amusement stretched a piece of horseskin over it and after it was dry had taken the skin off. I then cut two holes for the eyes, and others for the nose and mouth. I had thus formed a rude mask of it, which, when a candle was placed behind it, made a very horrible appearance.

We had suspended a blanket over our effects to conceal them from the Indians; and, after eating, they commenced pointing to it, and, as we supposed, asking what was hidden there, which alarmed me still more. So I determined to resort to the mask to get clear of them if I could. As this sat upon a shelving rock that projected from the wall, in a dark corner of the house, I lighted a piece of candle and placed the mask over it with the face pointing towards the door. On the Indians' again pointing to the blanket suspended from the ceiling, I beckoned them to come and see. When two or three came to where I was standing, I drew the blanket aside.

The Indians saw the form of a man's head with the light streaming from his eyes and mouth, and the one nearest to me gave a jump back, knocking the next one to him down, when all gathered their bows and arrows and fled from the house much frightened. We ourselves stood outside the house and laughed at the speed at which they ran. I then told Big Elk that we had better leave there, as I had no doubt a larger party was camping in our vicinity, and they might attack us that night. So we all commenced preparing to leave. We cooked some meat, which we carried in a kind of knapsack made by throwing a blanket over our shoulders and girding it around our waist with a belt, and in this we also placed such effects as it was necessary for us to have. In the dusk of the evening we departed. We walked all night without stopping and found it very fatiguing. We walked through several drifts of snow which came up over our knees, but on reaching the open plain, we discovered that much of the snow had melted. The next morning each of us took some of the meat out of our knapsacks and ate it as we walked along. After walking nearly twenty-four hours without rest, we came to a place where there was a little wood and camped, and after eating supper we concluded that we must by turns keep awake all night for the Indians might follow our tracks. So I told Alfred to take the first watch and after two or three hours to wake one of the Indians, who was to wake up another after a watch of the same time, and so on, all through the night till it came my turn, and I to have the last watch. I preferred the last watch, for the Indians, when they do attack invariably do so about daybreak. But I did not awake until the sun shone in my face, and I found all fast asleep. Alfred had gone to sleep without waking up an Indian. When I awoke, I was very cold, and so were all of us, and our fire was nearly out. So, replenishing the fire, we thawed our frozen meat and ate our breakfast. We concluded to descend the creek valley in which we had camped until it entered a larger stream. Big Elk said he knew where we were, that we were on a tributary of the Platte and that he was familiar with the country to the Pawnee villages, which gave us much relief.

We reached the Pawnee villages, I think, about the middle of February (for I had lost all computation of time). Here I witnessed an awful scene. On the three Indians' telling the others the fate of their friends and relatives who had been killed by the Mexicans, such a howl was raised as I had never heard before, particularly among the squaws. When they cried they do not sit down and shed silent tears as white women do, but howl at the top of their voices like a pack of wolves, and this was kept up for half the night.

I remained at the Pawnee village for several days, resting myself. Then, borrowing two horses from these Indians, for we had no use for a pack mule now (as our baggage consisted of the clothes we had on our backs), Alfred and myself started for Council Bluffs. On arriving at the place, I found that the military had built a cantonment on top of the bluff, because the river had washed about one-half of the one built in the bottom, as well as our first trading house, and our company had also built houses on the bluff. My friends scarcely knew me, and I was informed that they had long since given me up for lost.

The first night I washed myself from head to foot in warm water and put on civilized clothing. As soon as it was known in the cantonment that I had returned, a number of the officers came to see me, and they laughed heartily at my dirty, ragged appearance.

My arrival was about the first of March [1821], and Captain Bissell informed me that I might take a week or two of rest, which was acceptable [to me]. About the last of March, I told Captain Bissell that my engagement had expired and that I wanted to return home by the first boat that descended the river, as letters from home had arrived during my absence, urging me to do so. To this he said that he couldn't do without me, and that I must stay another year, and that the military had determined to reoccupy Fort Osage,[15] three or four hundred miles below, and that Major Ketchum, who was to command, would descend the river as soon as the ice disappeared. He [Major Ketchum] would go with two companies of soldiers, and he had selected me as their sutler, and that he [Captain Bissell] wanted me to accompany those troops and act as sutler and open a trade with the Osage[16] and Iowa Indians. He said that if I would do so, he would increase my salary to $500 the next year, to which proposition I assented.

15 Fort Osage was about forty miles below the mouth of the Kansas near the present Sibley, Missouri. The site was selected by William Clark in 1808 as a suitable site for a military post. It was permanently abandoned May 8, 1827, when Fort Leavenworth was founded. Jacob Fowler, who visited Fort Osage in July, 1822, reported: "The garrison at this time was commanded by one officer of the United States Army—having two men under his command both of them having deserted a few days ago and carried off all his ammunition." Jacob Fowler, *The Journal of*, 173. See also Chittenden, *Fur Trade*, II, 923; and James B. McCrellis, *Military Reservations*, 59.

16 The Osages lived on the Osage River in Missouri. The first notice of the tribe is on Marquette's map of 1673, which apparently places them there. This remained their principal location until they were removed westward by the government in 1825 and the years following. They were one of the first tribes in the Missouri Valley to have a regular trade with the whites, many years before the Louisiana Purchase. See Hodge, *Handbook of American Indians*, II, 157–58.

VII
Indians and Trade

Soon after this, we commenced selecting and packing suitable goods for such a trade, and as soon as the ice ceased running, which was in the latter part of April, the military as well as myself, commenced loading our boats. This was accomplished a few days before I was ready, by the soldiers, when they started down the river in two keelboats under the command of Major Ketchum. As soon as I was ready, I started after them, with four hands to row the boat and my interpreter to act as pilot and steersman. On passing the mouth of the River Platte, I looked up it and discovered a party of Indians in bark canoes descending the river. Not knowing whether they were hostile or friendly, we plied our oars vigorously but soon found that the Indians were fast gaining on us.

On their near approach, one canoe was paddled up alongside of our boat, when the headman, recognizing my interpreter, stepped on board. The interpreter, after a little talk with the Indian, told me that they were Iowa Indians returning from an unsuccessful war party against the Otoes, and that it was always dangerous to encounter an unsuccessful war party. This made me quite uneasy, as we would have to land that night, as no boat in those days attempted to navigate the Missouri River after night. So we concluded that instead of landing we would round to alongside a snag and make fast to it. The Indians coming up with us landed, but the Indian who had boarded us before came alongside and asked why we didn't go ashore. I told him through the interpreter, that I had a place on the boat where I could build a fire and cook our meals, and there was no necessity for going ashore. We then determined to keep a watch all night for fear they might board us in their canoes, the Indians numbering about twenty men, and we only six. Nothing occurring however, during the night, we started at daylight the next morning, leaving the Indians still in their camp. Between nine and ten o'clock, a head wind coming on compelled us to hitch on to another snag, when we saw the Indians coming on behind us. They could keep near the shore and avoid the wind and waves, while we could not. On coming up with us, the Indians again landed, and the headman told me that they were out of provisions and were going to make a hunt that day, also that the river made a very short bend just below us, and they intended to form a line across the narrow neck of land and make a drive down the river, where they would have a few men in canoes to shoot the deer as they approached, and if the deer got into the river, they would catch them with the canoes. He invited me to join in the drive, which the interpreter strenuously opposed, but thinking it best to show confidence in them I went ashore in the Indians' canoe and joined the drive.

Before I had gotten far, I stopped on a pretense of fixing my moccasins and let the Indians pass on ahead, when I concealed myself in the top of a large tree that had fallen down. About an hour after, I heard a tremendous hallooing, and at once knew that the drive had commenced. I remained in my hiding place until I saw a cub bear passing by me, when I whistled, and when the bear stopped, I shot and killed it. This formed a pretext for my returning at once to the boat with my game, which, by means of one of the Indians' canoes, I got to our boat. One of two Indians who had been left in charge of their camp expressed great surprise at my returning so soon. I told them that I had got as much meat as I wanted, and there was no use in my remaining any longer. In the evening the remainder of the Indians came to camp, well loaded with game. The wind continuing to blow, we had to stay where we were all night, still maintaining a watch, as we had done the night before.

The next morning we departed at daybreak, leaving the Indians in camp, and we saw no more of them. On reaching Fort Osage,[1] I found that it occupied a high point of land, probably a hundred feet high, which jutted into the water's edge on the western side of the river and was about two or three miles above the mouth of Fire Prairie Creek.[2] I think the little town of Sibley now occupies its site.[3] We arrived at the fort in the evening, and on going up the hill I found Major Ketchum and his command in possession. The Major informed me that a vacant house was on the lower side of the fort and I could take possession of it. I had no team to haul my goods up the hill, so I employed a number of soldiers; and the next morning I began unloading, carrying the boxes and rolling the barrels up the hill, which was a laborious job. By nightfall, however, all was in my house. This house consisted of a single room about twenty feet long and fifteen wide, with a counter running across the center, and was situated about fifty yards from the southern gate of the fort, so I found myself the only person within a hundred miles residing outside of the fort, except one family, consisting

[1] The Duke of Württemberg described the location of Fort Osage in June, 1823, as follows: "Fort Osage is on a high point at the end of this chain of hills and commands the surrounding prairie. The Fort is in good position for military purposes, but at present there is left only one log house which is occupied by a single family."—South Dakota Historical *Collections*, "First Journey to North America in the Years 1822–24," Vol. XIX (1938), 308–309.

[2] Fire Prairie is on the south bank of the Missouri, in the present Lafayette County, a creek of the same name entering the river at this point. It is said to take its name from the death there of several Indians in a prairie fire.—Maximilian, *Travels in the Interior of America*, 247, n. 192.

[3] Sibley is about one mile away. The old post is now undergoing extensive restoration and has become an attraction for excursions from Kansas City.

of a man named McClelland and his wife and daughter, eight or ten years of age. They resided about a quarter of a mile above the fort.

Major Ketchum with his wife and two or three children, the oldest a daughter of about ten years of age, and his sons resided inside the fort. I found there an interpreter employed by the military who was half Indian and spoke the language of all the Indians with whom I expected to trade. My own interpreter desiring to return to St. Louis, I discharged him, and he took charge of the boat in which I had descended from Council Bluffs and he departed down the river, I arranged with the military that I would pay one-half of the salary of the interpreter employed by them and that I should have his services when needed.

Shortly after my arrival, I dispatched this interpreter to the Osage villages, situated eighty to one hundred miles west on the Osage River, to inform the Indians that the trading house at Fort Osage had been opened again and ready for a renewal of traffic. On the interpreter's return, he was accompanied by the head chief of the Osages named Sans Oreille,[4] which means, "Walk in the Rain," and with him also came a small party of the tribe, who examined my goods and appearing to be satisfied with the prices, the chief said he would go back to his tribe and return soon with a large party, bringing large quantities of furs and peltries to trade. He stayed about a week around the fort, coming to my house every day and holding a long talk each time.

Shortly after his departure, a party of eleven Iowa Indians came in. They told me that they had crossed over to the west side of the river to hunt, as game was very scarce on their side (the

[4] Brackenridge describes a meeting with this chief, accompanied by Manuel Lisa: "I went to deliver a pipe to Sans Oreille (a warrior and principal man of this tribe) sent by General Clark. Sans Oreille, literally, 'without ears,' a name given him in consequence of his being unwilling to listen to the advice of the sober part of his people."—Henry Brackenridge, *Journal of a Voyage Up the River Missouri Performed in 1811*, 58.

eastern) side. They remained all day, and early the next morning were crossed over to their own side of the river by means of a large canoe belonging to Mr. McClelland. Two or three days after this, on opening my door in the morning, I found sitting on the door step a wounded Indian whom I recognized as one of the party of Iowas who had been at my house a day or two before. As I understood very little of the Iowa language, I asked a passing soldier to send the interpreter who occupied a room in the fort, out to me. On his coming, the Indian informed me that on crossing the river a few days before, the Indians had traveled all day until evening, when they came to a white settlement and camped near it, and that the next morning, before daylight, they had been fired upon by the whites, and he thought every Indian had been killed except himself; also that he managed though badly wounded, to reach the river a little above the fort, and, rolling a small drift log into the water, had with its assistance, crossed the river the night before, and, knowing that I was friendly, had reached my doorstep just before day. He was very weak and hungry.

I immediately dispatched the interpreter for the surgeon of the post and directed the interpreter to tell his wife to prepare some soup. On arriving and examining the Indian's wound, the surgeon said it was severe but not dangerous. We then proceeded to dress it and [saw] that the wounded man needed nourishment and rest. I spread a blanket on the floor and made signs to the Indian to lie down upon it.

Soon after this the interpreter arrived with a tin cup of rich soup, which the wounded Indian drank with great relish, and lying down, fell asleep. At dinnertime I gave more soup, and again he went to sleep. Shortly after this three armed men came to my door where I was sitting and asked me if I had seen anything of a wounded Indian. I said, "Yes, he is lying down in my room." Then one of the white men, who seemed to be the leader of the party, said, "Yes, damn him, I intend to kill him." I said, "'You cannot do so, for the Indian is under my protection and you must not harm him." Then he began to prepare his gun to shoot the Indian as he lay on the floor, when I immediately closed the door and barred it. The man then said, "If you don't give him up, I will kill him and you too," and with that he fired a ball through the door. This, I knew, would quickly bring me relief, as strict orders had been given that there should be no firing near the fort. In a few minutes the sergeant of the guard appeared and wanted to know what the firing meant. I called loudly, "Tell Major Ketchum to come here." In a short time the Major arrived, accompanied by the sergeant and Lieutenant McCray. On hearing their voices, I opened the door and explained matters to them.

The man who had fired the ball through the door, I found to be named Palmer, and he gave a very different version of the fight between the whites and the Indians a day or two before. He said the same party of Indians had camped in his neighborhood a few nights before the fight and had stolen some of the settlers' horses, and he had no doubt that they had come back to get the remainder, which was the cause of the difficulty. I asked him if he could recollect the night the horses were stolen, and he named the night. I then asked him if he was sure it was on that night, when he said, "Yes, I am positive." I told him some other Indians must have stolen his horses, as these had camped near my house on the night he had specified. To this he replied, "You are a liar." Major Ketchum told him to leave the fort and never to return. This Palmer refused to do, when Major Ketchum directed Lieutenant McCray to bring the guard there, and very soon the sergeant appeared with five or six soldiers. Major Ketchum then told Palmer and his companions that if they didn't leave he would have all three shot, and he directed the guard to march them down to the river and cross them over in the canoe, which was promptly done.

On re-entering the house, I found the Indian had crawled under the counter and concealed himself. I suggested to Major Ketchum that Palmer's party might return some night and forcibly take the Indian from me and kill him, therefore I desired to have the Indian taken inside the fort and placed in the hospital, to which proposition the Major at once assented. Then the interpreter was directed to explain matters to the Indian, who was taken into the hospital. That night or the night after, the interpreter awakened me and said the Indian was crazy and he could do nothing with him, and that he frequently asked for me, repeating my Indian name, "Men-par-wara" (A name White Cloud had given me, meaning White Feather). I immediately arose and accompanied the interpreter to the hospital, and on entering it, I found the Indian sitting on the side of his cot and singing his death song. I approached and shaking hands with him asked what was the matter. He responded through the interpreter that a spirit had appeared to him and told him we only wanted to cure him of his wound and then burn him. I told him that such was not the case, that his wound had caused him to have a fever and this was only a feverish dream. He soon became calmer and lay down and fell asleep once more. I continued to visit the hospital two or three times a day and gave the Indian assurances of protection, and he soon began to mend rapidly. Three or four weeks after he was taken into the hospital, the interpreter came to me and said the Indian was gone, that he had made a rope of his bedclothes, by which he had descended from the upper window and made his escape. This he could easily do because the back wall of the hospital formed a portion of the outer wall of the little stockade fort. The doctor was of the opinion that he could not get far, as his condition would not permit it. Detachments of soldiers were sent out in different directions to try and find him, but they returned without success.

Probably a month after this, Doctor Nicholson,[5] the surgeon of the post, was relieved by Dr. Craig,[6] who brought an order from St. Louis for the former to join the regiment at Council Bluffs. Doctor Nicholson soon procured two horses and a mule, one horse for himself and one for his Negro man, and the mule to carry their baggage, and started by land for their destination some three or four hundred miles up the river. About a week after his departure, they returned accompanied by a wounded Indian. The Doctor said that, waking up in camp one morning, he discovered both horses and mule gone and their camp surrounded by Indians, who, however, made no hostile demonstration. He also said that shortly after daylight, one of the Indians laid down his gun and walked up to him, when he at once recognized him to be the wounded Indian. The Indian appeared glad to see him and commenced hallooing to the others, when pretty soon both horses and mule were delivered up to him, and the Indian accompanied him back to Fort Osage.

On the interpreter's being called, the Indian said that his party had accidentally camped near the Doctor's camp, and the next morning, on going out to hunt for their horses, they discovered the Doctor's camp but did not know it was his. He therefore had taken the horses and mule, and a boy who was was him returned for the remainder of the Indians, who surrounded the

[5] It appears that Meriwether has confused Dr. Nicholson with a Dr. William Howard Nicholl. Heitman lists no Dr. Nicholson of the Sixth Infantry or rifle regiment of that period. The doctor mentioned is William Howard Nicholl, of New York; surgeon's mate, Sixth Infantry, February 19, 1817; post surgeon, January 28, 1820; assistant surgeon, June 1, 1821; major surgeon, July 28, 1830; died March 5, 1831. See Heitman, *Historical Register U.S.A.*, I, 748.

[6] This is Presley H. Craig, of Pennsylvania; surgeon's mate, 22nd Infantry, July 6, 1812; resigned, February 28, 1814; surgeon's mate, Sixth Infantry, April 12, 1820; assistant surgeon, July 1, 1821; major surgeon, July 13, 1832; died August 8, 1848. See *ibid.*, I, 333.

Doctor's camp, thinking it might be the party who had wounded and killed his comrades, and if so, they intended to kill the whites; but, not being certain who they were, they returned to wait until it was light enough to see. Then he recognized the Doctor and his Negro and had brought them back safely to the fort. The Doctor purchased of me some tobacco and other things and gave them to the Indian as a present, upon which the latter departed well satisfied he had repaid an act of kindness.

Some time after this, a young man came from Palmer's settlement and said that one of the settlers was very sick and desired the doctor to come and see him; that he had brought two horses, one for the doctor to ride and he had hitched them on the opposite side of the river.

He had hallooed over and the canoe had been sent for him. This was after Dr. Nicholson's departure in a boat up the river. Dr. Craig accompanied the boy to the sick man's house. On his return the next day, the Doctor said that the settlement was about twenty miles distant, and he found the man very sick. The sick man frequently moaned and muttered to himself, "Poor Indians, poor Indians." The next morning, the sick man appeared more calm, and he told the doctor that he was one of the party that had killed the Indians, which fact weighed heavily on his mind. He told him also that a few days after Palmer's return from Fort Osage, a hunting party had found the missing horses, which had not been stolen at all. He then went on to give the Doctor a version of the Indian slaughter which was even worse than the wounded Indian's statement. He told him that another Indian was wounded and ran into one of the settlers' houses and shut the door, as all the family were out, and, that on the parties returning to their houses, a little white boy told them that the Indian was there. Then all surrounded the house and told the Indian to open the door and come out, which, of course, the Indian did not understand. He came to the window and held out his hand to shake hands with them, instead of doing which, Palmer raised his shotgun and blew out his brains.

This tragedy had a singular sequel. Major [George C.] Sibley had arrived at the fort the spring before as agent for the Indians in that vicinity, and, on hearing Doctor Craig's statement, reported the facts to Governor Clark, who was also superintendent of Indian Affairs, and the Governor had Palmer and several of his party arrested, but they were promptly acquitted. At this time, Governor Clark, who was territorial governor, was a candidate for state governor, as Missouri had been admitted as a state into the Union. Immediately the hue and cry was raised against him in the frontier counties, that Clark was more friendly to the Indians than he was to the white people, which caused him to be defeated by an inferior man, I think, by the name of McNair.[7]

In the fall of this year [1821], I wrote to Colonel O'Fallon at St. Louis that my second term of engagement would expire the next March, and that I desired to be released at that time. I think it was about the first of March following that a young man arrived, bringing instructions to me to take an inventory of all goods on hand, turn them over to him, and take his receipt for them, and informing me that I could ride the same horse down to St. Louis that he had ridden up, and to bring all money I had on hand with me. This last order would have been very difficult of accomplishment, as a large portion of the money was in specie, and it was both dangerous and difficult for one man to carry such a sum through that wild and sparsely settled country. The inventory was soon taken, but the difficulty of carrying the money still remained. Before leaving, however, Captain [Alphonso] Wetmore, a paymaster in the army, arrived at

[7] Alexander McNair, first governor of the state of Missouri (1821–25), was born in Dauphin County, Pennsylvania, in 1774, receiving a majority of 4,020 votes over former Territorial Governor William Clark. He died at St. Louis on March 18, 1826. See *National Cyclopaedia of American Biography*, XII, 302.

the fort, stating that he had started from St. Louis in two canoes with a small detachment of soldiers, and that in one of the canoes was an iron chest containing a large amount of silver money. Unfortunately this canoe had been sunk and his iron chest and money could not be recovered until the river fell, hence he applied to me for what money I had to pay off the troops, which relieved me very much. I handed over to him six thousand dollars for which he gave me a draft or check on St. Louis.

I then packed all my heavy baggage in a box, marked it to the care of Colonel O'Fallon, St. Louis, and requested the young man who had relieved me (his name I have forgotten) to ship by the first boat down the river to me at St. Louis. About a week after I was relieved, I started alone for Franklin, mounted on Dr. Nicholson's horse, which I had purchased not knowing my successor would bring one for me, and leading Colonel O'Fallon's horse, which proved to be a most incorrigible beast. It broke away from me within a few miles after leaving and returned to the fort, so I proceeded on without it.

Several settlements had been formed between Fort Osage and Arrow Rock, and I got comfortable accommodations at these places. The third or fourth evening after my departure, I arrived at Arrow Rock, and here crossing the river in a little ferry boat, proceeded to Franklin, where I met two gentlemen who were going to St. Louis. One of these gentlemen was Major Owen of the U.S. Army, and the other was a Mr. Fisher, from Kentucky. On our arrival at St. Louis, I informed these gentlemen that I might be detained there for a day or two and that I was sorry to lose their company, to which they responded that if it was not more than one day, they would wait for me. I immediately inquired for the residence of Colonel O'Fallon, as I knew he had married a year or two before and set up housekeeping. I was directed to a large splendid house which the Colonel had recently purchased, in the back part of the city. I arrived there late in the evening and handed him the list of goods, wares, and merchandise left at Fort Osage, and unripping the crown of my otterskin cap, produced Captain Wetmore's draft. We then proceeded to settle accounts, for my salary. The balance due me was a little over seven hundred dollars, out of my salary of one thousand for my three years' service.

He then told me it was dangerous traveling through Illinois carrying so much money, that he had some money in Louisville, and if I was willing, he would give me a draft on Judge Fitzhugh, who I think was his stepfather. This proposition I gladly accepted, and he handed me a draft for seven hundred and paid me the remainder. He then informed me that several of the fur traders had combined to fit out a large expedition which was to be divided into different parties, for trapping and trading in the western wilds, and that probably one party might go to Santa Fe. I think he said Michael Immell or Captain Ashley, I do not recall which, would be chief captain; and if I would accept, he would procure for me the third position.[8] But I told him, "My father, as you know, is an old man and has written me some pressing letters to come home and assist him in his business." This I felt myself bound to do. I then told the Colonel that I was anxious to go, but I would return home and see if my parents could do without me, or if my younger brother was old enough to manage the farm. He then said he would try and keep the place open for me until the first of May, at which time I could return to St. Louis or inform him by letter if I could not [accept]. He gave me a fine letter to my father, informing him how well I had

[8] By this time Becknell had returned with the news that the Santa Fe trade was now open with the collapse of Spanish authority, and expeditions were being feverishly fitted out to exploit the golden opportunity. At the same time William H. Ashley was advertising for young men of enterprise to collect furs around the source of the Missouri. It is obvious that David Meriwether at the age of twenty-two had won the confidence of the seasoned mountain men directing these expeditions. See Chittenden, *Fur Trade,* II, 498–99; and Morgan, *Jedediah Smith,* 62–64.

discharged my duties. On receiving it, I returned to the hotel where I had left my companions and told them that I would start the next morning, and we all left together.

Next morning, crossing the Mississippi River, we proceeded through the state of Illinois, which was then very sparsely settled, and on arriving at the Wabash or White River (I have forgotten which) we came to a low piece of bottom land, where logs had been cut and placed across the road, then a ditch dug on each side, and the earth thrown on the logs. The river being very high, this embankment, which was many miles long, was submerged in several places. When about half way across it, we came to a covered spring wagon, the hind wheels of which had gotten into a hole where a log had been washed out. The gentleman in charge with his driver could not extricate it, but on his appealing to us for assistance, one of my friends and myself dismounted in the water over our boot tops, the other holding our horses. Each taking hold of one of the hind wheels, and the driver vigorously applying his whip, we extricated the wagon. The gentleman informed us that he was an agent of a Bible society and was traveling through that wild country distributing Bibles gratuitously, when the recipient was either unwilling or unable to pay for them. He proffered each of us a New Testament, but as we were going to an older country where we could procure them easily, we declined the present. Then turning to me he said, "My young friend, can you tell me what this place is called?" I replied, "I have heard it called Purgatory." He said, "I have often heard and read of Purgatory, and if it is any worse than this, I never want to get into it."

On reaching the White River, I saw immense forests of beech trees, which were entirely new to me, though I had been raised in Kentucky where such timber and also cane were abundant. It always appears singular to me that, west of the Missouri River to the head of the Gulf of California, I have never seen a beech tree or stalk of cane on the borders of the little streams; while I have found cottonwood and sycamore from Canada to the Colorado of the West.

On our arrival at Corydon, Indiana, I separated from my traveling companions, they proceeding to New Albany and I to Newman's Ferry across the Ohio, which was opposite the upper end of my father's farm. My horse being very much worn out and the roads deep, I was traveling along slowly, when a gentleman overtook me whom I at once recognized as Mr. Newman the ferryman, but he seemed not to know me. I asked him if he thought I could get to the ferry in time to cross that evening, when he responded, "Yes, I think so." He then asked me where I was going to stay that night if I got across. I told him that my father lived nearly opposite the ferry. At this, he held up his hands and said, "Golly, David, is that you? You have been gone so long that all of us had given you up for dead, and now I have found out who you are, I will ferry you across the river if it is midnight when we get there."

On placing my foot once more on Kentucky soil, I rode down to my father's house and, arriving at the yard gate, saw my brother, Albert, standing on the porch. It had commenced raining a little, and he hurried out to the gate and asked me if I wouldn't get down and come in out of the rain, to which I assented. Then calling a Negro boy, he directed him to take my horse to the stable and invited me into the house. He took me into my father's room, where I found my father, mother, sister, and younger brother sitting around the fire. They immediately made room for me, as it was chilly, inviting me to take a seat close to the fire. I knew every one of them and was surprised that none of them knew me. Supper being placed on the table, I was invited to take off my overcoat and leggings and eat supper with them. With my outer coat and leggings off, I thought they would know me, but no one seemed to do so. We took our seats at the table, and then, for the first time on such an occasion in three years, I heard a blessing asked, my father having practiced this act of devotion from my earliest recollection. After supper we all gathered around the fire again, when my father asked me where I was from. I responded, "From Missouri." He then asked me, "What part of Missouri?" Then I said, "Up the Missouri River." Then he asked, "Have you ever seen or heard of a young man named Meriwether there?" To this I responded, "Yes, several times." Then he said, "I have been waiting a year or more for the young rascal to come home." And he asked me if I had heard anything of him doing so. To this I replied, "I heard him say he was coming home some time this spring." Here the subject was dropped, and we conversed about various matters until bedtime, when I was conducted by my brother, into a back room in which were three beds. I was then shown one to which I could retire, my two brothers occupying the others.

On getting up the next morning, we all proceeded to a porch, where a basin of water and a towel were offered me for washing and drying my face and hands. Just as I had commenced wiping my face, a young man named Byers, the son of a neighbor, stepped onto the porch and immediately called me by name and shook me by the hand. At once the whole family congregated on the porch, and the house was in a turmoil. A general shaking of hands took place, in which all of the old Negroes on the place joined. Mr. Byers was then asked how he came to recognize me. He said that once when he and I were coon hunting, the dogs treed a coon up a large bush which stood on the bank of "Cane-run," when he proposed that I take the dogs down into the bottom to prevent the coon escaping up a larger tree while he cut down the bush with the hatchet we carried with us. While he was cutting, I was looking up at the coon, when the hatchet flew off its handle and struck me at the corner of my eye. The blood flowed freely, which frightened us much. And he added,

"When I came on the porch this morning I discovered the scar which I had cut in the corner of your eye and recognized you instantly."

The preceding night had been spent by me in meditating on what I should do, as I was very anxious to accept the offer made by Colonel O'Fallon in St. Louis and take another trip on the plains. I had pretty well come to the conclusion, as nobody knew me, to remain at my father's house on some pretext or another for a week or two, and, if I found my brother, Albert, was able to attend to my father's business without assistance, I would return to my roving, wandering life on the plains. But the recognition by Mr. Byers spoiled all my plans. This is the same Dillard Byers who afterwards married and settled in Shelby County near the town of Simpsonville and died there but a few years ago, a prominent member of the Methodist church, and said to be founder of the Methodist church in our neighborhood.

A few days after this I went to Louisville and collected my money, bringing it home and giving it to my mother to keep for me. I think it was about a month after my return, when going to Louisville again, I received a letter from Colonel O'Fallon requesting me to return to St. Louis in haste, as the new trading expedition of which I have previously spoken was preparing to depart, and he wished to confer with me about the route. The same day, I met on the street Captain Silas Craig, who commanded the old Steamboat Expedition, and I engaged passage for St. Louis and asked him if he would call at my father's and take me aboard, to which he agreed and said he would start the next day.

On returning home and informing my father and mother of all this, they appeared dissatisfied, but made no remark. The next morning I packed up a few clothes in saddle bags, and going into my mother's room, found her lying on the bed, and told her I wanted some money. Immediately her eyes filled with tears, and she said, "David you are going among the wild Indians again." But I assured her I was not and told her I only wanted twenty-five dollars to meet the expense of my trip to St. Louis, and if I did not return in two weeks, she could have all my money. My promise to go no farther than St. Louis appeared to satisfy her, and she handed me the money I wanted. During the day the boat passed down and stopped for me. Captain Craig asked me if I could assist his chief clerk if necessary, as his second clerk had been taken sick and was left behind. I answered, "Yes with pleasure, for old acquaintance sake." Steamboats were differently constructed then from what they are now. There was only one deck above the guards; the cabin was on the lower deck, and aft the boilers. The pilot did not steer the boat but stood on the front part of the boiler deck and, during the daytime, waved his right or left hand in the direction the boat was to run. But in the night he waved a small lantern for the same purpose, while the steersman stood near the stern holding the tiller in his hand and keeping a close lookout on the pilot. This was pretty hard on the steersman, and I frequently relieved him of his task and assisted the clerk whenever occasion required.

On reaching St. Louis, I called on Colonel O'Fallon, who informed me that neither Captain Ashley or Mr. Immell were in town, but they had left a young man who understood surveying, to make from my directions a rough map of the country over which I had traveled, as I had told Colonel O'Fallon long since that I could not embark in this expedition. Being somewhat of a surveyor myself, the young man and I soon constructed a rough map of the country, laying down the water courses and mountains from my memory, also marking where wood, water, and grass were to be found and noting what tribes of Indians might be expected to be encountered. I advised this young man who was to accompany the expedition, to employ Big Elk or some other Pawnee Indian familiar with the country, as guide. While in St. Louis, I assisted the clerk of the boat and slept on board at the invitation of Captain Craig.

About three or four days after our arrival in St. Louis, we again started down the Mississippi and up the Ohio. On getting near home, I asked the clerk what was my bill, when he informed me that he had been instructed by the captain to charge me nothing. One dark rainy night about ten or eleven o'clock I was put ashore in the yawl at my father's house. Approaching the house, a dog ran at me, but as I had after my return home had several hunts with him, I called him by name, and he came up to me in a friendly manner. Seeing no lights in the house, I thought it unnecessary to awaken the family, and, as the window of the boys' room was very low, I determined to creep in without, if possible, disturbing anyone. So, hoisting the window and placing the saddle bags on the sill, I crawled in. Knowing that three beds were in the room, and the situation of each, though it was very dark, I groped my way to one of them. I found it occupied, so proceeded to another bed, which I also found occupied. Then I went to the third and found that too had a tenant, but in feeling with my hand to see if there was room for me in any on the beds, my hand passed over the face of one of the occupants, when a female voice screamed, "Murder," in which cry several others joined. I immediately jumped out of the window, seized my saddle bags, and went rolling down the hill. This aroused the dog again, but, on calling him by name, he became pacified.

My father immediately came out on the porch fronting the river, holding a candle in one hand and his gun in the other. By this time I had ensconsed myself under a large rosebush. My father hissed at the dog when the animal would run down to where I was, barking furiously, but on my calling his name, would cease barking. Pretty soon the lights were extinguished in the house, and about an hour after this, supposing that everyone was asleep again, I marched up to the door and knocked. On my fathers' asking who was there, I told him, and as he always had a little Negro boy asleep in the room with him and my mother to make fires in the morning, he awoke Dennis and told him to open the door and let me in.

On entering the room of my father and mother, I discovered three beds on the floor beside each other, and all occupied. My father told me that a number of young ladies had visited my sister the evening before, and as all wanted to occupy the same room, and since no room but the boys' contained three beds, my mother had let them occupy the boys' room and the boys had been sent upstairs. He also told me that somebody had hoisted the window and crawled into the room and frightened the girls so much that they had insisted on having their beds brought into his room. Then he told Dennis to light a candle and conduct me upstairs.

At the breakfast table next morning, I listened to some of the most horrible tales. One of the girls declared that the man had a knife at least a foot long in his hand and had put his hand on her face to cut her throat, but her screams had awakened the others and he had jumpd out the window. They described him and his knife as most horrible looking objects, when in fact it was so dark that if I had a dozen knives, no one could have seen them, nor could any have told whether I was a Negro or a white man.

I did not attempt to correct them for several years, but after I was married, a number of these same girls were at my father's house, together with myself and wife. The girls commenced giving the latter a detailed account of this horrible occurrence, when I forebore no longer and told them it was I, and related the circumstances under which it happened.

VIII
Farming and Politics

On my return home I busied myself in settling up my father's old affairs and going to New Orleans every fall in flatboats, taking the produce of his farm as well as that of some of our neighbors. On one occasion I extended my trip to the island of Cuba and brought back in exchange for the produce, sugar, coffee, and other groceries, which I disposed of in Louisville.

In February, 1823, occurred the happiest incident of my checkered life, when I married Miss Sarah H. Leonard. This happy union continued about thirty-six years, during which time there were born thirteen children, six of whom still survive. My mother-in-law, Mrs. Mary Leonard, was the widow of the Reverend David A. Leonard, who had purchased a farm on the Indiana shore, nearly opposite my father's residence. In the June following, my father gave me one hundred and fifty acres of land, on part of which I now reside. As this land was covered with woods, I commenced building a small frame house and clearing off the timber. My father also gave me a Negro man, woman, and three children, the oldest of which was fourteen years of age. I purchased another Negro man, hired another, and began building and clearing land, which I found to be a laborious job, as we had to saw all the lumber by hand with a whip saw. But we succeeded in getting into a house of our own on the day before Christmas of that year. Before that we had lived at my father's and Mrs. Leonard's, a week on one side of the river and a week on the other side.

I opened a large wood yard and had the trees cut into cord wood for steamboats, and the sale of this wood just about paid for clearing the land. We had to use great industry and economy in order to keep out of debt. Indeed the produce of farms at that time scarcely paid the cost of its production. For instance, I purchased my corn the first year at 12½ cents per bushel and my pork at $1.50 per hundred net. The first crop of wheat I raised sold for 37½ cents per bushel and the first crop of tobacco at $3.37½ per hundred pounds, although my tobacco took the premium for being the best delivered in the Louisville markets. At the same time we had to pay twenty cents per pound for sugar, fifty cents per pound for our coffee, and such calico as you now buy for from five to seven cents per yard, cost us twenty-five cents per yard, and salt was one dollar per bushel.

Upon my return from Missouri, I found people of the state divided into two parties, relief and anti-relief. During the War of 1812, which closed in 1815, the cost of all farm produce was very high, hence the farmer went into debt to purchase more land and lived in an extravagant manner. By the time of my return, produce had fallen so low that they could not get out of debt, hence they called upon the legislature for relief, and at one session the legislature incorporated forty-two banks which issued an immense amount of paper money, and pretty soon the banks began to fail. Then the legislature incorporated what was called the Commonwealth Bank, with a number of branches in different sections of the state. This bank was not prepared to redeem its paper when presented, but the state had pledged its faith and credit for the final redemption of the bank's currency, which soon fell to fifty cents on the dollar. In order to bolster up this currency, it was made receivable for taxes and other debts due the state. An act was also passed by the legislature, providing that if a creditor did not receive it in payment of his debts, the debtor should have the right of extending such debts for one year, which was afterwards extended to two years. The Court of Appeals of the state promptly declared these laws unconstitutional, on the ground that the Constitution of the United States prohibited the state from issuing bills of credit, and that if they could not issue bills of credit themselves, they could not authorize a bank to do so. This created an immense prejudice against the Court of Appeals, and as the relief party had elected a majority in both branches of the legislature and also the governor, what was called the Reorganizing Act was passed. This act provided for the removal of the judges of this court from office and authorized the governor to appoint other judges, out of which arose the old and new court parties.

The old judges denied the power of the legislature to pass such an act and refused to surrender their offices, whilst the new court, sustained by the governor and the legislature, maintained the power of the legislature to pass such an act. Hence we had two courts in session at the same time, one reversing the decisions of the other, and anarchy reigned supreme. But finally the good men of both parties prevailed and effected a compromise by which it was agreed that all the judges would resign, and the governor agreed that he would appoint a court, the judges of which would consist of both parties; and this effectually settled the vexed question.

In 1824 a heated contest for the presidency arose between John Quincy Adams, General Jackson, Mr. Clay, and Mr. Crawford, and political feeling ran very high. When the returns came in, it was found that neither of the candidates had received a majority of the electoral votes, hence the election devolved upon the House of Representatives in Congress, and, Mr. Clay, having turned all his forces, as far as he could, in favor of Mr. Adams, the latter was elected President of the United States.

Immediately after his inauguration, President Adams appointed Mr. Clay secretary of state. Then arose a hue and cry against these two gentlemen, who were charged with bargaining, intrigue, and corruption, and parties became still more embittered against each other. In 1828, General Jackson and Mr. Adams were the opposing candidates, but Jackson swept everything before him and was triumphantly elected. Soon after this, the Bank of the United States began to agitate the question of its recharter, when it soon developed that General Jackson was opposed to this measure and Mr. Clay favored it. Hence the recharter of this bank became a disturbing element in our politics.

In 1832 Jackson was renominated for the presidency by the Democrats, and Mr. Clay was nominated by the Whigs and bank parties. At this time parties were equally balanced in Jefferson County. In 1831, the county having two representatives then, Samuel Churchill and Robert Tyler were elected by the Democrats, one by about twenty-five and the other by fifteen majority. On the eighth day of January, 1832, the Democratic convention at Frankfort nominated Colonel John Breathitt[1] for governor, but it was very difficult in some of the counties to get county candidates on the Democratic side of the legislature. In Jefferson County a convention was held at Jeffersontown, and Colonel Churchill and Mr. Tyler were nominated for re-election, but both promptly declined the nomination. Then another convention was called at the same place and the nomination offered to Captain Henry Robb, Captain John Woodsmall, Mr. Allan Rose, Mr. Alfred Luckett, Major John Hughes, and others, but they all declined to accept a nomination.

A little after this Colonel Breathitt came to Louisville and, getting the Democratic state central committee together, told

[1] Breathitt was born in Loudin County, Virginia, on September 9, 1786. In February, 1810, he was admitted to the bar and settled in Frankfort, where he was a successful lawyer. He served several terms in the state legislature and in 1828 was elected lieutenant governor of Kentucky as a Jacksonian Democrat. He was the eleventh governor of the state, serving from 1832 to 1843, not completing his term because of his death at Frankfort on February 21, 1834.

them that unless the counties brought out local candidates to sustain him in the canvass, he would certainly be beaten. Early in the month of June, I think it was, a bill was passed in Congress, rechartering the United States Bank, and it was generally believed that General Jackson would veto it. Some prominent Democrats were heard to say, "If he vetoes the bank bill, we will veto him." In due time, the veto came, which struck many Democrats with consternation. Another Democratic convention had been called to meet at Jeffersontown, and the day appointed was shortly after General Jackson's veto measure appeared. Both parties at this time had become violently aroused, and on the day of the convention the little town was literally filled with Democrats, but no one seemed willing to become a candidate for the legislature and sustain the veto. We were about to adjourn without accomplishing anything, when finally Mr. Harry Churchill, a brother of the Colonel, said he would nominate me if I would consent to run. About this time the convention adjourned for dinner, at which time Mr. James Guthrie,[2] William Pope,[3] Matthew Love, Major John Hughes, and a few others took me into a room and insisted on my making the race with Mr. Churchill.

I declined, however, on the ground that both of us resided in the lower end of the county and but five or six miles distant

[2] Guthrie was born in Nelson County, Kentucky, on December 5, 1792. He was admitted to the bar and in 1820 moved to Louisville where he was active in politics, serving in various capacities, including nine successive years in the lower house of the legislature and six years in the state senate. He was one of the principal founders of the Kentucky railroad system and was later president of the Louisville and Nashville Railroad. In 1853 he was secretary of the treasury in the Franklin Pierce cabinet, serving to the end of that administration. He died in Louisville on March 18, 1869.

[3] Colonel William Pope, of Virginia, is credited in history with having laid out the town of Louisville in 1780. William Pope, George Meriwether, and six others were named as trustees to survey the town on a tract of one thousand acres, which had been granted to John Connolly by Great Britain, which he forfeited by his allegiance to England. Collins, *History of Kentucky*, II, 360–71.

from each other, while, at the same time, a large majority of voters were in the upper end. I also informed them that I had that spring purchased my mother-in-law's farm in Indiana and had given notes for six thousand dollars. I told them, moreover, that I knew Mrs. Leonard had sold this farm for the express purpose of raising money with which to start her two oldest sons in business, and therefore I must decline as a duty to my creditors required me to attend to my private business, for otherwise I would not be able to meet my indebtedness. Later these gentlemen called on me again and asked me when my notes would become due, and I told them the time. Then they said, "We will remove this obstacle to your becoming a candidate; for, if you have not the money when your note becomes due, call on us and we will furnish it." Upon this assurance, I consented to accept the nomination. When we met in convention again after dinner, the hundreds of Democrats looked moody and disappointed, but when our two names were proclaimed as the candidates, they were received with great applause. Mr. Churchill, being unwell, merely arose and accepted the nomination. Then the crowd called upon me for a speech, and now, for the first time in my life, I arose to make a political speech. I don't know what I said or how I said it, but I sustained General Jackson's veto of the bank charter, the grounds he had taken against internal improvements in the state by the general government in favor of a strict construction of the Constitution of the United States, and all the other measures of his administration. When I concluded, the Democrats present (to say the least of it) appeared well satisfied, and I was congratulated by many.

It was well known that I had voted for General Jackson in 1824, in 1828, and had assisted in his nomination in 1832, and it may not be improper for me to say that I afterwards voted for Van Buren, Mr. Polk, and every other Democratic candidate for the President down to Mr. Cleveland, the present occupant of the White House, except Mr. Buchanan, and I would have voted for him if I had been at home. But I was a resident of a territory at that Presidential election, and the citizens of territories cannot vote [in] Presidential elections.

On my return home after my nomination, I told my wife what I had done and the circumstances under which I had accepted. She said she was sorry I had been forced to do so, but as some Democrat had to make the sacrifice, she didn't see why it shouldn't as well fall on my shoulders as on anothers.

The nomination was made on Saturday, and I mounted my horse on Monday morning to commence the canvass. I would continue riding over the country until Saturday night, when I would return home (for I never electioneered on the Sabbath), start again Monday morning, to return Saturday night, often at midnight. This kept up until the close of the election. As I was well known in the lower end of the county, I did little electioneering there. I left that neighborhood to be attended to for me by Issac P. Miller, Harry Shively, old Robert Miller, and other friends. When I went out on the Preston Road, I had the assistance of Captain Henry Robb, who had once before represented the county, and Captain Murphy. On the Bardstown Road I was ably assisted by Colonel John Doup, William Thixton, Mr. Finley, and others. Thence going up Floyd's Fork, I was assisted by Captain John Woodsmall, Mr. Pomms, Thomas Waller, Thomas Stafford, and others. Higher up, I was assisted by Tom Meddis, John Gillaland, Allan Rose, and others. About Boston I had the assistance of old Mr. Conn, his sons, and others. At Middletown I was aided by Captain John Wommack and others. On Harrod's Creek and that vicinity I had the help of Colonel John Shrader, Alfred Luckett, Mr. Hinley, and others.

We then had three days' election, and I left home at three o'clock in the morning of the first Monday in August and scarcely slept an hour until I returned home late Wednesday night, the last day of the election, when I lay on the bed with my clothes on while my wife prepared some supper for me, and I didn't awaken until sunrise the next morning. My wife was always a good Democrat, as her father before her, and she was anxious to know the result, and I replied, "Doubtful," but when the returns came in, I found that Breathitt had carried the county by eighty-one majority, Mr. Churchill, by eighty, and I by eighty-three. I think it probable that Mr. Churchill would have done better had he not been taken sick a few days after his nomination and was scarcely able to do anything during the canvass.

Our Whig opponents were two highly honorable gentlemen, Mr. Seaton and Mr. Galbreath, but neither of them, nor Mr. Churchill, made a speech during the canvass, whilst I had to meet on almost every other public occasion some distinguished lawyer from Louisville, particularly Colonel Frank Johnson and Mr. James W. Denny.

When the returns came in from the several counties of the state, it was ascertained that Colonel Breathitt was elected, but Mr. Morehead, the Whig candidate for lieutenant governor, was also elected, and a majority of both branches of the legislature were Whigs. Unfortunately for the Democratic party, Colonel Breathitt died during the second year of his incumbency of the gubernatorial chair, upon which the Democrats found themselves in the minority in every branch of the state government. But Jackson had been elected President by a triumphant majority.

Our success in the election of 1832 rendered it impossible for me to keep out of politics, and I was nominated and renominated repeatedly for the legislature, but the state continued under Whig rule for many years thereafter.

I think it was in 1847 that I was nominated a candidate for Congress in opposition to Mr. Garnett Duncan, a distinguished lawyer of Louisville. At this time our congressional district was not such as it is at present. It then consisted of the city of Louisville and the counties of Jefferson, Oldham, Trimble, Henry, and Shelby. A very vigorous and laborious though pleasant canvass ensued between Mr. Duncan and myself, and, as the Whigs had a majority in the district of from eight hundred to one thousand, I was beaten, as I and all my friends expected, but by a reduced majority. I had been nominated only to assist the Democratic candidate for governor and to bring the Democratic voters to the polls. But the Democratic governor was also defeated. The excitement and labor of the canvass prostrated me with sickness.

In 1849, delegates had to be elected to frame a new constitution for the state, and Mr. William C. Bullitt,[4] a Whig, and myself, a Democrat, were nominated as the anti-Emancipation candidates and were elected by large majorities. And here I desire to say, that if there ever was an honest, candid, and fair man in politics and in every other respect, it was William C. Bullitt. We roomed together for several months at Frankfort, from which I had a fair opportunity of forming an opinion of him. And all the harm I wish of any of his posterity is that, on dying, they may leave a reputation for integrity, honor, and fairness equal to that of their ancestor.

In 1851, I was again nominated for Congress against Colonel Humphrey Marshall,[5] who had returned from the Mexican War with all the honors attached to his position of colonel. I

[4] Bullitt was a descendant of a colonial family which emigrated from France to the United States in 1665, settling in Charles County, Maryland. He represented Louisville in the legislature of 1851–53, and in 1861 he was elected judge of the Court of Appeals. While chief justice of Kentucky in July, 1864, he was arrested by order of General William Tecumseh Sherman and later exchanged by General Nathan Bedford Forrest. He died in Louisville on February 16, 1897.

[5] Marshall was graduated from West Point on July 1, 1832, and was commissioned 3rd lieutenant in the Mounted Rangers; colonel, 1st Kentucky Cavalry, June 9, 1846; honorably mustered out, July 7, 1847. During the Civil War he was a brigadier general in the Confederate service and served from 1861 to 1865. He died March 28, 1872. Heitman, *Historical Register, U.S.A.*, II, 690.

strenuously resisted being nominated again for Congress, but the nomination was forced upon me. Old Dr. Bell,[6] who had been my family physician for years, told my wife that if I consented to make the race, to prepare my shroud and coffin, for I would never get through it. I therefore prepared a letter declining the nomination and went to Louisville for the purpose of having it published, when I found myself surrounded by Democrats who said that Dr. Bell had said this to my wife because he was a Whig and didn't want Colonel Marshall to have opposition.

Finally it was suggested that the matter should be referred to Dr. Flint, an eminent Democratic physician of Louisville. On agreeing to this, I requested Dr. Flint to confer with Dr. Bell, and then examine me and give his opinion. Some days after this he gave me a thorough examination and gave as his opinion that he could give me a prescription which would enable me to undergo the excitement and labor of the canvass. Immediately after this, Colonel Marshall and myself entered upon a heated canvass, in which I made about sixty speeches. L. W. Powell,[7] who had been nominated by the Democrats for governor, came into the campaign, and I went with him into every county of the district and gave him a most cordial support. But I was again beaten, as was expected, but by a still reduced majority. On the close of the polls I returned home, and the next morning I found my-

[6] Dr. Theodore S. Bell, of Louisville, was a journalist as well as a physician. He is described as a distinguished writer for the press and one of the editors of the *Louisville Journal*: "A physician of high standing and a professor in several Louisville medical schools."—Collins, *History of Louisville*, II, 280.

[7] Lazarus Whitehead Powell, born near Henderson, Henderson County, Kentucky, on October 6, 1812, was a prominent lawyer practicing at Henderson. He served as a member of the legislature in 1836, presidential elector on the Democratic ticket of James K. Polk and George W. Dallas in 1844, governor of Kentucky in 1851–55, and United States senator, 1859–65. He was appointed with Major Ben McCulloch, of Texas, as one of the peace commissioners to treat with Brigham Young in 1858. He died near Henderson, Kentucky, on July 3, 1867. See *ibid.*, II, 681.

self unable to get out of bed. Dr. Bell was immediately sent for, and on his arrival, the first words he said, were, "Didn't I tell you so?" He returned the next day accompanied by Dr. Flint, and they continued to visit me daily for over a week; after I got well, I paid Dr. Bell his bill and then went to Dr. Flint to pay him, but he refused to receive a cent, saying that he had been the cause of my sickness, and that by right, he ought to pay Dr. Bell's bill.

Mr. Powell was the first Democratic governor elected in Kentucky for about twenty years, and the Democratic party felt greatly rejoiced. About a week after the inauguration was to take place, I was one of the committee of Democrats appointed to go to Henderson, where the Governor-elect resided, and escort him to the seat of government. On our arrival there, we were told that he was still confined to his bed with an attack of inflamatory rheumatism, which had prostrated him a week or two before the election. Hence it was decided that a subcommittee of three, consisting of Levi Tyler, Alexander P. Churchill, and myself should wait upon the Governor-elect and see whether he was able to be removed on board the steamboat on which the committee had gone down to Henderson. On entering his bedroom, he at once exclaimed, "Here's my secretary of state," pointing to me.

We managed to get him on board the boat that evening and started on our return trip. During the next day, he asked me if I would accept the office of secretary of state, which I declined, saying, "You had better get some lawyer of reputation." To this he responded, "It is probable that I will not be able to enter on the full discharge of the gubernatorial duties for some time, and I want you in my office because you are familiar with legislation and the politics of the state." I then assented to his proposition, provided I might be permitted to resign when he had entirely recovered from his illness.

Arriving at Frankfort, Governor Powell had to stand on his crutches while taking the oath of office and delivering his inaugural address. He then directed the assistant secretary of state to make out my commission, and I took the oath of office and entered upon the discharge of my duties. That evening the Governor was removed to the house furnished by the state for the residence of its governor. The Governor was unable to enter his office until, I think, sometime during the month of November. This made it necessary for me to tramp backwards and forwards between the state house and the Governor's residence whenever it was necessary for the Governor to affix his signature to an official paper. But this only continued a short time, for, one day on coming into his room to get his signature to a paper, he said, "Meriwether, this won't do, for the state has furnished me with a house containing half a dozen rooms, and there is nobody to occupy them except myself and my little son, Henry. So select a room for yourself and live with me; then when you come home to dinner, you can bring the papers needing my signature, and at suppertime the same thing can be done, and you will be company for me at night." This was a great accommodation for me as the distance from the statehouse to the Governor's house was three or four hundred yards. I continued to reside with the Governor until I resigned my office.

I think it was early in the month of June following, that the death of Henry Clay,[8] then senator in Congress from Kentucky, was announced. This did not surprise me, for it was known that he had been long confined to a sickbed in Washington City. The

[8] Henry Clay died on June 29, 1852. David Meriwether's great-granddaughter, Mrs. Betsy Graves O'Neill, states that although the two men had been political opponents throughout their careers, Meriwether, learning of Clay's illness, called on him before his last trip to Washington, a few months before his death, to bid him goodbye. At the termination of their visit, Clay shook his hand and said: "In spite of our political differences, Meriwether, you have come to see a tired old man return to die, you are a man of heart, and I admire you."—Interview, Mrs. Betsy Graves O'Neill, September 28, 1963.

evening that this news arrived the Governor asked me to whom I thought he ought to appoint to the vacant senatorship. To this, I replied, that "If I had the appointment, I would give it to Mr. James Guthrie of Louisville." And he replied, "I agree with you, and I want you to write him a letter, tendering him the appointment in my name." This I did. The next day I received Mr. Guthrie's answer, in which he desired me to thank the Governor for his tender of the appointment, but he begged leave to decline it on the ground that he had several important suits on hand, and duty to his clients would not permit him to accept the appointment, and he closed his letter by saying, "Why [doesn't] the Governor appoint you?" After reading this letter I handed it to the Governor, when at once, he asked, "Will you accept it?" To this I replied that I wanted to get out of my present office, and this would afford me a pretext for resigning, whereupon he directed the assistant secretary to make out my commission.

That evening I came down to Louisville, and understanding that Mr. Clay's remains would arrive that night escorted by a committee of senators, I remained in the city and joined in the escort to the depot next morning. I then returned home, made a little preparation, and joined the committee on their return to Washington. My credentials were presented, the oath of office was administered, and I took my seat in the Senate of the United States. But I must say how diminutive I felt on occupying the seat of so great a man as Mr. Clay. Congress did not adjourn that session until about the first of September, at the close of which I returned home and took an active part in the Presidential campaign then in progress between General Pierce and General Scott, in which the former was elected.

Congress met on the first Monday in December following, when I again repaired to Washington, and the legislature of Kentucky having assembled about the same time, Mr. Dixon of Henderson was elected to the Senate, I think early in February.

Many senators doubted whether Mr. Dixon could take his seat before the fourth of March, but, on hearing of the election of Mr. Dixon, I immediately addressed him a letter in which I stated that, in as much as the legislature had expressed a preference for him, he could come on and take the seat, as I would not consent to hold it a single day after his arrival. He accordingly arrived in Washington and presented his credentials, which were referred to the Judiciary Committee, when a good deal of discussion arose in that committee and in the Senate as to whether he could take his seat before the fourth of March ensuing. It was finally decided that, in as much as I did not claim the seat, the oath of office should be administered to Mr. Dixon.

When Mr. Dixon arrived, I escorted him into the Senate Chamber, introduced him to a number of senators, and did not again enter the chamber until the question of his eligibility was decided. The fourth of March was near at hand, and as I desired to be present at the inauguration of General Pierce, I remained in Washington until that ceremony was over. General Pierce arrived in Washington two or three days before the inauguration was to take place, and I was introduced to him by Mr. Guthrie, who had been invited by General Pierce to take a seat in his cabinet. A day of two after this, I called upon the President in company with Mr. Guthrie to take my leave of his Excellency, and return home.

IX
Territorial Governor

SOME TIME IN THE MONTH OF MAY following, I received a telegram dispatch from Mr. Guthrie, who had been appointed secretary of the treasury, requesting me to hasten to Washington as soon as possible. I started the next day, arriving in Washington City at six o'clock one morning. Immediately after breakfast, I called upon Mr. Guthrie at his private residence to inquire what he desired. He informed me that the President desired to appoint me governor of New Mexico. I told him I could see no object in the world to my going to that country, as I had a large family of children at home, in whose rearing and education I desired to assist.

He then told me that we were about to have another war with Mexico over the boundary line[1] between the two countries, and the President had told his cabinet to select a man for whose prudence and firmness one or more of them could vouch for and to present his name the next day. Mr. Guthrie said further, that on the assembling of the cabinet the next morning, Governor Marcy,[2] the secretary of state, was asked by the President if

[1] The Treaty of Guadalupe Hidalgo, which ended the Mexican War in 1848, had provided for a survey of the new boundary between the territory remaining to Mexico and the huge tract acquired by the United States. The survey began in 1850, but many disputes and difficulties had developed within the mixed Mexican–American commissions that attempted to run the line. See John R. Bartlett, *Personal Narrative of Explorations and Incidents in Texas, New Mexico, California, and Chihuahua . . .* ; Report of the Secretary of the Interior, 32 Cong., 1 sess., July, 1852 ("Mexico and U.S. Boundary Survey"); William H. Emory, *Report of Wm. H. Emory Major First Cavalry and U.S. Commissioner*, Vol. I, 28; and 34 Cong., 1 sess., *House Exec. Doc. 135* ("U.S. and Mexican Boundary Survey").

[2] William L. Marcy served in the War of 1812 and filled important posts in

he had a suitable name to present to him to go out as governor of New Mexico. To this Governor Marcy replied in the negative. He then asked Mr. Guthrie if he had a name to present to him, and Mr. Guthrie responded that he knew a man for whose prudence and firmness he would vouch, but he did not know whether he would accept or not. Mr. Guthrie told me that he then presented my name, when the President asked if he hadn't introduced me to him, and Mr. Guthrie responded in the affirmative. The President said, "I recollect Mr. Meriwether now, and I liked his looks. Telegraph him to come here immediately." After telling me all this, Mr. Guthrie added, "It is proper for you to go around and thank the President, whether you accept the office or not, and as I am going to see him this morning, I will go with you."

On arriving at the White House, Mr. Guthrie said to the President, "Mr. Meriwether has come, in obedience to my dispatch, but I don't believe he will consent to go to New Mexico." The President asked, "Why." Then I told him the reasons I had given to Mr. Guthrie, and added that I once was a prisoner in New Mexico and was released upon promising never to return there. The President asked me if I had been in the Mexican War, to which I responded in the negative but told him of my being captured about thirty years before. "Well," said the President, "the statute of limitations bars your promise."

The President and Mr. Guthrie then began discussing the boundary question and the probabilities of war growing out of it, when I remarked, "Gentlemen, I don't think you understand that question." I was asked "How do you understand it?" To this I replied, "The treaty by which New Mexico was ceded to

---

New York State, including associate justice of the Supreme Court and three terms as governor. During 1831–37 he served one term as a United States senator. He became secretary of war in 1845 and was secretary of state in the Pierce cabinet. He displayed notable ability as a statesman and diplomat.

The Plaza at Santa Fe
a Short Two Decades after Meriwether's Governorship.
St. Francis Cathedral, in background, was built
by the Reverend Jean B. Lamy.

Courtesy Museum of New Mexico

David Meriwether (in rocking chair)
on His Ninetieth Birthday, Surrounded by Friends
and Relatives, October 30, 1890.

the United States provided that each government should appoint a commissioner, an astronomer, and a surveyor to locate the line, and when the line was complete and a map made of it, and signed by all parties, it is then to become a part of the treaty." "Now," said I, "this line has never been finished, for, after progressing some distance, the American surveyor protested that they were not running the line right, and he said he never would affix his signature to a map of that description. This line is no part of the treaty until it is finished." This appeared to surprise the two gentlemen, and I was asked where I got this information. To this I replied, "When in the Senate of the United States, a committee was appointed to investigate this subject, and I was placed upon that committee." I was then asked if the committee had made a report. To this I replied that I had drafted[3] the report myself. I was also asked if the report had ever been printed. I said, "Yes, I read the report in the *Daily Globe* a few days after the committee had made it."

The President summoned his private secretary and asked me to give him as near as I could the date of the printing of this report, and the secretary was directed to hunt it up. In a short time the secretary returned with the report of the committee and proceeded to read it to us. When the reading was finished, the President turned to me and said, "You have got to go to New Mexico, you know more about this matter than any one of us do."

I then consented to accept the office, on the condition that I might be permitted to resign whenever this boundary question could be settled.

I was then directed to accompany the private secretary of the President to the Secretary of State's office, and the private secretary told Governor Marcy to make out my commission as

[3] Report from the Secretary of the Interior (in relation to fixing the initial point in the boundary line between the United States and Mexico), 32 Cong., 1 sess., *Sen. Rpt. 345*, August 20, 1852, 1–5.

governor of New Mexico. I was asked the place of my birth, my age, and present residence, the answers to which were duly recorded. My commission was then made out and sent to the President for his signature. Governor Marcy then said, "I suppose you are aware that you will have to take the oath of office." To this I responded in the affirmative. "And you will have to go to the Secretary of the Treasury," he said, "and execute a bond with security." I asked him who could administer the oath of office, to which he replied, "Any judge of the U.S. District or Circuit Court." He then told me that I would have to deposit a duplicate copy of the oath in his office, and directed a clerk to to make a copy of the oath on the back of my commission and to write a duplicate of it, both of which were handed to me. I then went to the office of the secretary of the treasury and asked what would be the penal sum of the bond, and I was informed it would be twenty-five thousand dollars. I told Mr. Guthrie that there was no person in Washington whom I could ask to go my security for that amount, upon which he asked me whom I proposed to get when home. I mentioned probably half a dozen names, when he said, "Any two of them will be sufficient. I will have the bond made out, leaving the names of the securities blank. You can execute it here now, take it home with you, and return it to this office by mail." I then applied to Colonel Peter C. Washington, assistant secretary of the treasury, to know where the nearest U.S. judge resided. In answer to this he told me that Judge Taney[4] resided at Baltimore but might not be at home, so he sent a dispatch to a friend in that city, and in response

[4] Roger Brooks Taney was born in southern Maryland on March 17, 1777. A strong supporter of Andrew Jackson, he served as attorney general in 1831–33, secretary of the treasury in 1833–34, and was confirmed as chief justice of the United States Supreme Court on March 15, 1836, succeeding Chief Justice John Marshall. In the last position he handed down the celebrated Dred Scott decision in in 1857 upholding the rights of slave owners. See *Dictionary of American Biography*, 289–94.

was informed that the Judge was holding court at Richmond, Virginia.

I proceeded to Richmond and had the oath of office administered to me in duplicate by the Judge, who impressed me as being one of the great men of the nation. Returning to Washington the next day, I deposited the duplicate with the Secretary of State and asked for instructions, Governor Marcy informed me that he would send them to me by mail at Louisville. I then called on the Commissioner of Indian Affairs for his instructions, which were also to be forwarded to me by mail. I also called on President Pierce to take my leave of him, when he asked me, "How soon will you leave for New Mexico?" I replied, "In five days." "Why," said he, "you can't get your baggage ready in that time." I told him that the Mexicans had robbed me of my baggage once, and I determined then never to encumber myself with much again. The President sent for Jefferson Davis, the secretary of war, to inquire how soon he could have an escort ready for me. Mr. Davis informed him that he had determined to supercede Colonel Sumner,[5] then in command in New Mexico, and send out General Garland to take his place, and that General Garland[6] would call on the President in a

[5] Colonel Edwin Vose Sumner arrived at Santa Fe on July 19, 1851, and and assumed command of the district of New Mexico. He was born in Boston, Massachusetts, on June 30, 1797, and entered the army in 1819 as 2nd lieutenant of infantry. He served in the Black Hawk War and was on General Stephen Watts Kearny's staff with the Army of Occupation in New Mexico in 1846. He was breveted lieutenant colonel in 1847 for gallantry and meritorious conduct at the battle of Cerro Gordo, Mexico; colonel, September 8, 1847, for gallantry at the battle of Molino Rey, Mexico; and major general, May 13, 1862, for gallantry in the battle of Fair Oaks, Virginia. While in command in New Mexico he strengthened the discipline and made a number of changes in disposition of troops. On August 17, 1851, he led four troops of horse, one company of artillery, and two companies of infantry into the Navaho country but failed to quell the hostile spirit of the Navahos. See William A. Keleher, *Turmoil in New Mexico*, 58; and Heitman, *Historical Register, U.S.A.*, II, 936.

[6] General John Garland, a native of Virginia, entered the army as a 1st lieutenant on March 31, 1813. He was promoted through the various grades and was

few minutes. On the arrival of General Garland, I was introduced to him, and we were directed to consult together and make arrangements for an early departure. As the General had to get his outfit at Fort Leavenworth[7] and I at Kansas City, fifty or a hundred miles below, it was agreed that we would meet at Council Grove,[8] which is about one hundred and fifty miles west of the Missouri River.

About this time I received a letter from my son-in-law, Captain Graves,[9] requesting me to procure for him the appointment of Indian agent for New Mexico. I handed the letter to the Secretary of Interior and referred him to Mr. Guthrie, secretary of the treasury, who was well acquainted with the Captain, for information as to the propriety of his appointment, upon which

---

awarded the rank of brigadier general on August 20, 1847, for gallant and meritorious conduct in the battles of Contreras and Churubusco, Mexico. He succeeded Colonel Sumner in command of the Ninth Military District of New Mexico on July 20, 1853. See Heitman, *ibid.*, I, 446; and Colonel Joseph K. F. Mansfield, *Mansfield on the Condition of the Western Forts, 1853–54*, 30.

[7] Fort Leavenworth was established on May 8, 1827, on the west side of the Missouri River, in the present Leavenworth County, Kansas. It had a well-chosen location near the mouth of the Kansas River as a starting point for Santa Fe; military escorts were furnished there for the early commerce over the trail. McCrellis, *Military Reservations*, 56–60.

[8] Council Grove, now the county seat of Morris County, Kansas, was one of the most important stations on the Santa Fé Trail. There the caravans assembled to form an organization for protection in passing through the Indian country beyond. It had good facilities for camping—thickly wooded bottom land nearly one mile in width extending a considerable distance along the Neosho River. It received its name when the commissioner surveying the trail in 1825 met the Osage Indians in council there and secured their agreement to the unmolested passage of American and Mexican traders through their country. William Elsey Connelley, *Doniphan's Expedition and the Conquest of New Mexico and California*, 156–57.

[9] Captain Edmund A. Graves was born November 3, 1818, near Lebanon, Kentucky. He studied law at Harrodsburg, Kentucky, and later practiced at Lebanon. He was elected to the Kentucky legislature in 1844 and 1846. In March, 1847, he was appointed captain of Company F, Sixteenth Infantry Regiment, and served under General Zachary Taylor in the Mexican War. On January 20, 1849, he was married to Catherine Hardinia Meriwether, the daughter of David Meriwether. He was appointed Indian agent on May 21, 1853, and accompanied the Meriwether party to Santa Fe, where he served for a brief time as agent to the Utes, and later at Doña Ana in the southern part of the territory. Meriwether Papers.

the Secretary of the Interior said, "If Mr. Guthrie says so, he will be appointed." On returning to my hotel, I found a Mr. [James M.] Smith, who had recently been appointed an Indian agent for New Mexico Territory, who desired to go out with me. I told him to be in Louisville in a week from that day, and, giving him Captain Graves's address in that city, told him to call on the Captain and get information as to when I would be ready to start.

That night I started for home, and arriving at Louisville, strongly advised Captain Graves not to accept the appointment if sent to him, as he had but recently commenced the practice of law, and I thought he had much better stick to it, which he finally agreed to do.

Relatives of Dr. Jacobs, a brother of the late mayor of the city of Louisville, called on me saying that the doctor desired to visit New Mexico and wished to know if I would take him out with me. To this I at once assented and told them that he must be ready in less than a week. In five or six days all preparations were made, and having purchased four mules and a horse, I boarded a steamboat and was off down the Ohio, together with my son Raymond. I was glad to meet several acquaintances on board the boat, among them whom were the Honorable Richard W. Thompson,[10] of Indiana, afterwards secretary of the navy during the administration of President Hayes; Captain Gunnison,[11] of the U.S. Army, Lieutenant Beckwith, Dr. Jacobs, and others, all of whom were going to Kansas City, Missouri.

[10] Richard Wigginton Thompson was born near Culpepper Court House, Virginia, July 9, 1809. He was elected as a Whig to the 30th Congress from Indiana and served two terms, 1847–51. He was appointed secretary of the navy in the cabinet of President Hayes and served from March 12, 1877, until his resignation on December 21, 1880. He died at Terre Haute, Indiana, on February 9, 1900. *Biographical Dictionary of the American Congress*, 1709–10.

[11] John Williams Gunnison graduated from West Point and was appointed 2nd lieutenant in the Second Artillery on July 1, 1837, and 1st lieutenant, Topographical Engineers, on May 9, 1846. He served as astronomer in the Stansburg

On arriving at St. Louis, I met Dr. Connelly,[12] an old trader in New Mexico who rendered me great assistance in procuring a suitable outfit. He went with me to a carriagemaker's establishment and selected a carriage with three seats, which, by letting down the backs of the seats, furnished a mattress to sleep on, which would protect me from rattlesnakes and other vermin; and by letting down the curtains, I would be protected from the weather. The carriage had a large boot behind, in which to place by baggage. While here I was called upon by my old friend, Colonel O'Fallon, and my young friend Issac Sturgeon, who was born and raised in the county of Jefferson, but who had removed to St. Louis. Mr. Sturgeon informed me that Captain Bissell resided but a few miles out of St. Louis and proposed to call that evening in his buggy and take me out to visit one of my earliest and best friends. I found the Captain quite advanced

---

Expedition of 1849. On March 3, 1853, he was commissioned a captain and ordered to survey a route for a Pacific railroad farther to the south than that made by the Stansbury Expedition, by way of the Huerfano River and Cochetopa, and thence through the valleys of the Grand and Green rivers. On October 24, 1853, he left the encampment of the expedition on the Sevier River to explore the lake of that name. At daybreak of the twenty-sixth his party was attacked by a war party of Utes, probably of Chief Walkara's (or Walker's) band, and only four of the party escaped. The victims, including Gunnison, were badly mutilated. See Hubert Howe Bancroft, *History of Utah*, 463–71; Heitman, *Historical Register, U.S.A.*, 483; and 33 Cong., 1 sess., *House Exec. Doc. 1*, 57–58.

[12] Dr. Henry Connelly was a practicing physician in Kentucky prior to his moving to Chihuahua, Mexico, in 1828, where he lived and conducted a business for many years. He was imprisoned by the Mexican authorities in Chihuahua prior to Doniphan's capture of that city, during the Mexican War. At the close of the war he came to New Mexico, residing at Santa Fe and also at Peralta, Valencia County. At Peralta he married Dolores Perea, widow of José Chaves, the father of Colonel J. Francisco Chaves, who was prominent in New Mexico affairs. He was appointed territorial governor by President Lincoln in 1861 and reappointed in 1864. According to Twitchell, credit was due Governor Connelly that the Confederacy secured no permanent foothold in New Mexico. Hubert Howe Bancroft describes him as "A man of good intentions, of somewhat visionary and poetic tempermanent, of moderate abilities and not much force." Bancroft, *History of Arizona and New Mexico*, 633. See also Ralph Emerson Twitchell, *The History of the Military Occupation of the Territory of New Mexico . . .*, 365–66.

in years but hale and hearty, and he received me with great cordiality. That evening we returned to St. Louis and the next morning boarded a Missouri River boat for Kansas City. I found great changes had taken place on the river since I passed up and down it about thirty years before, particularly at the place where old Fort Osage had stood, where I had resided the last year I was in the fur trade. Instead of the old fort, I found a village called Sibley.

On reaching Kansas City, then consisting of only a warehouse and probably a dozen dwellings, we were advised to go back a few miles to the town of Westport,[13] where we could get better accommodations. Here I received a letter from Captain Graves, informing me that Mr. Smith had called on him in Louisville and persuaded him to change his mind and accept the commission of Indian agent, and that they would join me in a few days. He requested me to purchase for him a good horse, saddle, and bridle, and the necessary outfit for traveling across the plains. Here I met Judge Davenport,[14] of Mississippi, who had recently been appointed chief justice of New Mexico by the President. Captain Gunnison and party were also here, purchasing outfits for the long trip over the plains, as the Captain had been detailed to survey the route for a railroad from the Missouri River to the Pacific Ocean.

A brisk trade in mules soon commenced, as Captain Gunnison required about fifty; with our additional ones and Mr. Smith

[13] Independence, Missouri, began as an outfitting point for western expeditions as early as 1827. During the following six years the steamboat landing was destroyed by the erosion of the Missouri River, and as a consequence Westport came into existence, the town itself being several miles back from the landing. Laid out in 1833, it grew rapidly, diverting much of the trade from Independence. It was the true beginning of Kansas City. See Chittenden, *Fur Trade,* I, 464.

[14] Judge J. J. Davenport, of Mississippi, "was the newly appointed Judge of the First District of New Mexico, thereby Chief Justice of the Territory."—John Ward, "Indian Affairs in New Mexico, from the Journal of John Ward," Ed. by Annie Heloise Abel, *New Mexico Historical Review,* Vol. XVI (July, 1941), 3, 356.

and Judge Davenport's four, it consisted of quite a herd. The last two gentlemen determined to travel together and make a joint outfit. About this time, Captain Graves arrived and I found it necessary to purchase a baggage wagon and four more mules to transport our provisions and baggage. When we were about ready to start, I received a telegram from General Garland, dated at Fort Leavenworth, stating he would be ready to leave the next day; and, if he arrived at Council Grove before me he would wait for me, if I arrived first, for me to wait for him.

We departed the next morning, accompanied by Mr. Thompson and his two little sons, they desiring to look upon the broad plains of the West by traveling with us a few days. Our party, in addition to Mr. Thompson and his boys, consisted of Judge Davenport and Mr. Smith with a wagon and driver, Captain Graves, Dr. Jacobs, and Raymond on horseback, a baggage wagon and driver, and my carriage, which was driven by a free Negro who I had hired to go and who was to act as cook for the mess. On reaching Council Grove, we found that General Garland had not arrived but that Captain [Nathaniel Chapman] Macrae with about two hundred soldiers were camped about a mile below the little settlement, awaiting the arrival of the General. In a day or two General Garland arrived with his staff and a detachment of troops, among whom I found Major [Cary Harrison] Fry, a paymaster in the army who had recently married a Louisville lady; Colonel Miles[15] and his wife and family, Lieu-

[15] Dixon Stansbury Miles entered West Point from Maryland, graduated, and was appointed 2nd lieutenant, Fourth Infantry, on July 1, 1824. After rising through the various grades he was promoted to lieutenant colonel on September 23, 1846, for gallantry at Monterey, Mexico. He died on September 16, 1862, of wounds received in the defence of Harpers Ferry, Virginia. When Meriwether met him at Council Grove he had recently figured in the boundary trouble between the United States and Mexico. William Carr Lane, Meriwether's predecessor as territorial governor, issued a proclamation claiming the Mesilla Valley, a disputed tract about El Paso; but Miles, who was in command of nearby Fort Fillmore, refused to take possession without orders from Washington. Lane angrily expressed his feelings in a letter of March 19, 1855: "And some 300 U.S. troops who are unemployed and

tenant [Wylly C.] Adams and his wife, and Captain Macrae also had his wife and family with him. All were pleasant traveling companions, especially Dr. DeLeon,[16] who was going out as chief surgeon.

Our train, consisting of a hundred or more wagons and carriages, departed the day after the arrival of General Garland. With us also was Captain Gunnison and his surveying party, Mr. Ben O'Fallon, son of the Colonel, and another young gentleman, both of whom had joined us for a pleasure trip on the plains.

On arriving at the Pawnee Fork[17] of the Arkansas River, we found it too swollen to be forded, so camped. We also found at this point awaiting the falling of the river, a Mexican train, the conductor of which informed me that plenty of buffalo were five or six miles up the stream.

The next morning a party of us started out for a chase. As my son Raymond had never seen such a thing before, I let him ride the horse, and I mounted a mule, as a buffalo chase was no new thing to me. On arriving in sight of the buffalo, all except myself dashed off in pursuit, for it was no use for one on a mule to attempt to catch a buffalo. I followed up the dry bed of a stream a mile or two, when I found a hole of water where buffalo

are within 5 miles of the scene of activity, fold their arms in frigid tranquility and thereby sustain the enemies of their country." Heitman, *Historical Register, U.S.A.*, I, 708; and Mansfield, *Western Port*, 57–77.

16 David Camden DeLeon, of South Carolina. Assistant surgeon, August 21, 1838; major surgeon, August 29, 1856; resigned, February 19, 1861; surgeon, C.S.A., 1861–65; died September 3, 1872. Mansfield said of him: "His skill as a physician entitles him to a high standing in his profession. Although the number of cases that he administered to amounted to 361 exclusive of officers families and servants, he did not lose one, and in several instances to my personal knowledge his subjects were very sick."—Mansfield, *Western Forts*, 31. See also Heitman, *Historical Register, U.S.A.*, I, 366.

17 The Pawnee Fork of the Arkansas empties into the Arkansas at the present town of Larned, Kansas. See Perrine, "Military Escorts on the Santa Fe Trail," *New Mexico Historical Review*, Vol. III (July, 1928), 277.

were in the habit of drinking. As no rain had fallen here but only on the upper waters of the Pawnee Fork, I concealed myself and mule under the banks of the creek, thinking probably some buffalo might come through there for water.

In about an hour I discovered a small drove of buffalo approaching, and on their coming up within seventy-five or a hundred yards, I fired and dropped one in his tracks. I cut off large quantities of the meat, and placing it on the back of the mule, I tried to lead him, but he went backwards instead of forwards. I then tried to drive him before me, but with no success. After working with him an hour or two, I mounted and got him started with the meat, but on going a few miles he gave out. I wore my switch out on him, but to little purpose, and, as it was an open prairie, I could get no other switch. I again tried to lead him without success. I finally then tried to drive him, but to no purpose, so I had to throw off all the meat and again mounting, by a vigorous application of my ramrod, I got him in motion again, but only in a slow walk. On reaching a gradual descent in the prairie, I succeeded in raising a trot, but very shortly the mule stepped in a gopher hole with his forefoot and pitched me clear over his head. I thought that my thigh was broken, but on laying down a while and examining it, I found that the hammer of my gun had stuck into it about an inch and there was no fracture of the bone. The mule's foot was still in the hole, so I had to take my knife and cut away the hard ground to make the hole large enough for the animal to extricate himself. On arising, the mule appeared to be very lame, and I once more essayed to lead and drive him, but to no purpose, so mounting again, by vigorous application of my ramrod I once more got in motion.

I was proceeding down the valley of the Pawnee Fork, upon which I knew our camp had been made but probably half a mile from the river, when about sundown I discovered campfires upon its bank. Supposing that this was General Garland's camp, I turned in that direction. In a few minutes, I discovered an Indian galloping towards me, who approaching, made signs by putting his fingers to his mouth and working his jaws in imitation of a person eating, which I understood to be an application for something to eat. But I had nothing to give him, and he became very importunate, as I thought, and seeing another Indian coming, I drew my pistol, thinking it better to settle matters with the first before the second arrived, but at this, he threw up his hands, showing me that he had no arms and therefore was not dangerous. On his arrival the second Indian commenced speaking to me in the Osage language, all of which I had not forgotten, and informed me that the other Indian wished to know if I wanted anything to eat, and if so, to go with him to his camp and he would feed me. I felt much relieved at this, for I was on the point of shooting a man who wished to befriend me.

The Osage Indian accompanied me until I arrived in sight of the military campfires, which I could see at some distance, as it was then getting late. On arriving at a line of sentinels, who had been placed around the stock belonging to the military, and telling who I was, they permitted me to enter camp. I was heartily tired of the stubborn, obstinate mule and turned him in with the government stock and left him. Some little time before this I had heard the firing of guns and saw a bonfire on top of the hill, and I at once conjectured this would indicate that they thought I was lost and were signalling for me. As I passed through the camp, the wife of Lieutenant Adams hailed me and asked if I wouldn't take a cup of coffee, whereupon I entered their tent and found they had just finished supper. I was soon helped to a good supper for which I felt grateful, as I had eaten nothing since sunrise that morning, and it was now one or two hours after sunset of a long June day.

On coming out of the tent, I fell in with Captain Graves, who told me they had all given me up for lost, and he accompanied me to camp, where I slept that night without waking. That night General Garland issued orders that no officer or soldier should indulge in a buffalo chase, for fear of breaking down horses. The next morning the water had subsided sufficiently for us to cross. Before the middle of the day we encountered large herds of buffalo, and the first thing I saw was General Garland with several officers in full chase in disobedience of his own orders of the night before. So I thought I would join them, and mounting Raymond's horse for that purpose, I directed the train to proceed on to a good camping ground.

The others had gotten a long ways the start of me, so I proceeded slowly in a different direction, and, after going a few miles, saw a herd coming at full speed directly towards me. Quickly dismounting, I forced my picket pin into the ground as far as I could with the heel of my boot and ran about one hundred yards to get a shot. This changed the course of the buffalo a little, and they headed directly for my horse, whereupon he jerked up the picket pin and took after them, and as far as I could see, remained in full chase. So here I was, by myself and on foot, about fifteen miles from camp, without a drop of water on a hot summer day. Pretty soon, however, I discovered a man in chase of a small buffalo cow coming in my direction; within a few yards of us the buffalo was shot dead, and on reaching the spot where she lay, I found Colonel Mansfield[18] of the army. I at once inquired if he had any water, and he answered,

[18] Colonel Joseph King Fenno Mansfield graduated from West Point as brevet 2nd lieutenant of Engineers on July 1, 1822; he was made colonel on February 23, 1847, for gallant conduct at the battle of Buena Vista. Secretary of War Jefferson Davis, who served with Mansfield in the Mexican War, appointed him to the Inspector General's Department on April 22, 1853. Colonel Mansfield wrote an illuminating report ("Report of Inspection of the Department of New Mexico, 1853." National Archives, Washington, D.C.) on the installations and personnel of the district. See Mansfield, *Western Forts.*) In the Civil War he was commissioned major general of volunteers commanding the Twelfth Army Corps, with permanent rank of brigadier general. He died on September 18, 1862, of wounds received at the Battle of Antietam. Heitman, *Historical Register, U.S.A.*, I, 688.

"Not a drop." When I explained my condition to him, he suggested that he gallop after the train, procure a wagon, and return for his game, while I would remain and keep the wolves off until his return. So I sat down on the buffalo's carcass in a very melancholy mood, but shortly after I saw my horse coming back at a very slow pace, as he had his picket rope around one of his hind feet. I greeted his arrival with pleasure, as this horse had become a great favorite with us all. On examination, I found the fetlock badly chafed by the lariat rope and a number of holes in his hip, some half an inch deep, where the picket pin had struck him while galloping after the buffalos.

Pretty soon I discovered Colonel Mansfield coming back with a party of soldiers and a wagon for his meat. He also brought with him a canteen of water, which I promptly emptied. After cutting up the buffalo meat and placing the meat in the wagon, we commenced our pursuit of the train, which we overtook about camping time.

We struck the Arkansas River at the Big Bend[19] and followed up the valley of that stream to Fort Atkinson,[20] where we were cordially received by the officers of that post, who invited us to dine with them; but, as there was no wood and but little grass there, we sent the train ahead to find better camping ground. Here we were informed that a new and better route had been

[19] The present town of Great Bend, Kansas, is located at this place.

[20] Fort Atkinson was a small one-company military post of short duration on the Arkansas River west of the present Dodge City, Kansas. It was described by James A. Bennett in September, 1850, as follows: "Arrived Fort Atkinson, garrisoned by 1 company for the protection of travelers from the Indians. The company is in constant fear of an attack from a nearby camp of 1,500 hostile Indians. This company has to send 35 miles for firewood and are obliged to send 12 to 15 men in company to get it. Passed in sight of the Indians and crossed the Arkansas River 1½ miles in width, without bridge."—Bennett, *Forts and Forays: A Dragoon in New Mexico*, 1850–56, 12. In a petition to Congress, February 25, 1854, the New Mexico legislature protested the abandonment of Fort Atkinson and requested its reestablishment for the protection of the mail route and wagon trains. 33 Cong., 1 sess., *House Misc. Doc. 47*, 1–2.

discovered across the plains, by a man named Aubrey,[21] and hence it was called "Aubrey's Route."[22] If we followed the old route, we would have to pass a plain eighty miles wide, without either wood or water, but by continuing up the valley of the Arkansas about two hundred miles, and then crossing the stream, the longest distance without wood or water would be only forty miles.

So procuring a guide who had traveled this new route and could show us the best places for camping, we determined to take it. A day or two after our departure from this post, I, being in advance of the train, discovered on coming to the top of a hill a merchant's train ahead of us surrounded by Indians, whooping and yelling like demons. I immediately called to General Garland, who was a short distance in the rear, informing him of what

[21] Francis X. Aubry (often spelled "Aubrey") was a French-Canadian by birth. He was prominently known in Independence, Missouri, and was identified with the Santa Fé Trail as a freighter in the early forties. He was a dynamic, adventurous individual, who pioneered the Aubry Cutoff in 1849–50; to win a wager in 1850 made a famous ride for Santa Fe to Independence in eight days with a few hours to spare, and cut the time to five days and some hours on a thousand-dollar wager in 1852; and drove five thousand sheep from Santa Fe to California in 1852–53, incidentally exploring the feasibility of a rail route along the thirty-fifth parallel. He was killed in a Santa Fe barroom in 1854 by Richard H. Weightman. territorial delegate to Congress from New Mexico, in the course of an argument over his California route. See William E. Connelley, ed., *Doniphan's Expedition*, Appendix F, 628–29; Twitchell, *The Military Occupation of New Mexico, 1846–51*, 302; and Walker D. Wyman, "F. X. Aubry: Santa Fe Freighter, Pathfinder and Explorer," *New Mexico Historical Review*, Vol. VII (January, 1932), 1–31.

[22] The original Santa Fé Trail followed the Arkansas River into Colorado and entered New Mexico from the north over the Raton Pass. Later the freighters began using the Cimarron Cutoff; they crossed the river above Dodge City, where the present Kansas town of Cimarron perpetuates the name, and cut southwest across the Plains. The Aubry Cutoff as described by Robert M. Wright, the well-known freighter and dealer in buffalo hides, left the Arkansas above the Cimarron Crossing and followed a middle course between the Raton and Cimarron routes; and was "less dangerous [than the latter] because less subject to Indian attacks and water was more plentiful."—Kenyon Riddle, *Records and Maps of the Old Santa Fe Trail*. Robert M. Wright, *Kansas Historical Collections*, VII, 51. The greatest distance without water on this route was about thirty miles, as compared with sixty miles on the Cimarron Trail. Meriwether obviously overestimated these distances.

I saw in the valley below, and he quickly hastened to the relief of the train.

As soon as the Indians saw the military crossing the crest of the hill, they scampered off. On coming up with the merchant train, I found that it was in charge of a Mr. Cooper,[23] who had left Westport a short time before us. He informed me that two little Mexican girls who had been made prisoner of the Indians had made their escape the night before and come into his camp, telling him that they had escaped from the Indians. When he was about to start the next morning, the Indians surrounded his train and demanded to search his wagons to see if the girls were in them. He said also that a fight would soon have occurred but for our timely arrival, but he did not intend to give the girls up.

I informed General Garland that our treaty with Mexico required the United States to liberate and return to the Mexican authorities all prisoners from Mexico held by the Indians on our side of the line, and that I desired him to give the girls a passage in his train to Santa Fe, which he at once consented to do. The girls were then brought out of Cooper's wagon and delivered to us. They said they belonged to the province of Chihuahua and that they had been captured several years before by the Comanches and had been traded off to the Indians from whom they had escaped; they said also that on the evening before, as usual, they had been sent out with some Indian boys and girls to herd ponies at some distance from the Indian camp and had seen Cooper's train pass along the road and they determined, if possible, to make their escape. When the time arrived in the evening for driving the ponies into the Indian camp, instead of doing so, each mounted a pony and followed in to Cooper's camp.

[23] It is probable that this was one of Braxton Cooper's trains. Cooper was a contemporary of Captain William Becknell and was identified with the Santa Fé Trail as a freighter and trader as early as 1824. W. W. H. Davis said that a Mr. M'Carty was conductor of the train, and that the Indians from whom the girls escaped were Kiowas (*El Gringo*, 249).

Both of these girls appeared quite bright and greatly rejoiced at their rescue. One was about thirteen or fourteen years of age, the other ten or twelve. On our arrival at Santa Fe, I sent them down to El Paso, where the governor of Chihuahua[24] spent some of his time, as this was near the disputed boundary. Shortly after this I received a letter from the governor, thanking me for the return of the two prisoners and expressing great satisfaction at the United States government's having at last a representative in New Mexico who appeared disposed to comply with the treaty stipulation between the two countries.

But to return to our march across the plains. On our reaching the crossing of the Arkansas on this new route, I saw places that appeared familiar to me and which I recognize as points upon the route which I had traveled with the Pawnee Indians about thirty years before. The next day after crossing the river, I saw two conical hills, which I at once remembered as having seen on that occasion. I asked the guide if he knew any name for them when he said, "They are called the 'Spanish Peaks.' " I think on my former trip we passed nearer to them than this time, as they looked much higher than now. We now judged them to be from fifty to seventy-five miles distant, and they looked no larger than haystacks.[25]

On reaching the Colorado [Canadian], I recognized it as the stream on which the Indians were defeated, but think this defeat occurred much higher up the river. In due course of time we reached Fort Union,[26] a military post of the United States,

[24] Governor Angel Trias, a staunch supporter of General Santa Anna, was later deposed by a revolution headed by G. Casavantes and removed from office in August, 1879. See Bancroft, *North Mexican States and Texas,* II, 617–18.

[25] The Spanish Peaks (altitude, 12,708 feet) were noted landmarks in the days of the Santa Fé Trail. They lay to the east of the Sangre de Cristo and Culebra ranges. The present highway passes some miles to the eastward over a portion of the old trail.

[26] Fort Union was established by Colonel Edwin V. Sumner shortly after his taking command of the military district in April, 1851. It was primarily a depot

Buffalo Hunting on the Plains, One of Meriwether's
Activities, Here Depicted in a Water Color
by Peter Rindisbacher.

Courtesy Joslyn Art Museum, Omaha

Early Portrait of Kit Carson, Who Served as Indian Agent under Meriwether.

Courtesy Kit Carson Museum

a little more than one hundred miles east of Santa Fe. As we had now arrived at the settlements and thought ourselves safe from Indians, we left the military here and proceeded with our own company alone, as General Garland would be detained until next morning.

On arriving about ten or twelve miles from Santa Fe, and it being late in the evening, we encamped; but General Garland, having procured fresh mules from Fort Union, overtook us and passed into the city that night. The next morning as we were about to start, we were waited on by a delegation consisting of Mr. Messervy,[27] who had recently been appointed secretary for the territory, Judge Houghton,[28] who had been judge under the military government of New Mexico, Hugh Smith,[29] who had

for the distribution of military supplies and a western terminus for the military escorts. It was situated in the Mora Valley, north of Las Vegas. W. W. H. Davis described it as "an open post without either stockades or breastworks; much the appearance of a frontier village."—*El Gringo*. See also Mansfield, *Western Forts*, 32–38; and Robert M. Utley, "Fort Union and the Santa Fe Trail," *New Mexico Historical Review*, Vol. XXXVI, No. 1 (January, 1961), 36–47.

27 William S. Messervy was a native of Massachusetts. He had come to Mexico prior to the Mexican War and engaged in business in Santa Fe where he built up a large fortune. He was a man of fine talents and enjoyed the confidence of the people. He was secretary of the territory under Governor William Carr Lane and acted temporarily as governor upon Lane's retirement; he then became secretary of the territory under Meriwether.

28 Judge Joab Houghton, born in New York in 1811, came to Santa Fe in 1844. He was appointed chief justice of New Mexico during the American military occupation in 1846. He was a leading merchant of Santa Fe and also operated a monthly stage line to San Antonio, Texas. He and Elias Brevoort entered into a contract July 2, 1854, to carry a monthly mail between Santa Fe, Albuquerque, Socorro, Doña Ana, and Fort Fillmore, New Mexico; and Frontero, El Paso, San Elizario, Magoffinville, Leona, and San Antonio, Texas. See Keleher, *Turmoil in New Mexico*, 22n., 263.

29 Hugh N. Smith was sent to Washington by popular demand in 1849 as an unofficial delegate for the principal purpose of seeking statehood for New Mexico. In July, 1850, by a vote of 92 to 86, the House of Representatives refused to admit him. He was nominated for secretary of the territory in 1851, but his appointment was not confirmed. Governor James S. Calhoun characterized him as "an immensely clever man." He advocated force in the subjugation of the Indians. See *ibid.*, 38.

been raised in Jefferson County, Kentucky, and whom I had known in his boyhood; and several prominent Mexican citizens, together with a Catholic priest. The last informed me that he had been sent by the bishop[30] of that diocese to request our party to proceed immediately upon our arrival to the cathedral, whereupon he would sing a Te Deum in honor of our safe arrival.

This was the first time in my life that I had ever witnessed this imposing religious ceremony, and at its conclusion we proceeded to the old Mexican Palace, which seemed entirely familiar to me. Here a temporary platform was erected upon which I mounted and delivered my inaugural address.[31] Although the address was brief, its delivery took some time, as I spoke to a mixed audience of Americans and Mexicans, and when I had uttered a sentence in English, I had to stop until Mr. Messervy interpreted it into Spanish, and this proceeding had to be followed until its close. At the end of the address, we were all taken into the Senate Chamber, where a handsome collation had been prepared for us. Here I was introduced to the few Americans present, and also to the principal Mexicans of the city. That night a grand fandango was got up in honor of our arrival, and a delegation of citizens escorted us to it.

We found the ballroom filled with ladies and gentlemen, and I witnessed among the ladies some of the most graceful dancers that I had ever seen in my life. But I was a little disgusted at seeing the ladies puffing away at cigarettes. I stayed at the fan-

[30] Bishop John Baptist Lamy (originally Jean Baptiste l'Amy) was born at Lempedes, France, on October 11, 1814. In 1853 he was consecrated Bishop of Santa Fe. During the early years of his jurisdiction he had difficulties with the Mexican clergy. In 1885 he retired to his country place, now known as the Bishop's Lodge, on the Río Tesuque. He is the protagonist in the well-known novel by Willa Cather, *Death Comes for the Archbishop* (New York, 1922).

[31] This was August 8, 1853. According to tradition the roof of the cell at the west end of the Palace in which Meriwether had been confined as a prisoner in 1820 collapsed on that very day. This was taken as a favorable omen by the people of Santa Fe. *San José Mercury-Herald,* April 7, 1893.

dango but a few hours, when returning to the Palace and spreading my blanket upon the floor, went to sleep.

INAUGURAL ADDRESS OF GOVERNOR MERIWETHER

FELLOW CITIZENS OF NEW MEXICO:

I appear before you today, by virtue of the commission from the President of the United States, which I now hold in my hand, appointing me to the office of governor of this territory; and allow me to present my acknowledgments for this flattering reception. In the commencement of my administration, I would have it distinctly understood, that so long as the chief executive power of the Territory may be wielded by me, no distinction will be known, between the different classes into which this population may be divided. The elevated and the lowly, the rich and the poor, the native-born citizen and the immigrant who had or may settle in our midst, are all alike entitled to the protection of the laws, and must be held answerable to their behests.

It will become my duty to guard and protect, as far as lies in my power, the interests of each citizen, and to see that the laws are enforced; the first will at all times afford me pleasure, and the latter may at times become irksome and a painful duty, but it is one which must be performed at every hazard. It will afford me pleasure to contribute my mite towards the development of the resources of the territory, with her wide expanded plains, her genial and salubrious climate, her mineral resources and geographical position. If we are but true to ourselves, the day is not far distant when New Mexico may claim her position as an equal in the glorious sisterhood of States composing the American Union. To accomplish this end, however, it becomes necessary that there should be a united and harmonious action on the part of the several departments of the territorial government, as well as the military power of the general government stationed here; and above all, that we should receive on all proper occasions, the cordial support of the community at large.

A stranger in a strange land, I am aware that unaided my feeble arm can accomplish but little towards the preservation of order and the enforcement of law; but relying as I do upon the smiles of divine providence, and the aid and assistance of the several co-ordinate departments of the government; together with that of the virtuous and intelligent portion of the community, I now say to you, the laws of the land must, and shall, be impartially enforced.

Having therefore taken the oath prescribed by law, I now enter upon the discharge of the duties of the office of governor of New Mexico.[32]

The following is an extract from the *Santa Fe Gazette*, published in an eastern paper, giving an account of our arrival and the reception:

We are indebted to Mr. E. A. Graves, Indian agent, for a copy of the *Santa Fe Gazette*, containing a full account of the reception of the new Governor and his address, which we publish in another column. It is brief and in good taste. The Territory appears to be in a satisfactory condition.

The canvass for delegate to Congress is on hand. The Nominee of the Democratic party is a Mexican. Some object to him because he does not speak the English language, and charge that he has been suspended by the Catholic Bishop from the functions of the Christian ministry on account of licentious conduct.[33] Ex-Governor Lane[34] is the opposing can-

[32] The territory of New Mexico, etablished under the Organic Act of 1850, embraced the present states of New Mexico, Arizona, and southern Colorado. Two governors had preceded Meriwether: James S. Calhoun, who died in office, and William Carr Lane.

[33] José Manuel Gallegos was formerly a priest of the Albuquerque parish. The charges against him were largely the result of disagreement between Bishop Lamy and the Mexican clergy. The evidence of any wrongdoing on the part of Gallegos is meager and questionable. See Bancroft, *History of Arizona and New Mexico*, 650.

[34] William Carr Lane, a native of Virginia, entered the army as surgeon's mate on September 15, 1814, and became post surgeon on April 24, 1816, resigning in 1818. He was the first quartermaster general of the state of Missouri as well as the

didate, and he is generally popular with the American residents.

New Mexico is said to be one of the most healthy countries in the world; and should the Pacific railroad pass through it, and infuse some American enterprise into that region, it may become an important state of the Union. It doubtless has no inconsiderable mineral resources, which time and industry may develop.

It has been known for some time that the Government at Washington had made important changes in the offices of this Territory. In our last issue we announced the arrival in our town of Captain Graves, Indian agent in the place of Dr. Steck,[35] and Dr. Jacobs as the private secretary of the newly appointed Governor, in place of Governor Lane. In this announcement, we have to correct a misapprehension in relation to Dr. Jacobs. It seems that the present Governor has no private secretary, the law not allowing him one, as it should be in our humble judgement.[36] Dr. Jacobs, however, is a

first mayor of St. Louis. He was appointed by President Fillmore and assumed office as territorial governor in September, 1852. He resigned the following year to carry on his campaign as delegate to Congress. Heitman, *Historical Register, U.S.A.*, I, 164; and Prince, *History of New Mexico*, 192–93.

[35] Dr. Michael Steck was a native of Hughesville, Pennsylvania, in which state he practiced medicine. He had been appointed agent to the Mescalero Apaches by President Fillmore. This newspaper mention indicates that he was the victim of the change in the national administration from Whig to Democratic at the accession of President Pierce. He was, however, reappointed by Pierce the following year and went out with Governor Meriwether when the latter returned to his post after a brief visit at home and a conference in Washington (see Chapter XI). He was subsequently appointed superintendent of Indian affairs in New Mexico by President Buchanan. During the Civil War he became embroiled with General James Henry Carleton over the latter's action in rounding up the Navahos and holding them on the arid Bosque Redondo in eastern New Mexico. His position was vindicated in 1868 when the Navahos were released and permitted to return to their homeland—a measure for which he had faithfully labored at his own expense. Throughout his career he was a dedicated agent genuinely interested in the Indians' welfare. Bancroft, *History of Arizona and New Mexico*, 731–32; and Keleher, *Turmoil in New Mexico*, 506, 137n.

[36] Governor Meriwether, however, did acquire a private secretary. Young William Watts Hart Davis, a lawyer by profession, who had served as first lieutenant and then captain of a Massachusetts infantry company during the Mexican

friend of the Governor, and a young man of wealth, who has paid us the compliment of a visit with a view to become acquainted with our people and the resources of our Territory. We hope he will use a part of that surplus wealth in some of the enterprises which are now almost open to our view; which if successful, will form the ground work of a solid and substantial prosperity.

We have now to record the arrival of Governor Meriwether, of Chief Justice Davenport, who succeeds Judge Baker, and of James M. Smith, as Indian agent in place of

---

War years, came to New Mexico in December, 1853, as United States attorney for the territory. In addition to his prescribed duties he served on a voluntary basis as private secretary to the governor and accompanied him on several of his excursions over the area. Obviously he enjoyed listening to Meriwether's accounts of early life on the Plains and recorded them in his diary and in his book, *El Gringo; or, New Mexico and Her People*, published in 1857. These writings constitute a valuable source not only for Meriwether's life but for contemporary New Mexico. Davis soon returned to the East and settled in Doylestown, Pennsylvania, where he published a newspaper.

Davis' book records one incident not mentioned in Meriwether's autobiography. Although it does not seem to fit the known facts of the Governor's life, it should be noted that elsewhere Davis has presented his career consistently.

According to this story Meriwether and some companions were returning from a trapping expedition loaded with packs of furs when they saw a party of mounted Indians approaching. The trappers made for a grove of timber, where they tied their animals and took off the packs to make a rude breastwork. Then Meriwether and a few of the men rode out to meet the Indians, Meriwether and a chief riding in advance of their respective parties. "The Indian Chief came up with his lance at rest, while Meriwether rode tomahawk in hand; and when within proper distance, the former made a lunge with his lance, which the latter struck down with his hatchet, but not with sufficient force to prevent it piercing his thigh and giving him a severe wound. The shock jostled the Indian, and before he could recover his position, the Negro boy rode up to him, and with a single stroke of his hatchet on the head, killed him. The Chief having fallen, the other Indians turned and fled. As soon as Meriwether was wounded he fainted and fell to the ground, from loss of blood, and when he came to he found himself lying beside his dead foe. The trappers resumed their march in a few days, and reaching their trading post without further molestation. For this gallant act of the Negro boy in saving the life of his master he was set free as soon as they returned to Kentucky."

See Davis, Diaries and Papers, thirty-three pieces, Negative photostats of originals in possession of Clinton P. Anderson, Bancroft Library; Twitchell, *Leading Facts of New Mexican History*, Vol. II, 314; and Heitman, *Historical Register, U.S.A.*, II, 361.

Major Winfield. Not of the least importance among these arrivals, we record that of General Garland and his aide, Major Nichols,[37] of the United States Army, sent out by the administration with some three or four hundred recruits to strengthen the various military posts of this Territory. General Garland and Major Nichols arrived on the evening of Sunday last and reported the Governor as in camp at Arroya Honda, some five miles' distance. A Deputation of the citizens was immediately sent out to assure him of the friendly disposition of the people of this town, and to know of him at what hour of the next day he would be willing to accept an escort into Santa Fe. The hour of 9 A.M. of Monday last having been fixed upon, the deputation returned.

Agreeable to this understanding, the town of Santa Fe on the next morning presented an unusually interesting appearance, everywhere could be seen the carriage, the buggy, or horse, caparisoned for the gallant rider; soon the road, in the direction as above indicated, was alive with the moving throng or the anxious spectator. Much to his honor, Governor Lane (though now an Ex) was foremost in this demonstration of respect for the newly appointed Governor and his co-adjutors in this Territory.

The Secretary of the Territory, Mr. Messervy, the Attorney General, Mr. Amhurst,[38] General Garland with other officers of the Army, the church represented by a priest at the instance of the Bishop, who is most deservably popular in this town, and a large number of the most influential and respectable citizens without any party distinction whatever followed in the train and paid all honor to the new appointees by mak-

[37] Major William Augustus Nichols, of Pennsylvania, was graduated from West Point in July, 1838; was commissioned major on September 8, 1847, for gallant conduct in the battle of Molino del Rey, Mexico; served on the staff of General Garland at Albuquerque as assistant adjutant general; became major general on March 13, 1865; died April 8, 1869. Heitman, *Historical Register, U.S.A.*, I, 747.

[38] Merrill Amhurst, attorney general under the William Carr Lane Administration, was later active as a practicing attorney in New Mexico.

ing their advent, as it were, a grand gala day, full of hope and trust in the wisdom and patriotism of their rulers at Washington; not with standing it severed relations of a personal nature at least, which years of acquaintance and public service had cultivated the fullness of friendship and confidence.

The procession would have been a creditable one to any city of the States; having formed on the road between this and the arroya, it moved on in calm and stately dignity to Santa Fe, through the principal entrance to the city until it reached the plaza in front of the Palace, or, speaking more democratically, until the cortage was drawn up in front of the State, or Governor's house. Here the procession debarked, and thousands congregated to witness the formality of a public introduction of distinguished officers and the inauguration of the new Governor. The first duty was performed by Mr. Messervy in a manner that was creditable to that officer.

When the Governor was introduced, he arose in a calm, steady, firm, positive and inflexible voice, announced by what authority he was there, and the policy by which he would be governed in the administration of the laws. The welkin rung with the shouts and the huzzas of the people, thus to say most emphatically that the Territory so far as they were concerned, was to be a land of law and order.

General Garland was next introduced, who gracefully recognized the plaudits of the people by the politeness and civility which invariably makes the true American officer. It was gratifying to behold for the first time in this Territory that mutual respect which has always prevailed between the civil and military authorities.

The ceremony out of doors having been brought to a close, the Governor and other officers repaired to the Governor's room of reception, where all were introduced to him who desired it. After this formality was over, another door was thrown open, and all invited to partake of a splendid collation which had been prepared for the occasion under the direction of now ex-Governor Lane. The meats and fruits of the season, the choice pic-nics of the tropics, the wines and brandies of far distant countries, all contributed to enliven the scene and make all joyous. At the head of the table stood Governor Meriwether, ex-Governor Lane, General Garland, and Judge Davenport. Appropriate toasts were drunk by all, and responded to in bumpers full of wine; the civil, military, and judiciary, were each separately toasted, and each responded to in a manner to show that the three powers of the State would be a unit in order to protect "the life, liberty, and happiness" of the people of the Territory.

X
Dragoons and Hostiles

NOW MY TROUBLES AND VEXATIONS COMMENCED. The Democrats at once raised a howl similar to that now raised against the Executive of the United States, "to turn the rascals out."[1] This was easily done, as I had but little patronage to bestow, but the great difficulty was where to bestow it. There was a great clamor raised by the applicants for office, but little material to fill them. Some wanted the attorney general removed, and persons who had never read a lawbook in their lives were recommended to fill his place. Indeed there was one American, by trade a blacksmith, who pushed his claim with great vigor for that office. The two Indian agents who had come out with me, both wanted to be stationed near the seat of government. There were but three Indian agents in the territory (I was entitled to five) and between fifty and sixty thousand Indians to be attended to, and the two agents who went out with me had probably never seen a wild Indian in their lives. But it was my duty to locate them, and I determined to station one agent in the northern end of the territory and the other in the southern end, leaving myself to attend to the Indians located in the central part. Then there arose a contest between the two agents, as both wanted the southern agency. I first tried argument and persuasion, but finding this to no avail, I gave Captain Graves preemptory orders to proceed to the town of Taos in the north and

[1] Meriwether, dictating his memoirs in 1886, was referring to the political change that came with the accession of the Democrat, Grover Cleveland, after twenty-four years of uninterrupted Republican rule.

take possession of the agency there, and ordered Smith to Fort Massachusetts[2] in the south.

Here another embarrassment awaited me. I found nearly the whole [Indian] appropriation made by Congress had been expended by my predecessor [Lane], leaving me without sufficient money to pay the traveling expenses of the two new agents and the hire of interpreters.[3] Then again I found a great deal of

[2] This is a slip of speech or transcription for Fort Webster. Fort Massachusetts was the most northern post in the department of New Mexico, on Utah Creek about twenty miles from the Río Grande in present Colorado. It was founded June 22, 1852, but abandoned in 1858 and replaced by Fort Garland, about six miles to the south. Smith was assigned to the southern part of the territory, with headquarters at Fort Webster. In the fall of that year the military planned to abandon the site, and Meriwether then notified the Indian Office that it would be unsafe for the agent to remain there. Apparently he moved his office to Doña Ana, for he died there on December 15. Captain Graves appears on the records as agent for the Capote and Moache Utes at the Abiquiu Agency in 1853. He was sent to succeed Smith at Doña Ana in 1854, resigning in June of that year. The noted Kit Carson took over the northern agency in January, 1854, with his office at Taos. See Letter, Meriwether to Commissioner of Indian Affairs, November 30, 1853, National Archives, New Mexico Superintendency, 1849–80, Microfilm 234, Roll 547. See also Carson Papers, quoted in Bancroft, *History of Arizona and New Mexico*, 668; and Mansfield, *Western Forts*, 17.

[3] Congress appropriated $10,000 for Indian administration in New Mexico during the fiscal year 1853–54. Possibly this had not yet become available, but in any case it was—to quote Meriwether—"practically equivalent to no appropriation." A much larger sum had been granted in previous years.

On August 31, slightly more than three weeks after he entered upon his duties, the governor summarized the situation and submitted recommendations to the Indian Office. He said that there were "upwards of thirty thousand hostile Indians subject to the immediate jurisdiction of this superintendency, embracing the Gila and Cohila Apaches and Mescaleros in the south and southwest, the Navahos on the west, the Utahas and northern Jicarilla on the north and east, to say nothing of the fierce and warlike tribes of the Kiowas, Cheyennes, and Arapahoes, on the northeast, and the Commanches on the southeast, that press upon its borders, and often invade the Territory, committing frightening depredations, both upon its citizens and property. . . . I will venture to submit the opinion . . . that the government must either feed and clothe these Indians to a certain extent, or chastise them in a decisive manner. . . . If the pacific problem be resorted to, it should be carried out upon a large and liberal scale, such as to embrace the entire Indian population in this section, for if one tribe, or a band of any particular tribe, be fed, and the same relief be withheld from the others, it but serves to endanger discontent and dissatisfaction. Then if the more stringent and vigorous policy be adopted, it should

hostile feeling existing between a portion of the American population and a part of the Mexicans. The territory had been under rigid military rule before a civil government was established, and as this was done under Mr. Fillmore's administration,[4] every officer was politically opposed to me. Mr. Messervy, an old merchant of Santa Fe, had a few months before been appointed secretary of the territory and was the only Democratic officer, except those who went out with me, whom I found in the territory.

Mr. Lane, as soon as relieved from the office of governor by me, announced himself a candidate for the office of delegate in Congress, and Mr. Gallegos was nominated by the Democrats, though those in the territory calling themselves Democrats knew little or nothing of the principles of the Democratic party.

On my arrival I found Mr. [Merrill] Amhurst acting as attorney general for the territory. Not considering him a suitable person to fill that office, and he having deceived me on two occasions, I notified him that he would be removed as soon as I could find a suitable person to take his place. This gave umbrage to the Whig party, which soon became very hostile to my administration.

About this time, Gallegos came to me, and I found him to be a shrewd, intelligent man, well educated in the Spanish language, but he frankly confessed to me that he knew nothing of the principles of the Democratic party and desired to be informed

---

in my opinion be persisted in and carried to an extent which would leave a lasting impression upon their minds as to the power of the government. Neither policy will be found to be effective if partially carried out."—33 Cong., 1 sess., *House Exec. Doc. 1*, August 1, 1853, 429–39 (Report to George W. Manypenny, commissioner of Indian Affairs, Santa Fe.) See . . . Commissioner of Indian Affairs, *Annual Report, 1853*, pp. 189–201, for complete reports from Governor Meriwether and Agent E. A. Graves.

[4] That is, civil government was established under Millard Fillmore's administration. Since Fillmore was a Whig, the advent of Pierce and his appointees meant a change to the Democratic party.

concerning them. I told him that we had a written constitution of the United States, which extended all over the states and territories and was the supreme law of the land; that the Democratic party was in favor of a strict construction of this instrument, whereas the Whig party was in favor of a more latitudinous construction; that the Democratic party was in favor of a tariff or tax upon imported goods, only sufficient to raise a revenue which would defray an economical cost government; that the Democratic party was in favor of allowing both slaveholders and those opposed to slavery to emigrate into the territories with their property and leave each territory to settle the question of slavery, when it becomes a state, but that a majority of the Whig party and a minority of the Democratic party were in favor of excluding slavery from the territories until they were admitted as states into the Union. I told him that these were the principal points of difference between the two parties, upon which he then asked me to write the foregoing down for him and said he would have it translated into Spanish so that he could read it. Shortly after this, a meeting was announced to be held in Santa Fe, at which Mr. Gallegos would address the people, and that evening a committee waited on Judge Davenport and myself and invited us to attend, which we both consented to do. Mr. Gallegos could not speak English, [so] I got a friend who spoke both languages to sit by us and interpret Gallegos' speech as he delivered it, but told him to do so in a low tone, so as not to interrupt the speaker. I found that Gallegos had comprehended the points of difference between the two parties and had expounded them with cleverness, and that the speech had made a very favorable impression upon the audience. Both Judge Davenport and myself were called upon for speeches but declined.

Seeing the effect of Gallegos' speech upon the people of Santa Fe, the Whigs became greatly exasperated, and the next morning, when "Wash," my Negro servant, came into my room, he kept muttering to himself, which I did not understand. On asking him what was the matter, he said, "They have done hung you and Judge Davenport, for, as I came across the plaza this morning, I saw you both hung up to the flagstaff." I went to the front door and saw two suits of clothes stuffed with straw, one with my name on it and the other with the Judge's hanging by the neck to the flagstaff. A large crowd soon collected around these effigies, among whom I discovered the persons whom I judged to be responsible for them. Judge Davenport soon arrived, and became very indignant at the outrage, when I remarked in an audible voice, "Judge, I wouldn't mind this thing, for I have no doubt that in less than a year, you will have an opportunity of pronouncing sentence of death against its authors, and I will have the satisfaction of ordering their execution in reality. They can hang suits of clothes stuffed with straw, but you and I can cause them to be hung in reality."

This was interpreted to the Democrats present and appeared to give them great satisfaction, and they began to make preparation to tear the effigies down, when I interferred and told them to let the effigies remain as a monument of the author's folly. That evening a man by the name of Collins,[5] who controlled the *Santa Fe Gazette,* came to my office and advised me not to attempt another Democratic meeting, as there was real danger of my assassination. Believing him to be one of the authors of this attempted indignity, I said to him, "Collins, if you expect to intimidate me or make me swerve from the principles of Democ-

[5] James L. Collins was born in Crab Orchard, Kentucky, on February 1, 1800. He crossed the plains to Santa Fe in 1826 and two years later moved to Chihuahua, there engaging in the mercantile business until the Mexican War, when he returned to Santa Fe. In 1852 he established the *Santa Fe Weekly Gazette* and continued as its publisher until 1858. Under the Buchanan administration he was appointed superintendent of Indian Affairs for New Mexico, and reappointed by President Lincoln. In May, 1866, he was appointed receiver of the land office and custodian of United States funds, at Santa Fe. He was shot to death during a robbery of his office on June 6, 1869.

racy, you will find that you have waked up the wrong passenger." To this he replied, "I hope you don't think I had a hand in this thing." And I answered, "As Nathan said unto David, verily thou art the man," upon which, he picked up his hat and departed.

The next issue of Collins' paper gave an account of our being hung in effigy and attributed it to the fact of the Judge and myself having attended the Democratic meeting. One of these papers I transmitted by the next mail[6] to Judge Casey,[7] with a request that he show it to the President, to Mr. Guthrie of the Treasury and to Governor Marcy, secretary of state, and to tell them that if they thought I had acted wrongly, I would at once tender my resignation. To this letter, Judge Casey replied, "All these officers said they could not see that I had done anything improper, but they were glad to find that I had gone to work to organize a Democratic party in that distant Territory."

The campaign for delegate from the territory and for members of the legislature soon became very bitter. Collins' paper espoused the cause of [former Governor] Dr. Lane, and Major Weightman[8] who had been a volunteer officer in the Mexican

[6] A monthly mail and passenger stage was maintained between Independence, Missouri, and Santa Fe. In view of the vast expanse of territory covered, considering Indian raids and the monumental task of livestock replacement and station maintenance, the service was reasonably good. On February 25, 1854, the New Mexico legislature petitioned Congress for an improvement in communication facilities. See 33 Cong., 1 sess., *House Misc. Doc. 53*, 1–2.

[7] The Judge Casey referred to was no doubt Joseph Casey, born at Ringgold Manor, Washington County, Maryland, on December 17, 1814, who was elected to the 31st Congress, in which he was seated on March 4, 1849. After his term in Congress he was engaged in private law practice until 1856, when he was appointed reporter of decisions of the Supreme Court of Pennsylvania. *Congressional Dictionary*, 671.

[8] Richard Hanson Weightman was born in the District of Columbia and entered West Point on July 1, 1835; he either was dismissed or resigned April 28, 1837. It is said that he was dismissed from the Academy for stabbing a fellow cadet; however, the editor has been unable to verify this act. Meriwether was not far amiss in his estimate of Weightman's character; he was a brave popular officer with a tendency toward hot headedness. In the Mexican War he was elected captain of

War, started what he called a Democratic paper in Albuquerque,[9] which espoused the cause of Gallegos. I soon found that Collins was a shrewd, cunning, and designing man, and Weightman, bold, indiscreet, and defiant. Collins did not appear to understand the principles of the Whig party, nor did Weightman expound the principles of the Democratic party with any degree of force. Both papers indulged more in personalities than in argument.

The election was to come off in September, and the returns were to be made to the Governor, who jointly with the Secretary, was to count the votes and give a certificate to the candidate elected as a delegate in Congress. For some time it seemed doubtful as to which of the two candidates was elected, but finally there came in a poll book from an Indian village, containing between two hundred and three hundred votes for Dr. Lane. Upon the propriety of counting these Indian votes, Mr. Messervy and myself differed. I contended that no Indians were allowed to vote, that there was no precinct established at this

---

Battery "A," Missouri Light Artillery, upon its formation May 28, 1846, and served under Doniphan. At the end of the war he settled in Albuquerque, where he practiced law and conducted a small newspaper with indifferent success. He was delegate to Congress from New Mexico, serving from 1851–52. Most accounts of the killing of Aubry (see note 21, Chapter IX) state that Weightman threw a glass of brandy into his victim's face and then stabbed him. Prior to this incident he had difficulty with Lieutenant Edmund Chouteau, and a duel was prevented by intervening friends. Later in Santa Fe he fought a duel with Judge Joab Houghton, which resulted in no fatalities and was settled by Weightman's apologies. He was colonel of the Missouri State Guard, Confederate States of America, and was killed at Wilson's Creek, Missouri, on August 10, 1861. See Prince, *History of New Mexico*, 193–94; Heitman, *Historical Register*, I, 1014; Twitchell, *Military Occupation of New Mexico*, 381–94; and Connelley, *Doniphan's Expedition*, 262–63.

9 Albuquerque, originally named San Francisco Xavier de Albuquerque, was founded in 1706 and named in honor of the viceroy of New Spain. The military post of Albuquerque was originally established on November 17, 1846, by American troops. At this period it was department headquarters of the New Mexico Military District, with General John Garland in command. See Lansing B. Bloom, ed., "Albuquerque and Galisteo, Certificate of Their Founding, 1706," *New Mexico Historical Review*, Vol. X (January, 1935), 48–50; and Mansfield, *Western Forts*, 20.

village, nor officers to receive the votes. Mr. Messervy contended that he and myself were bound to count all the returns made to us. But we soon came to an amicable understanding with each other, I agreeing that if Lane was elected without counting the Indian vote, I would sign his certificate; Messervy agreeing that if Gallegos was elected, after counting the Indian vote for Lane, that he would sign the certificate of Gallegos; but if Lane was elected by counting the Indian vote for him, he would give Lane the certificate, and I saying that if Gallegos was elected by excluding the Indian vote for Lane, I would give Gallegos the certificate, and let Congress decide the question. When the vote of the last county was received and all the votes summed up, it was found that Gallegos was elected by about three hundred majority, even though the Indian vote was counted for Lane. So we had no difficulty in giving Gallegos our joint certificate.

Dr. Lane immediately gave notice to Gallegos of his intention to contest his election, and both parties proceeded to take testimony. It was supposed that the testimony should close by the first of November and both parties would proceed in the stage which left on the first day of each month for Washington. A day or two before that time, Gallegos, who lived in the southern portion of the territory, arrived in Santa Fe and, the day before the stage was to leave, went to the conductor to pay for and engage his passage for Independence, Missouri. He was told that the stage was full and he couldn't go. When Gallegos called upon me to know what he was to do, I told him, "You have your carriage and two mules here; purchase two additional and your provisions, and keep up with the stage and travel in company with it." This he at once agreed to. The hour for the stage to leave was twelve o'clock the next day. But lo and behold! The next day all the mules were gone. Then Gallegos came to me again, and I told him that I had no doubt that this was a made-up plan to prevent him getting to Washington, for I had placed a man to watch when the stage left, and the stage was not full.

I thought in a few days he would get his mules again and then he could hire a man who knew the road and an interpreter to accompany him; and, as the Indians were all quiet and peaceable, and a few or none were to be found at this season[10] of the year near the traveled route, he could proceed with safety. This he agreed to do. About the second day after the stage had left, the lost mules were found grazing near the city, and Gallegos prepared for his departure. I gave him letters of introduction to several Democratic members of Congress with whom I was acquainted and one to the veteran Democratic senator from Missouri, Colonel [Thomas Hart] Benton, who then resided in Washington City. I also gave him a sort of way-bill. I advised him, on arriving at Independence, to sell his mules, as he was sure to get his seat in Congress and hence would not return until after the second session of Congress was over. If navigation on the Missouri River was not obstructed by ice, I advised him to take a boat for St. Louis; but, if no boats were running, there would be a stage going between these two points, and on his arrival at St. Louis, to take a boat for Louisville, Kentucky, and there take another boat for Wheeling, Virginia, and then by stage to Washington City. There he would employ some Democratic lawyer to attend to his case for him. I then had the above translated into Spanish so he could read it for himself, and thus equipped, he started on his journey.

On his arrival in Washington, his credentials were presented, he took his seat, and the contest between him and Dr. Lane began. The committee of Congress soon reported in Gallegos' favor, which action was confirmed by the House of Representatives, and his troubles ended.

[10] During the winter season, the Indians seldom ventured forth on hostile expeditions, primarily because of the lack of forage for their ponies.

On the first morning in December following, the legislature of the territory met, and I think there were but five members in both branches who could understand or speak a word of English. I was glad to find that my old friend, Dr. Connelly, had been elected to the territorial senate, for, although a bitter Whig, I regarded him as an honest man, and he had long been a resident of the territory and spoke both languages fluently. I prepared a brief message to the legislature, entirely avoiding politics, and confining myself exclusively to the local interests of the territory. The only written law which I found in the territory was a military code by General Kearny[11] when he conquered the territory. This might have been suitable to a military government but was not adapted to a civil one, and I therefore recommended many changes in this code. One evening after my message had been translated and printed in the Spanish language,

[11] Upon the occupation of New Mexico, General Kearny drew up what was known as the "Kearny Code" for the establishment of a civil government under Acting Governor Charles Bent. The code was unpopular because of its severity and its limitation of private and property rights. Five hundred copies were printed in Santa Fe at Governor Bent's direction by Oliver P. Hovey. Upon receipt of the code, Secretary of War Marcy on the instructions of the President wrote Kearny, January 11, 1847, reprimanding him and advising that rights conferred upon the people required the action of Congress; however, he was upheld in the setting up of a civil government. 30 Cong., 1 sess., *House Exec. Doc. 60*, 179.

Further light is thrown upon the legal situation by some handwritten pages found among the Meriwether Papers. They are captioned "Reminiscences of Gov. D. Meriwether" and without doubt were written by John A. Graves, the son of Captain Graves. The writer said the governor told the following story of beautifully chased solid silver waiters of Mexican workmanship that graced his mantel:

"Since the treaty of cession provided that all laws of New Mexico not in conflict with the laws of the United States would remain in force until superceded by the legislature, Meriwether was anxious to acquire a copy of them. He was unable to find any in Santa Fe, and so called on General Manuel Armijo, the last Mexican governor, hoping to obtain one. He found the former official in bed—his deathbed as it proved. Asked for a copy of the laws, he replied, 'There is but one copy of these laws in existence, and that is in my possession.' Then after a few minutes he raised his head slightly, and pointing to his forehead, he said, 'Here is that copy; my will was the law of the land.'

"Passing the place three weeks later, Meriwether stopped to see Armijo again and found that he had died and had left him the two waiters as a memento."

Dr. Connelly waited on me and said that my message had given great pleasure to the Mexicans, who had become restive and tired under the military code, and they wondered how I had become so familiar with the wants of the territory. "Now," said he, "I will forget the words Democrat and Whig; although I am a Whig, I will support your administration; but whenever you say Democrat, you will find me opposed to you."

Here my serious labors commenced. So few understood the manner of writing bills that I was applied to almost every day to draft bills for different members, all of which bills I had to have translated before being presented to either house.

Shortly after my arrival at Santa Fe, I had succeeded in releasing two more Mexican children from the Indians and sent them down to the governor of Chihuahua at El Paso.[12] Thinking this a favorable opportunity, I suggested to his Excellency that the United States and Mexico had expended a sufficient amount of blood and treasure without getting into another war, and I proposed to him that, as he had possession of a part of the disputed territory,[13] and as our two governments were negotiating a new treaty and boundary, that things should remain in status quo until the question of the boundary was settled by negotiation, to which he responded favorably.

On having thus quieted all difficulties on the Mexican boundary for the present, I made application to the President at Washington for a leave of absence for the purpose of visiting my

[12] Don Juan de Oñate crossed the Río Grande at El Paso del Norte (the later site of El Paso, Texas) on May 4, 1598. The first settlement consisted of Coons's Ranch, Magoffinville, and Stephens' Ranch. Bartlett describes Coons's Ranch, established in 1848, as the first settlement on the American side of the river. Benjamin Franklin Coons is credited with its first Anglo name, Franklin. What was first known as El Paso del Norte was the later Juarez, named in honor of Benito Juarez. George P. Hammond and Agapito Rey, eds., *Oñate*, 315; W. W. Mills, *Forty Years at El Paso*, Introduction and notes by Rex W. Strickland, 7; and Bartlett, *Personal Narratives*, I, 192–98.

[13] The area later included in the Gadsden Treaty, which encompassed a portion of the fertile ground of the Mesilla Valley, along the Río Grande.

family and settling some private business that required my attention. On mentioning the fact to Dr. Connelly that I expected to return home in the spring, he informed me that he was going with a train of wagons about the first of the next March, and he would be glad if I would accompany him. This gave me great pleasure, as the government allowed me to keep the four mules and the carriage, by which I had first gone out, and which I could use for this trip. I at once assented to the Doctor's proposition, provided I got the leave of absence.

During the latter part of February, the Doctor, together with a Mexican[14] (I think his brother-in-law) arrived in Santa Fe on their way to Missouri. At this time my leave of absence had not arrived, but, as I expected it by the February mail, he told me he would be detained two or three days at Las Vegas,[15] which was immediately on our road, and where he had another mercantile establishment, and that he would even wait there some days for me if necessary. On the arrival of the February mail, I received an indefinite leave of absence, and immediately commenced preparations for my departure.

On learning this, the Baptist missionary[16] in Santa Fe called

[14] It is probable that the Mexican referred to was José Francisco Chaves, the son of Don Mariano Chaves, former governor under Mexican rule, and Dolores Perea, of Bernalillo. He was the stepson of Dr. Henry Connelly. Chaves was a major in the First Regiment of New Mexico Volunteers and was promoted to colonel upon the resignation of Ceran St. Vrain. He was later prominent in New Mexico politics, being elected as delegate to Congress in 1864 and 1866 and serving as district attorney of the Second Judicial District, 1875–77. He was murdered in an isolated cabin in Torrence County, New Mexico, November 26, 1904, under circumstances that seemed to indicate a plot on the part of bitter political opponents. His murderer (or murderers) was never apprehended. Keleher, *Turmoil in New Mexico*, 480–81.

[15] Las Vegas was first settled about 1835, on Gallinas Creek, a tributary of the Pecos River. It was the temporary capital of New Mexico during the Civil War when the Confederates under General Sibley captured Santa Fe. W. W. H. Davis described it in 1853 as "a dirty mud town of some seven hundred inhabitants; many of the houses were in ruins, and most of the others wore an exceedingly uncomfortable appearance."—*El Gringo*, 51–52.

[16] According to W. W. H. Davis, the Reverend Louis Smith "had been sent

on me and said his wife was very anxious to visit her relatives, I think in Ohio, and that the Baptist board of home missions was to meet in New York in the spring, which meeting she was anxious to attend and get permission for him to withdraw from that mission, and he wanted to know if I would give her a seat in my carriage. To which I responded, "I will do so with great pleasure." That evening Mrs. Smith called at my office to know the time of my departure and what preparations were necessary for her to make. I told her that I would leave the day after tomorrow, and that she would have but little preparation to make. I showed her my carriage, and how the backs of the seats could be turned down, which would afford her a mattress to sleep on, and, by letting the curtains down, she would be as secret as in a stateroom on a steamboat. At first she demurred at depriving me of my comfortable lodging, but on telling her that sleeping on the ground was no new thing to me and that my son, Raymond and myself would occupy a tent beside the carriage, and that all she would have to do would be to take a roll of blankets, she told me she was a good cook, and if I would take some flour along, whenever we camped at night where there was plenty of wood, she would make us fresh biscuits. She said she would be ready at my office on the morning of our departure. My old driver and cook not desiring to return to the States, I procured the services of a Negro named Louie. He had been in New Mexico for several years and wished to return.

I think it was the last day of February that we departed, and on reaching Las Vegas, we found Dr. Connelly would be ready to start the next day. Our train then consisted of about one hundred wagons and three carriages, together with about one hun-

out by the Baptist Board of Home Missions nearly three years before, and during this time he had labored faithfully in this new field, but with little success." He erected the first Protestant church in the territory at Santa Fe with the help of Joab Houghton, "who took a lively interest in it from the beginning."—*ibid.*, 238–72.

dred extra mules, which the Doctor and Mr. Chaves were taking along to bring out some wagons on their return. Dr. Connelly and myself laid in a supply of corn here, which Mr. Chaves declined doing, and filling his empty wagons with wheat straw, said his mules must be satisfied with this. Indeed, this was the invariable practice of Mexicans. I never knew one to take a bushel of corn with him.

On reaching a creek near what was called Barclay's Fort,[17] a nearby trading house, we camped with plenty of water and grass but no wood. We camped here early in the evening because it was fifteen or twenty miles to the foot of Turkey Mountain,[18] where we could get wood. This was a remarkably pleasant evening, and we could sit in the sun and be comfortable without any fire. When the time came to commence getting our supper, the boys picked up some little sticks, sufficient to boil a pot of coffee, so our supper that night consisted of coffee and crackers. But shortly after sunset clouds began to make their appearance over the mountains hard by, and pretty soon it commenced snowing, which drove us to our couches at an early hour. At about midnight the wind blew down the tent in which Raymond and myself were sleeping, so we had to be content to lie still, covered by the tent and snow. About daybreak we arose and found the snow five or six inches

[17] Alexander Barclay in the spring of 1848 in association with Joseph B. Doyle founded "Barclay's Fort" on Mora Creek not far distant from its junction with Sapello Creek, near the present Watrous, New Mexico. It was described by W. W. H. Davis on his trip to Santa Fe in 1853 as "a large adobe establishment, and like the immense caravansaries of the East, serves as an abode for men and animals. From the outside it presents rather a formidable as well as neat appearance, being pierced with loop holes and ornamented with battlements."—*El Gringo,* 51. Barclay was an Englishman who first settled at the Maitland Concession of Upper Canada in 1833. He was a bookkeeper and storekeeper at Bent's Fort on the Arkansas in 1838 and in 1842 became a trader. After the American conquest of 1846, he was Acalde for the Upper Arkansas area. See Alexander Barclay, Correspondence and Papers, 1823–58, Bancroft Library.

[18] The Turkey Mountains are west of the present U.S. Highway 85, north and a few degrees west of Watrous, New Mexico.

deep, and, as we had no wood and it had been quite cold, we at once hitched up and started for Turkey Mountain.

During the morning's travel I was thinking of telling Mrs. Smith what an uncomfortable camp we would have, for, as soon as we would build a fire, the snow would melt, and, as the ground was not frozen, we would soon be in mud up to the tops of our shoes. But on reaching the wood, I discovered a flat rock, probably twenty feet long and ten or fifteen wide, and raised about a foot from the ground, and off the surface of which the wind had blown all the snow. On Louie's driving the carriage up close to the rock, we stepped out on it without getting our feet even dampened from the snow. We soon had a good fire built at one end of the rock, and Mrs. Smith's culinary art was called into requisition. In due time she had some warm biscuits baked, a good pot of coffee ready, together with some fried meat, and we all had a comfortable breakfast. At night we could not pitch the tent because we could not drive the tent pins in the rock, when Mrs. Smith expressed her fears that we would have a hard bed. This brought to my mind the remark of the boy with the hard bread, and I told her that, "Although the bed might be hard, it would be harder if we had none."

Here Dr. Connelly, Mr. Chaves and myself held a council, and on my informing them of the advantages of the new route [Aubry Route], where we could get better wood, water, and grass, than on the old one, we agreed to go the new way. As none of the party had ever traveled that route except myself and Raymond, they elected me Captain with authority to regulate the march and time and place of camping.

Nothing occurred worthy of notice until one evening there came up a tremendous snowstorm, when I informed the other two gentlemen that we were fifteen or twenty miles from either wood or water, and proposed that we should drive under the protection of a steep hill, which would break the force of it, and camp. To this, Mr. Chaves demurred and said he would proceed by himself if we did not go with him. So he started off, and Dr. Connelly and myself drove under the protection of the hill and camped without wood or water, and giving our animals a good feed of corn, went to our blankets. In the morning we found our animals drawn up under the protection of the wagons and hill, and, as the weather was very cold, and snow covered the ground, we gave them more corn and started. On reaching Mr. Chaves' camp, he asked us how many mules we had lost. On telling him not one, he said that thirty-seven or thirty-eight of his had frozen to death the preceding night. He had driven so far the preceding day and night that the weaker portion of his mules became exhausted and, he having no corn for them, had lain down, and, being covered with snow, had frozen to death.

Nothing else occurred worthy of note, until we crossed the Arkansas River, where we found dry grass about knee high, and strict orders were given that no smoking was to be done in camp. One morning we found the wind blowing up the river with extreme violence, and, turning off the road to reach the river where we could water our animals, camp, and get breakfast, orders were renewed prohibiting smoking. At this time Mr. Chaves was with his train probably a mile behind us. The road was about a quarter of a mile from the river, and we had to cut the grass with our knives for a space sufficient to build our campfires.

Mr. Chaves passed by us, and, going five or six miles lower down the river, also went into camp. Then the cooks were all hastened up, for I told Dr. Connelly that Chaves' Mexicans would have the grass afire, before we could get breakfast. I saw a volume of smoke and flame arise near Chaves' camp and gave immediate orders to hitch up and get to the opposite side of the road, which was well beaten and about twenty feet wide. We had scarcely reached this place of safety, when the flames, ten or more feet high, passed our late camp. On reaching Mr. Chaves' camp, we found that he had driven his stock below it to graze, and, as the fire originated at his camp, it proceeded very slowly against the wind, while it ran with great speed toward our camp, which fact enabled him also to escape the flames. We proceeded down the valley of the Arkansas and found Fort Atkinson evacuated and in ruins.

After crossing the Arkansas, we encountered numerous herds of buffalo, all which appeared to be moving north. We found the finest veal I ever ate in my life, for the Mexicans would chase the calves, lasso them, and bring them alive into camp. I was astonished to find the calves so easily tamed, for, after being tied to a wagon wheel for a short time, they became so tame that they would let us go up to them and pet them with our hands. One day while Raymond was ahead of the train about one hundred yards, a herd of buffalo crossed the road between the train and myself, and a calf unhesitatingly trotted along behind his horse, while its mother trotted parallel to the road a few hundred yards distant, apparently much distressed on account of her offspring. On seeing this I hailed Raymond and told him to drive the calf back; although he whipped it with his quirt, it would not leave, so he dismounted, caught the calf, and threw it down and held it until the train had passed. Then pulling up some weeds and grass and covering its head, he quickly mounted and rode off—it is hoped the calf soon reached its distressed mother.

Mrs. Smith had often expressed a great wish to have it said when she arrived in the States, that she too had killed a buffalo on the plains. To gratify her, one night when we had a calf in camp and were about to slaughter it, I got one of my pistols, and when I handed it to her, she placed herself within feet or four feet of the animal and shot it in the head. It dropped dead, upon which she exclaimed, "Now I can tell my people that I have killed a buffalo on the plains."

On reaching the Big Bend of the Arkansas River, where the

road leaves that stream for the Missouri, Dr. Connelly told me that all Mexican trains were in the habit of camping before leaving the buffalo regions, killing and curing sufficient meat to last them to the Missouri River and back to the Arkansas again, and that this would require a detention of about a week. He therefore proposed that he and myself should proceed alone in our carriages, as all danger from the Indians was then over, to which I at once assented.

On reaching the Little Arkansas River,[19] the wind was again blowing with great violence. At such time it was very difficult to strike fire with a match, or even to cook after we had started the fire. So I directed the driver to select a place where there was a steep hill under which we could cook breakfast; and, as all the curtains were closed except the one in front, I advised Mrs. Smith to remain in the carriage until breakfast was ready, when our breakfast would be brought up and we could eat together in the carriage. Such a place being found, the carriage was driven near the top of the bank, the animals turned out to graze, and the cooking of breakfast commenced. When our breakfast was ready, Louis and myself started up the hill with it, and, reaching the top, I discovered an Indian standing at the end of the carriage tongue looking intently at Mrs. Smith.

He could talk a little English and asked me if that was my squaw, to which I replied, "Yes." Then he said, "I have a squaw here that I will swap for her." And looking in the direction in which he pointed his finger, I saw two squaws, each sitting on a mule and holding the Indian's horse. I at once objected to his proposition to swap, when he said he would give me one squaw and a mule for her, and I rejected this proposition also. Finally he offered both squaws and both mules, which also I declined.

[19] The source of the Little Arkansas is in the present Ellsworth County, Kansas. It flows southeast through Rice, McPherson, Reno, Harvey, and Sedgewick counties and empties into the Arkansas at Wichita. The Santa Fé Trail crossed it in Rice County. See Connelley, *Doniphan's Expedition,* 158.

This colloquy seemed to amuse Mrs. Smith, but on starting, Louis told us that the Indian said that his people had a large camp a short distance down the river. This news frightened the lady very much, for she became seriously alarmed for fear the Indian might get a strong party and take her by force. As our party consisted of Dr. Connelly and his driver, Raymond, myself and driver, I did not think there was much danger. To quiet her fears, however, we agreed that each one should alternately stand watch that night, but no Indian appeared. On coming within about fifty miles of Council Grove, then the first settlement in Kansas, we left camp after supper, intending to travel a distance sufficient to enable us to reach that little village the next night. But before we had gone more than ten miles, it began to rain furiously and became so dark we couldn't see the road, so we were compelled to camp, and picketing our animals we all went to sleep.

A little before daylight, I awoke, and looking out, discovered that our horse and all the mules were gone. Now we were in a pitiful condition, particularly Dr. Connelly and Mrs. Smith, for the former was a large fleshy man and could not walk very far, and the latter was a delicate lady. We happened to have a little wood with us, so I directed Louie to boil a cup of coffee and told Raymond to make a half circle around the camp, on the southern side of the road, while I made a similar circle on the northern side, for the ground was so soft that one of us would be sure to discover the tracks of our animals. Pretty soon I saw Raymond diverge from his circle and start off in a direction from camp, from which I at once knew that he had found the trail, so I returned to the carriages.

About this time it had turned cold and began to snow and sleet a little, so I drank a cup of hot coffee and ate a few crackers with Mrs. Smith and sat in the carriage two or three hours, trying to devise some plan by which we could reach Council Grove if our animals were not recovered. I finally became uneasy on Raymond's account, fearing that the Indians had stolen our stock and that if he came up with them, they might kill him. These reflections induced me to follow on Raymond's trail as fast as I could walk, but on reaching an eminence in the prairie and looking ahead, I saw Raymond returning, riding the horse and leading Dr. Connelly's mules by their lariat ropes and our mules following. On his arrival, I asked him why he had ridden so slowly, and he told me that if he went faster, the loose mules wouldn't keep up, and he was afraid of losing them. He also said he was nearly frozen to death and asked me to ride the horse ahead at a brisk gait, while he would run along behind and keep the mules up, as this exercise would restore warmth to him. So mounting the horse without saddle or bridle, but with a lariat around his neck, I hastened toward camp.

When I came within twenty or thirty yards of where the carriages stood, I called out for Louie, who was fast asleep under the carriage, which had been his usual place for sleeping during the whole trip. Hearing my call, Mrs. Smith pulled back the curtain of the carriage and placing both her hands above her head, screamed out as loud as she could, "Glory to God! Glory to God!" We soon hitched up and started once more but found the roads so heavy that we gave up all hopes of reaching Council Grove that night, and on going about twenty miles and finding a place where we could get some wood, we determined to camp there for the night. Starting the next morning immediately after an early breakfast, we reached Council Grove a little before night. I had told Mrs. Smith that at this place we could get good quarters, as the government of the United States had established a mission there for the benefit of the Kansas Indians,[20] the young-

[20] The Kansas (or Kaw) Indians were of the Siouan family, related linguistically to the Osages. They resided along the Kansas River, a few miles above its mouth, numbering slightly more than 1,500 and living in dome-shaped earth lodges. Marquette's autograph map indicates that they were in that area as early

er portion of whom were to be taught in school, and taught also all the principles of the Christian religion. I had told her further that the man in charge was a minister of the gospel and occupied a large two-story house, which had been erected at the expense of the government. Dr. Connelly had an acquaintance living here, at whose house he intended to stop, so I determined to proceed to the mission house. I had gone but a short distance in that direction when I met the missionary coming to see who had arrived. Having made his acquaintance the summer before as I went out, I introduced him to Mrs. Smith, the wife of a Baptist missionary in New Mexico, and told him that we were coming to claim his hospitality for the night. He promptly responded, "I can't entertain you." I said to him, "Here is Mrs. Smith, the wife of a missionary and who has traveled a thousand miles without seeing a house, and you certainly can give her a night's lodging, while I go to the little tavern and get accommodations there." To this he replied, "She doesn't belong to the same denomination that I do, and you had better go to the tavern." So we proceeded to a little log tavern where we were kindly received and ushered into a room where there was a good fire burning. Learning that we had eaten nothing since early in the morning, the landlord's wife and daughter hastened to get supper for us. When bedtime arrived I told Raymond to prepare the carriage for him and myself to sleep in, when the landlady said, "No Governor, I have a little room back here that you can occupy, and Mrs. Smith can sleep with my daughter."

Next morning, the weather still being unfavorable, we determined to remain, but after dinner the clouds broke away, and we started, knowing that we could get a good camp where there was wood and grass, about twenty miles distant. While Louie,

---

as 1673. In 1847 they were placed on a reservation at Council Grove, and twenty-five years later were removed to the present Oklahoma. See Muriel H. Wright, *A Guide to the Indian Tribes of Oklahoma.*

Raymond, and the landlord were hitching up our horses, I approached the landlady and asked her what I had to pay. She named a very moderate sum and said, "We never charge missionaries anything and wish they would always call upon us in going out or coming in."

This little episode strongly reminded me of the parable of the Pharisee and the Publican, but verily this man (the missionary) got his reward, for in reaching Washington City and telling Colonel [George W.] Manypenny, commissioner of Indian Affairs, he hastily asked me, "How soon can I get a man there in his place." I told him that there was a stage leaving Independence the first day of each month. He remarked, "Such a fellow cannot draw another month's salary from this department." When I went out some weeks afterwards, I found he had been relieved.

When we had reached about half way to where we could get wood, I was attacked by a violent congestive chill, and we were without means of procuring wood to make a fire. So I wrapped myself up in blankets, told Raymond to hasten forward on horseback with his hatchet, and have a good fire on our arrival. On reaching the camp ground, instead of a small fire made of sticks such as could be cut with a hatchet, I found a fire made of logs of considerable size, and on asking Raymond how he managed to cut such big wood with a hatchet, he told me in searching for some dry wood to start the fire, he had found a good axe which some camper had left there and with which he had felled a small dead tree, cut it into lengths, and made the fire in the place we camped. I immediately had my blankets spread out, told Raymond to get me some quinine out of the trunk, and took a heavy dose of it; and I soon had some hot rocks at my feet and lay down. Pretty soon, Mrs. Smith produced a tin cup full of hot coffee which I drank. At this time my pulse was very feeble and resembled a thread, but after a little while, reaction commenced, when I went to sleep and did not awaken before daybreak the next day, when I repeated the dose of quinine and a cup of hot coffee. The others got their breakfast, and we started once more.

About twenty miles or more from the Missouri River, the road forked, one fork leading to Kansas City, the other to Independence, and, as Mrs. Smith had told me that she had a friend living near the latter place, also a member of the Baptist church, at whose house she had remained several days when starting for New Mexico, and moreover as I had to get some person to care for my horse and mules, we determined to go to this house. After parting with Dr. Connelly, we determined to make another night's travel and reach a little village near Blue River, called Santa Fe, and remain there that night, as the weather was very threatening. But, on reaching within a few miles of this little town, it began to rain and became so dark that we couldn't see the road. So we had to once more camp without wood or water, but we did not trust our animals that night to the picket pins but tied Raymond's horse to the hind wheel of the carriage, feeling assured that the mules would not leave him. The next morning we found the snow three or four inches deep, and started for Little Santa Fe as soon as it was light enough for us to see the road, intending to get our breakfast there. On reaching the little place, we saw nobody astir and no smoke coming from any chimney, but seeing the woods on Blue River[21] a few miles distant, we proceeded there. As usual I sent Raymond ahead to get a fire made and thought as we rode along how uncomfortable it would be after the fire was made, from the melting snow, but once more we found ourselves agreeably disappointed, for we found a large fire with the snow all melted for eight or ten feet around. Asking an explanation from Raymond, he said that a train had camped there the previous night and had left but a short time before his arrival.

[21] One branch of the Santa Fé Trail crossed this stream west of the village of Hickman Mills, Jackson County, Missouri.

Here we gave our mules and the horse the last of the corn we had procured at Council Grove, and, starting after breakfast, we reached the house of Mrs. Smith's friend, which was but a few miles from Independence. To my surprise an old gentleman received us, whom I had known as a resident of Jefferson County, Kentucky, many years before. His name was Mickelberg. He received us very hospitably and soon had a good warm supper prepared for us. I soon made arrangements with him to keep my animals until my return, and on asking him as to the probabilities of our getting a boat to descend the Missouri, he told us he had been at Independence that day and had learned that a boat had passed up a few days before, bound for Fort Leavenworth, the captain of which had left word that all passengers and freight intended for St. Louis be ready as he would return the next day.

The next morning we proceeded to Independence, accompanied by Mr. Mickelberg and a boy, who would take our baggage and team back to his home. Independence was not immediately on the bank of the river but on the highlands some two or three miles from it. Mr. Mickelberg informed us that there was a little warehouse on the bank of the river, where we could remain until the boat's arrival, so we passed through the town without stopping, descended the high hill, and reached the landing where we had to wait but a few hours, when the expected boat landed, and we were off down the river that same evening. We had a good trip down this turbulent stream, and as we passed the site of old Fort Osage in daylight, I looked out on the site of my old residence of over thirty years before. We reached St. Louis in the night and were informed that a Louisville boat would depart in the morning. Transferring ourselves from one boat to the other, we once more started down the "Father of Rivers" and in due time passed up the Ohio and reached my old Kentucky home. We were put ashore a little before daybreak, and as Mrs. Smith had told me she had a brother-in-law, or brother, I forgot which, living at Madison, Indiana, I invited her to remain at our house until she could communicate with him. The next morning a dispatch was sent to Louisville directed to her relative in Madison, and a messenger brought back an answer that evening, saying that he would meet her on the mail-boat the next morning. So I took this amiable lady in my son's buggy the next morning and delivered her safely into the hands of either her brother or brother-in-law. I arrived at home about the first of April and very shortly after reported my arrival to the secretary of state by letter to Washington. He directed me to report to the President in person as soon as I recovered from the fatigue of my long journey.

About the middle of April, I accordingly proceeded to do so, and both the President and Secretary appeared well satisfied with the temporary settlement of the boundary question which I had made with the government of Chihuahua. I remained in Washington about a week, in consultation with the postmaster general as to the post routes to be established in the territory, with the secretary of the treasury as to appropriations to be made, and with the commissioner of Indian Affairs, relative to the condition of the Indians in that territory.

About the time these matters were concluded, the President sent for me, and, on presenting myself, he asked me how soon I could get back to New Mexico, as he had received information that the Indians had become hostile and were committing depredations on the frontier.[22] In answer I told him that it was impos-

[22] Shortly after Governor Meriwether left on his leave of absence in March of 1854, the Jicarilla Apaches and Utes began hostilities, raiding and plundering in the northern part of the territory. This was partly due to their dissatisfaction over the suspension of food supplies necessitated by the depletion of funds. The Governor hurriedly left Louisville about June 17, and upon his arrival in Santa Fe he endorsed a policy of force. In the meantime even before he had reached Kentucky, news of a military disaster reached Fort Union on March 31, 1854. About twenty miles from Taos in a canyon of the Embudo Mountains, Lieutenant Davidson en-

sible for me to start back before the first of June, when I could travel in company with the stage, which would leave Independence on that day. The President urging me to return to my post as soon as possible, I immediately sent a telegraphic dispatch to General Garland, directed to the care of the postmaster at Independence, requesting that gentleman to forward my dispatch to the General by the May stage. In my dispatch to the General, I requested him to keep the Indians in check as much as possible until my arrival, which would be in company with the June stage. I also wrote to Mrs. Smith, that I would leave home about the middle of May, and if she desired to return with me, to be in Louisville at that time. I then hastened home again and commenced preparations for my departure.

gaged the hostiles and suffered an overwhelming defeat. He was forced to retreat to Fort Burgwin, leaving between thirty and thirty-five dead. Kit Carson is said to have visited the field a day or so later, and he stopped long enough to help bury them. See National Archives, Microfilm 234, Roll 547, Letters Received by the Office of Indian Affairs, 1824–81. New Mexico Superintendency, 1849–80; and Blanche C. Grant, *When Old Trails Were New*, 156.

XI
Apaches, Utes, and Navahos

I ARRIVED AT INDEPENDENCE three or four days before the stage would start and immediately proceeded to the residence of Mr. Mickelberg to see the condition of my mules and horse, and I actually found them to be too fat for hasty travel. I found at Independence, Dr. Steck[1] from Pennsylvania, who had recently been appointed an Indian agent in New Mexico, and he informed me that he had spoken for a passage in the stage for Santa Fe. I at once told him that I was going out in company with the stage, and that Raymond would accompany me on horseback, also that his passage in the stage would cost him one hundred dollars, and for that sum he could purchase a horse and bridle at Independence, which he could sell in New Mexico for the same sum and probably more.

I told him further that I would take provisions enough for him and the trip would cost him only about fifteen dollars, which suggestion pleased him. He went to Hall, the proprietor of the stage, and told him he would not require the seat already spoken for but would purchase a horse, saddle, and bridle and would accompany the Governor on horseback. I also called upon Mr. Hall and told him of the fat condition of my mules, and that therefore I would start a few days ahead of the stage and let them get accustomed to travel before the stage overtook me. I also told him that I would purchase a sack of corn at Council Grove and offered to pay him to have it carried in the baggage

[1] See note 35, Chapter IX.

wagon which accompanied the stage, when he at once said he would direct the conductor to carry the corn for me without charge. I then saw the conductor, Booth, and told him I would purchase the corn and have it at the little tavern at Council Grove and would give him a dollar for his trouble in bringing it along until he overtook me. This he agreed to do. I started about three days before the stage and traveled leisurely along to Council Grove. Here I purchased the sack of corn and directed it to be delivered to Booth.

I continued traveling by short stages until I arrived near the crossing of the Arkansas, and, not knowing which road Booth would travel, I camped one evening to await his arrival. The next day he arrived, but instead of stopping at our camp, he passed, driving like Jehu. We immediately hitched up and started after him and found him in camp some eight or ten miles farther on, where I also camped. On asking him for my corn, he told me he couldn't find where I had left it. So I found myself without corn with which to feed my mules for the remainder of the trip, and on application he refused to let me have any of his, saying he had but a small supply for himself.

We soon crossed the Arkansas River, taking the old route,[2] which I had never traveled before, and he continued to drive very fast, so much so that I found it very difficult to keep up.

On reaching the Cimarron River, I met a sergeant with ten soldiers, who informed me that he had been sent out from Fort Union by General Garland's orders to protect me from the Indians, who were very hostile. We camped together that night, and I sent my driver to the sergeant's camp to see if he could supply me with a little corn. On his return he brought me about half

[2] Strictly speaking, the "old route" was the one that followed the Arkansas into Colorado and entered New Mexico over Raton Pass; but Meriwether is referring to the Cimarron Cutoff, which was older than the Aubry route.

a sack but said the sergeant did not want me to let Booth know that he had supplied me with corn. On asking why he did not want Booth to know it, the sergeant told Louie, my driver, that I had deprived Booth of a passenger, and he (Booth) wanted to break down my team and hoped the Indians would scalp me, to which I replied that this was a charitable wish to say the least of it.

The next morning when we came to their camp, we had to send our animals three or four hundred yards to get water, and, as soon as Raymond and Dr. Steck started for the water, Booth and the sergeant started off again without me. That night we all camped together, and I sent for the sergeant and asked him for whom he was sent out as an escort, and his reply was, "You, Sir." Then said I, "Why do you go off and leave me?" To this he replied that he did not observe that I was ready to start. I asked him if he had a corporal with him, and he said, "Yes." "Then," said I, "divide your men, and let me have the corporal and five men, and you and five remain with Booth."

At the next camp we made, when nearly ready to start, some antelope came down to the creek about a quarter of a mile ahead of us, when Booth shouldered his gun and went in pursuit of them. I then directed the corporal to mount his men, and Raymond to have our team hitched up and started, not so much with the intention of leaving Booth as to get into the next camp by the time he would arrive. But I saw nothing more of Booth and the sergeant until we arrived at Fort Union, which we reached early in the morning; Booth did not get there until late in the evening.

On my arrival at Fort Union, I immediately called on the commander to learn the condition of Indian affairs and to procure an escort from there to Santa Fe. The commanding officer informed me that the Indians were very hostile, even between

Fort Union and Santa Fe, but said he could not supply me with an escort for the remainder of the route, so I procured corn sufficient to give my animals a good feed that night and the next morning, knowing that I could secure an additional supply at Las Vegas and Tecolote.[3] I then called at Booth's camp late in the evening and told him that I thought we had both played the fool long enough, that neither could get an escort any farther, and added, "You let me know when you start in the morning and I will start with you, you camp when and where you please and I will camp with you." To this he replied, "I will get fresh mules here, and I will start when I get ready, and I will camp when I get ready, so you may shift for yourself."

The next morning I started by daybreak, and my mules moved off briskly, as they had had nearly twenty-four hours' rest and three good feeds of corn. Traveling about twenty miles, I watered and fed my mules and turned them out to graze. Shortly after this, Booth passed me by without stopping, pulling off his hat and bidding me "goodbye." I immediately hitched up and started after him. In about eight or ten miles I passed his camp and returned his salute, saying, "You won't see me again until you get to Santa Fe." On reaching Las Vegas, I got another supply of corn and more again at Tecolote, and I reached Santa Fe about half a day ahead of Booth. Immediately on my arrival at Santa Fe, General Garland called on me and told me that the Indians were harassing the frontier very much and that he had not enough men to pursue and whip them. He said that by the last returns he had about eleven hundred soldiers in the territory and six military posts to man, but if I would call out a regiment of volunteers to assist him, he would make quick work of

[3] Tecolote was founded about 1824 by Salvador Montoya. It served as a forage station for the army during the Indian wars. It was about twelve miles west of Las Vegas. Kenyon Riddle, *Records and Maps of the Santa Fe Trail*, 74.

the Indians. To this I responded, "General, sit down at my table here and write me an official letter, stating your inability to bring the Indians to terms and asking me to call out a regiment of volunteers to assist you." This he at once did. I then prepared a proclamation printed in Spanish and English, calling for a regiment of volunteers, informing the people that each company might select its captain and two lieutenants and that I would appoint the field officers, and that they should receive the same pay and allotments as regular soldiers and be armed and equipped by the U.S. government.

On the day appointed in the proclamation for these volunteers to rendezvous at Santa Fe, more appeared than I had called for, and here was trouble for me. I had a colonel, a lieutenant colonel, and a major to appoint, and everybody wanted to fill these offices. I appointed no applicant but tendered the appointment as colonel to Mr. St. Vrain,[4] who I think was a Frenchman by birth but who had resided for a number of years in the territory and spoke the English and Spanish languages well. On hearing this, a certain party in the territory commenced dissuading him from accepting the appointment, they having recommended another man, who I was determined not to appoint. But Mr. St. Vrain accepted. I then appointed a Mexican lieutenant colonel and an American major. The men were all mustered into the service of the United States,[5] and, together with such regular soldiers as could be spared from the military posts, were all

[4] Meriwether could not have made a better selection. Ceran St. Vrain was a descendant of a distinguished French family, whose parents migrated to the United States in 1790. He was born about 1797 at Spanish Lake, near St. Louis, and as a youth was employed by the fur-trading firm of Pratte, Cabanne, and Company. For nearly half a century he was a prominent figure in the Southwest, being actively engaged in the New Mexico as well as the Chihuahua trade, and a member of the firm of Bent and St. Vrain. He became a Mexican citizen in 1828, as did some of his contemporaries as a measure of expediency in Mexican relations. In later years he conducted a store and flour milling operation at Mora, New Mexico, where he died October 28, 1870, one of New Mexico's most respected citizens.

[5] Four companies of volunteers were recruited.

placed under the command of Colonel Fauntleroy[6] of the United States Army, and they took the field in search of the Indians.[7]

As the Indians had not been pursued after committing depredations, they became careless, and one morning before day, their camp was surprised and captured, a few being killed and some children taken prisoners. This was during the latter part of August or the first of September,[8] and about the middle of the latter month, my interpreter came to me and said that Chico Velasquez,[9] the head chief of the hostile Apaches, together with three or four of his men, were in the Indian office and very anxious to see me.

[6] Colonel Thomas Turner Fauntleroy, a Virginian, was commissioned major of the Second Dragoons on June 8, 1836; lieutenant colonel on June 30, 1846; and colonel of the First Dragoons on July 25, 1850. At the beginning of the Civil War he resigned and entered the Confederate service as brigadier general of Virginia Volunteers. He died September 12, 1883.—Heitman, *Historical Register, U.S.A.*, I, 415.

[7] Colonel Fauntleroy with two companies of the First Dragoons and two companies of the Second Artillery left Fort Union and arrived February, 1855, in Taos, where they were joined by the volunteers under St. Vrain, with Kit Carson as chief guide. The combined force rode from Taos to Fort Massachusetts, then followed the Río Grande into Colorado and cut north to Saguache Pass. Here in the San Luis Valley they encountered the Indians in great numbers and defeated them. The artillery and wagons were left at Saguache under the command of Lieutenant Lloyd Beall with one hundred and fifty men, while the Dragoons and Volunteers followed the Indians' retreat eastward. A number of skirmishes occurred as the troops advanced, handicapped by snow and mountainous terrain, finally engaging the hostiles on the headwaters of the Arkansas, where they were defeated and scattered. The expedition returned to Fort Massachusetts, arriving there about the first of March. Twitchell, *Military Occupation of New Mexico;* Letter, DeWitt C. Peters to family, as quoted in Grant, *When Old Trails were New*, 306; Banche C. Grant, ed., *Kit Carson's Own Story of His Life*, 117–20.

[8] Meriwether's narrative does not follow the Fauntleroy expedition into Colorado through the spring of 1855 but concentrates on events occurring nearer Santa Fe during the summer and fall of 1854.

[9] Chico Velasquez is classified by Meriwether and others as a Jicarilla Apache chief, a leader of hostilities in the northern part of the territory, though some accounts represent him and his people as Moache or Capote Utes. It is hard to distinguish, for the Utes and Jicarillas often joined forces in their forays against the settlements. It is probable that Chico Velasquez was the leader of the band that had killed the colorful mountain man, Old Bill Williams, and his companion, Dr. Kern in the Sangre de Christo Mountains some years before. Fort Sutter Papers, Docu-

I told him to tell Chico that I did not want to see him. On that night we had received returns of the election and found that the Democrats had carried both branches of the legislature, which caused great rejoicing among the Democrats. Bonfires were built and guns fired off, which frightened the Indians exceedingly. My interpreter returned after supper and again told me that the Indians were very much frightened and were anxious to see me, and I again told the interpreter to tell them that I didn't want to see them. The next morning, the interpreter came the third time and told me that the Indians were afraid to go away, for fear that they would be killed on the road, and afraid to remain for fear they would be killed in the house, and begged piteously to see me.

I then accompanied the interpreter to the Indian office, where I found four or five Indians sitting in a very despondent mood. I had seen Chico once or twice during my stay in the territory, and he immediately jumped up and reached out his hand to shake hands with me. But I placed my hands behind my back and declined shaking hands with him. He then asked through the interpreter why I refused to shake hands with him, to which I replied, "Your hands are stained with white peoples' blood, and I can't touch them." He then said he had been attacked by the white soldiers while peacefully encamped and had not disturbed a white man since our former interview, and, if he had not resisted when attacked, he would have been worse than a dog.

I had heard on my arrival in the territory that the Indians were not the aggressors, but I well knew that when the Indians and the whites once commenced fighting, the Indians never would make peace until whipped, and, therefore, necessity compelled us to whip them. I asked Chico why, after he had whipped

ments, 127–29, Huntington Library; Howard Louis Conard, *Uncle Dick Wootton: The Pioneer Frontiersman of the Rocky Mountain Region*, 200; and James H. Simpson, *Navaho Expedition: Journal of a Military Reconnaissance from Santa Fe, New Mexico to the Navaho Country, Made in 1849*.

the white soldiers, his people still continued to harass our frontier. To this he replied, "Your men have killed and wounded some of our people, and I could not control my young men." I then asked him whether, if I made peace with them, they would stop all depredations on our borders and restore the mules, horses, sheep, and cattle they had taken. He said he couldn't do this, that his people had eaten all the sheep and cattle but had some ponies that he would restore. I asked if he was willing to act as my captain and obey my orders when delivered to him. To this he replied, that he would as far as he possibly could. I then got a large silver medal with suitable devices and inscriptions on it and about as big as the bottom of a tin cup, several of which had been furnished me by the government for such a purpose, and suspended this around his neck with a ribbon. On one side of this medal was an Indian and a white man shaking hands, and underneath it was written, "Peace and Friendship." On the other side was a tomahawk with the pipe of peace lying on it. These devices I explained to the Indians, and they soon comprehended them. "Now," said I, "Chico, this is your commission, you are my captain and must obey my orders, and when the moon gets round and big, come to me and I will pay you your salary." This closed our conference, but the Indians said they were afraid to leave for fear they would be killed before they got out of the settlement, so I pulled out a white pocket handkerchief, and tying it to a stick, told him that this was the white man's sign of peace, and, "Whenever you carry this in your hand, no white man will harm you." On this assurance they mounted their ponies and departed.

About a week or ten days after this, Chico and a few of his men came again, bringing with them forty or fifty Mexican ponies, which I delivered to their owners, when I ascertained who they were. A few weeks after this, [Chico] came again, bringing me a letter from the commanding officer of Fort Union, stating that he [Chico] had returned to that post about forty head of beef cattle, which his young men had recently run off. On my asking him why his young men continued to do so, he said that his tribe had been broken up into small parties, and some of them were so far distant that he had been unable to inform them that peace was made.

Shortly after this event, a wealthy Mexican, who resided about thirty miles from Santa Fe, came and informed me that the Indians had run off fifty or sixty head of horses and mules belonging to him. I asked him what Indians had committed this act, and he said it was the Navahos. I then asked him if he was not mistaken, saying that the Navahos never came East of the Río Grande. He replied that he had followed after and came up within fifty yards of the rear party. I told him I would write to Mr. Dodge,[10] the Navaho agent at Fort Defiance,[11] and instruct him to try to procure the restitution of his stock, but that I still believed it was not the Navahos who had robbed him.

About a week after this interview, Chico again came in bring-

[10] Captain Henry Linn Dodge was a practicing attorney at the time of Kearny's entry into Santa Fe during the Mexican War and was named by the General to act as treasurer. He served with the New Mexico Volunteers in that war, and later as a captain of militia under Colonel John M. Washington in the expedition to the Navaho country in 1849. He was appointed agent to the Navahos in July of 1853. He was a most capable and energetic individual, a strong proponent of a new treaty, asking for a school, implements, and a few artisans to teach the Indians the rudiments of agriculture. He participated with Governor Meriwether in the treaty council at Laguna Negra on July 16–18, 1855. On November 19, 1856, he left the camp of a small detachment of troops under the command of Major Kendrick to hunt for game and never returned. A wide search was made, but his mutilated body was not recovered until the following summer. He was the victim of Coyotero Apaches. Frank D. Reeve, "The Government and the Navajo," *New Mexico Historical Review*, Vol. XIV (January, 1939); and Simpson, *ibid.*, 202–11.

[11] Fort Defiance was established September 18, 1851. It was situated at the mouth Canyon Bonita on the west side of Defiance Arroya, the present-day Black Creek, near the east line of what is now the state of Arizona. In 1853, Mansfield estimated the number of Navahos under Dodge's jurisdiction as one thousand warriors. "Their chiefs are numerous, and they sometimes commit depredations on the New Mexicans. In May last, eleven of them drove off five armed New Mexicans and captured 5,000 sheep."—Mansfield, *Western Forts*, 48.

ing the Mexicans' horses and mules with him, and told me the party who stole his stock was the last party of his people to be informed that hostilities had ceased. These horses and mules were restored to the owner at once, and the moon being about full, I paid Chico his salary, not in money, of which he did not know the value, but in tobacco and other articles, to the amount of between five and ten dollars, which appeared to be satisfactory to him.

Shortly after this, Mr. Head, an American gentleman who had resided on the frontier and had never been disturbed by the Indians because he treated them kindly and gave them something to eat when they were hungry, came into Santa Fe and informed me that a Mexican had killed an Indian and that Chico and all his band were in a very excited mood and desired him to come and see me and beg me to come to his [Mr. Head's] house, where they would meet me. I told this gentleman to return and tell the Indians to remain quiet until I arrived. As soon as I could get an escort ready, I started for Mr. Head's residence.

On my arrival there I found Chico and Tamouche[12] awaiting my arrival. They at once reminded me that I had told Tamouche that if the white people molested any of his people, to let me know, and I would give them satisfaction. "Now," said Chico, "A Mexican has killed one of my Indians, and we haven't disturbed any Mexican, and we desire to know whether you are as good as your word." I told him I would do all in my power to have the murderer arrested and punished. To this he responded, "You will never be able to catch him, for he has gone over across the mountains." Then I told him that he did not

[12] Tamouche, the Ute chief, was described by W. W. H. Davis: "His features were regular and classic, and appeared fashioned in nature's finest mold. He was dressed in a suit of buckskin, the coat highly wrought with beads, and his arms were the bow and arrow, which however, he laid aside before appearing in the presence of the Governor. Take him all and all, he was the finest specimen of a wild, untutored Indian I have ever met, and in personal appearance would compare favorably with his civilized white bretheren."—*El Gringo*, 283.

know how long my arm was, that I could reach over a mountain and catch a man, and that I would do so. This did not appear to satisfy them, and they returned to their camp near by, appearing very much disappointed. After their departure I told Mr. Head I would give one hundred dollars to have the murderer caught; and, as there were several Mexicans present, I asked him to give this information to them. In a few minutes, a Mexican constable came to me and asked if I would give him one hundred dollars if he caught the murderer. To this I replied, "Yes," and added, "I have one hundred dollars in gold, which I will give you on your producing the murderer." He said, "Well, I'll have him here tomorrow morning." I asked him if he was certain that he knew the man, and he said, "Yes, I have heard him boast of having killed the Indian, and he has shown me the Indian's blanket with a bullet hole in it and the Indian's blood upon it." And he immediately departed to find him. I then requested Mr. Head to visit the Indian camp and tell them not to leave before morning, at which time I desired Chico and Tamouche to come to see me.

Next morning shortly after breakfast, Chico and Tamouche came to my camp, apparently very much excited, when I told them that I would have the murderer there in an hour or two. Whilst we were talking, the constable arrived with the man tied on a horse. On my asking the fellow if he had killed an Indian at a certain time and place, he responded, "Yes." I asked him why he had done so, and he replied, "I didn't know it was any harm to kill an Indian." To this I replied, "By the time you get through my hands, you will find it is some harm to kill an Indian, when he is quiet and peaceable." I directed him to be placed under guard. Tamouche, who spoke the Spanish language quite well, understood all that had passed between me and the murderer and asked what I intended to do with him. I replied, "I will take him to Santa Fe with me, and a judge there who sits on the high seat in the court house will have twelve men brought in who will sit before him and will ascertain whether the Mexican is guilty or not; and if he is found guilty, the judge will inform me of it. Then it will be my duty to have a rope tied around his neck and have him hung up to a tree like a dog." To this Tamouche replied that he did not see any use of my going to all that trouble and said, "You heard the man tell you that he had killed one of our people. Just deliver him to us, and we will save you all that trouble." This I declined to do, telling him that if I myself had seen the man commit the murder, I would have to bring him before the judge and jury. I then gave Chico and Tamouche each a gray cloth coat, which I had made for them, decorated handsomely with red and yellow braid, a number of brass buttons in the front, and a rosette on each side of the breast. These were the first coats that either had ever had on his back and pleased them very much. I gave them also some presents for the family of the man who had been murdered and told them that when the murderer was to be hanged, I would send for them, so they could see it done. This pleased them well, and they departed.[13]

I took the prisoner to Santa Fe, but as no court would be held until the next spring, and having ascertained that the murder was committed in the county of Taos, I [decided to send] them there for trial. The next spring about a week before the opening of court in Taos, I got General Garland to detail a noncommissioned officer and a guard of soldiers to take the prisoner

[13] Meriwether reported this incident to Commissioner Manypenny and received an answer from the Commissioner's secretary dated December 29, 1854: "Returns letter of Governor of New Mexico relative to the arrest of a Mexican for the murder of a Utah Indian, and the rewards offered, for the murderer and his accomplices, with decision therein." The secretary went on to say there was no fund for that purpose, but he would pay it from other funds, "But it is not to be regarded as a precedent." See *ibid.*, *283;* and Letter, Commissioner of Indian Affairs to Meriwether, December 29, 1854, National Archives, New Mexico Superintendency, 1849–80.

to the town of Taos. But the soldiers returned in a few days, informing me that the prisoner had escaped, which I regretted very much, and although I made strenuous efforts to find him, I was never able to arrest him again.

During the following winter, Chico was taken sick with what proved to be smallpox, and he expressed a great wish to see me once more, as he thought I could cure him. But he was informed that the great council of the territory of which I was the head—meaning the legislature—was in session, and it was impossible for me to leave Santa Fe. He then asked to have a sheep killed, and be given as much as he could eat. This was done, and in a few days he died, and Tamouche became the head chief of the tribe.

Tamouche was the most gentlemanly Indian in his manners that I ever met with in my life, but unfortunately, he would get drunk whenever he could get whisky. Some time after this, he learned that I was going to visit the States again and made application to go with me, saying that he had heard of boats running there with fire built on them, and long trains of wagons also running by fire, and wanted to go and see them for himself. I at once consented to take him along with me and informed him when I would start. But, as he did not arrive on time, I departed without him.[14] A few days after my departure he did arrive at Santa Fe and followed several days with the hope of overtaking me, but finding that he could not do so, he returned to his people.

I think it was about February, 1855, that a small party of Mescalero and White Mountain Apaches ran off all the stock from a little village called, I think, Gallesteo [Galisteo], twenty miles south of Santa Fe, and immediately a runner was sent to Santa Fe with information of the raid. There were a few troops at Santa Fe at this time, and the messenger arrived about sunset,

[14] The Governor returned to the East in the fall of 1855 and spent the winter with his family. See Chapter XIII.

but Lieutenant Sturgis[15] got eight soldiers and eight citizens together and immediately after supper started in pursuit.

Now it must be recollected that the Indians had about forty miles the start, for the messenger had to travel twenty miles to Santa Fe, and Sturgis had to travel twenty miles to get where the Indians had started. But he followed them with vigor, traveling in three and a half days one hundred and sixty miles. He overtook the Indians, killed nine of the eleven of the party, recaptured the horses and mules, and turned them over to the owners. This expedition was energetically and skillfully managed, for the third morning, on reaching an eminence in the prairie, Sturgis discovered the Indians' campfires in a small grove of timber about one-fourth of a mile distant. Now, if he had attacked them while in camp, the Indians would have had the trees behind which to conceal themselves, but by concealing his men behind the little hill, while he lay down in the cold and watched the Indians' movements until they started, he and his men mounted and proceeded at a gallop after them. The grove of timber protected him from their sight until he got to the further side of it, when he discovered the Indians slowly driving their stock ahead of them, a few hundred yards out on the prairie. Then he made a dash, and, as before stated, killed nine out of eleven, also recovering all the stock, save one horse, which the Indians had killed for food. This exploit made Lieutenant Sturgis a captain, and he now holds the rank of a general officer in the United States Army, and the last I heard of him, he was stationed on the Pacific Coast.

This spring I determined to visit the Navaho Indians and instructed their agent, Henry Dodge, to assemble them at or

[15] Samuel Davis Sturgis, of Pennsylvania, graduated from West Point July 1, 1846, and was commissioned 2nd lieutenant, Second Dragoons. At this time he was a lieutenant of the First Dragoons. He had a distinguished military career during the Civil War and was promoted to major general. He died September 28, 1889. Heitman, *Historical Register, U.S.A.*, I, 934.

near Fort Defiance, for the purpose of meeting me.[16] It was arranged between myself and General Garland, who also desired to visit Fort Defiance, that he would start a few days ahead of me and go to Los Lunas,[17] where Captain Ewell[18] commanded, and would meet me west of the Río Grande where the roads from Los Lunas and Albuquerque came together. On arriving at the junction[19] of these roads, I discovered that a train had proceeded me in the direction of Fort Defiance; supposing that the General and Captain Ewell had gone on to the Puerco (Hog) River, I followed on but found the water of that river so bad

[16] In July, 1854, Congress had appropriated $30,000 for the expenses of making treaties with the Apaches, Utes, and Navahos.

[17] Los Lunas was a temporary post located at the town of the same name twenty-one miles south of Albuquerque.

[18] Captain Richard Stoddert Ewell, of Virginia, a grandson of Benjamin Stoddert, first secretary of the navy, graduated from West Point on July 1, 1836, and was commissioned 2nd lieutenant, First Dragoons. He was prominent in command of escorts on the Santa Fé Trail and was breveted captain in 1847 for gallantry at the battles of Contreras and Churubusco, Mexico. He resigned on May 7, 1861, and subsequently was commissioned lieutenant general in the Confederate service; died January 23, 1872. Heitman, *Historical Register, U.S.A.*, II, 410.

[19] Governor Meriwether left Santa Fe on July 5, 1855, accompanied by his son Raymond, W. W. H. Davis acting as his secretary, and two servants. They followed the approximate route taken by Oñate in October of 1598, up the present Río San Jose, named by him the Río de La Mala Nueva. The present U.S. Highway 66 follows closely the same route, crossing the Río Puerco about twelve miles west of the Río Grande and continuing up the San Jose. The Río Gallo does not appear on modern maps; however, on a map compiled by Lieutenant John G. Parke and drawn by Richard H. Kern in 1851 a Cañon del Gallo is shown on the east slope of the Zuni Mountains and opening into the stream now known as the San Jose, north of the present town of San Rafael. Farther up the San Jose is the village of Bluewater, perpetuating the name of Meriwether's Agua Azul. The trail then led past Ojo del Oso or Bear Springs, where Colonel Doniphan concluded a treaty with the Navahos, November 22, 1846. Unfortunately Meriwether gives a meager description of the country and people encountered, particularly the villages of Laguna; however Davis does give us an almost day-by-day narration of events in his book, *El Gringo*, in which he devoted forty-three pages to the chapter, "Trip to the Navajo Country." Davis, *El Gringo*, 389–432. See also Hammond and Rey, eds., *Onate*, 394; Simpson, *Navaho Expedition*, 194–200; and Letter, Dodge to Commissioner Manypenny, August 2, 1855, National Archives, Indian Records, New Mexico Superintendency, 1854–55, Microfilm, Roll 547.

that I supposed they had gone on to the Gallo (Rooster) River, so I proceeded there. But not finding them, I proceeded up the river and that night came to the camp of a supply train of heavily loaded wagons, on its way to Fort Defiance. The conductor of the train informed me that no escort had passed them.

Being now in the Indian country and not disposed to travel so slowly as the wagon train, and being assured by a Pueblo Indian, whom I tad taken along as guide and interpreter, that there was no danger, I determined to proceed with my small party, consisting of myself, one wagoner, my carriage driver, Raymond, and the Pueblo Indian. I found the valley of the Gallo River about twenty miles in length and a quarter of a mile in width covered with lava, which had flowed down from the mountains at its head. This was the most tantalizing place that I ever visited. The water flowed under this bed of lava, and we could hear it gurgling beneath, and where there were cracks we could look down and see it, eight or ten feet below, but without a possibility of getting a mouthful.

On reaching the mouth of the Agua Azul, or blue water, we ascended that stream, seeing large fields of lava here also, to the north of us. Finding a good place before we reached the foot of the mountains, we camped. At this camp a half-breed Indian, the interpreter for Major Kendrick,[20] joined us and said that he had been sent in pursuit of a deserter from Fort Defiance but not being able to find him, would return in company with us to that post. Both interpreters informed me that we would find a good spring of water on the top of the mountain, where we could camp the next night if we desired to do so. After ascending the valley of this stream six or eight miles, we commenced to climb

[20] Major Henry Lane Kendrick, of New Hampshire, entered West Point on September 2, 1831, and was commissioned 2nd lieutenant, First Infantry, July 1, 1835, and later, brevet major for gallantry at Pueblo, Mexico. He retired December 18, 1880, and died on May 24, 1891. Heitman, *Historical Register, U.S.A.*, II, 592.

the Rocky Mountains,[21] but the ascent was far from precipitous. On reaching the top, we found ourselves on a sandy plain, fifteen or twenty miles long and varying from five to ten miles in width, with mountains a thousand feet high on each side thereof, and the plain was so level that I concluded it had formerly been the bed of a large lake, which had been drained off by some volcanic eruption, which caused the lava before spoken of.

This valley was quite sandy, and on arriving at the spring, we found but little grass. Then the two interpreters informed me that on traveling ten or fifteen miles farther, we would find a a lake, with water, grass, and wood, and I determined to proceed. The sand caused us to travel slowly, so the two interpreters soon got ahead of us, and we could see Indian campfires on both sides of the valley, which caused us some apprehension lest the interpreters were playing false. After night these two men had gone so far ahead as to be entirely out of sight, and, fearing to be entrapped by the interpreters, I told Raymond to ride ahead, stop at the first suitable place where there was some grass for our animals, and we would camp. So he rode ahead and discovering a good place, halted until we came up. At this time I heard loud hallooing ahead of us and soon saw my interpreter coming in our direction. He informed me that he and his companion had reached the lake and built a fire, and he had returned to see what had become of us. So we proceeded to the camp chosen by them.

Although this was summertime, we found it quite cold and a fire very agreeable, and the next morning there was a heavy frost. As it was a long distance to the next camping ground, we determined to breakfast here. While this was in preparation, I took my gun and proceeded after a few ducks I saw at the edge of the lake. I had gone but a few hundred yards through the high grass and weeds, along the borders of the lake, when I came

[21] He was in fact climbing the Rocky Mountains, for the Zuni Mountains he ascended here form the Continental Divide.

upon the skeleton of a man, over which I nearly fell. He had evidently been dead a year or more, as the flesh was all gone and the bones bleached white. I suppose it was the skeleton of some poor fellow who had been killed by the Indians or who might have starved to death. This shocked me so that I returned to camp, and after breakfast we proceeded on our journey.

We found the western descent of the mountains very gradual, and in a day or two we arrived safely at Fort Defiance, where I found Dodge encamped with a large body of Indians. Major Kendrick, the accomplished commander of this post, met us at the gate and informed me that he had an empty barracks room already prepared for our reception and would expect us to eat our meals at the mess table of the officers as long as we remained. We arrived here early in the day, and that evening General Garland and Captain Ewell arrived also. The supply train which we had passed had informed them that we had gone on ahead.

As I had a wagonload of presents for these Indians, consisting of farming implements, tobacco, and other suitable articles, we spent the next day subdividing them, and the day after commenced their distribution.[22] On the morning of our arrival, Dodge brought the head chief of the tribe named Eschitchinee and introduced him to me. The old fellow claimed great credit to himself for having protected me and my small party while crossing the mountains and said if it had not been for his exertions, we would all have been killed, when in fact, he was

[22] Although Meriwether does not state the fact, his council with the Navahos was held on Laguna Negra, about twenty-five miles north of Fort Defiance. Under the escort of Ewell's dragoons the Governor and his party pitched camp on the shore on July 16 in the midst of two thousand assembled Navahos. On the second day of the meeting Zarcillas Largo, whom Meriwether calls by his Navaho name of Eschitchinee, turned over the leadership to the younger Manuelito. A treaty defining the tribal boundaries was drawn up and signed by the principal men on July 18. The council ended amicably, the Navahos being well pleased with their liberal treatment. They could not foresee that the treaty would fail of ratification by the United States Senate. See Davis, *El Gringo*, 389–432.

at Fort Defiance, at least one hundred miles' distance from us. He was riding a very fine horse, and, as they had a large number of horses and mules and I needed another, I asked to purchase this horse from him. But he said, "I won't sell him to you but will give him." But when we were about to depart from Fort Defiance and I proposed to pay him for the horse, he again repeated what he first said. He also said, "Next morning I have to fight with another Indian on horseback, and this is my favorite charger; if I am killed, I will tell my son to present the horse to you the next morning, but if I am not killed or wounded, I will give the horse to you myself." I saw no more of him or the horse afterwards during this visit.

As it rained heavily the next morning, we did not depart until after dinner, and, going about fifteen miles, we camped and picketed our animals where there was good grass. My Indian guide and interpreter did not start with us but said he would come into our camp that night, which he did after we had finished an early supper. I presented him, before leaving Fort Defiance, with a large red blanket, of which he seemed very proud, but coming into our camp with this blanket thrown over his shoulders and the wind blowing it about, Raymond's horse, seeing it, gave one snort, jerked up his picket pin, and started full speed back to Fort Defiance, followed by all the horses and mules in camp, amounting to about one hundred and fifty.

General Garland started a detachment of soldiers after the animals, accompanied by Raymond and our carriage driver, but they did not overtake them until they had reached Fort Defiance. After getting them all together they started back and arrived at camp about four o'clock in the morning, the horses and mules and those who had gone after them were all spattered with mud. This caused us to make a late start the next morning, as we had to let the animals eat grass, and ourselves to get breakfast. We proceeded to the eastern side of the mountain without any incident of note, but when we had descended nearly to the foot, being ahead of the escort, we saw a large number of Indians occupying our old camping ground, so I halted until the General and the escort came up, when the Indians began to move off. General Garland directed Captain Ewell to pursue and ascertain what Indians they were, while we proceeded on into camp on the Blue Water [Agua Azul].

Ewell soon returned accompanied by the head chief, Sanches, and two or three of his men. This was a small band of Navahos, who had separated from the main tribe long before and occupied the eastern slope of the mountains. On their arrival, I applied to Sanches to sell me a sheep, when he informed me that he couldn't do so without his wife's consent but that he would send one of the young men to the Indian camp and procure one for me. The young man soon returned bringing a fat lamb with him and said Sanches' wife wanted one dollar for it, which I gave him.

The Navaho tribe of Indians differs in some respects from any I have seen. They treat their women with more respect than any other Indians, are more cleanly in their appearance, and the women hold property separate from their husbands. All the sheep and wool belong to the women, and you can't buy either from any man in the tribe, they manufacture the most beautiful and substantial blankets that I have ever seen. These blankets are handsomely figured in red, blue, and white. One of them I now have; I have used it as a carriage blanket every winter for about thirty years, and it still has the colors as bright as when it was woven.

The missionaries in this country, and other learned divines, have a theory that these Indians are descended from one of the lost tribes of Israel, as all the figures on their blankets resemble the pyramids of Egypt, and the instruments used in making these blankets are precisely the same as the pictures of these instruments in the old English Bibles, which are spoken of in the Bible as the "Distaff and Spindle" used by the Jews. In addition to this, they do not bury their dead but place them in caves in the mountains, which brings to mind the cave of Machpelah and others spoken of in Jewish history. But the question arises, how did any of the lost tribe of Israel reach the continent of North America?

XII
Indians, Captives, and Boundary Problems

On arriving at Santa Fe,[1] I found the White Mountain and Mescalero Apaches had sued for peace, in consequence of a successful expedition made by Captain Ewell into their country in the spring before.[2] He had pursued them to the foot of the White Mountains and saw their campfires a little before day one morning. Then he concealed his men in a dry ravine, and, after daylight, sent Captain Stanton[3] with his company to engage them in their mountain fastness, after which Stanton and his men were ordered to hastily retreat down into the plain, where Ewell with his two companies of soldiers lay concealed. This was well accomplished, but at the loss of Captain Stanton and several of his men. The Indians pursuing the remainder were warmly received by Ewell and his men, and many of their tribe were lost before getting back to the mountains.

Captain Stanton had his young wife in the territory with

1 Meriwether is confused in his chronology here. His council with the White Mountain and Mescalero Apaches occurred in June before he went to the Navaho country in July.

2 Captain Ewell in command of eighty men of the First Dragoons left Fort Thorn on December 28, 1854, traveled east to the Sacramento Mountains south of the White Mountains, and joined Captain Henry W. Stanton's force on the Ruidoso on January 7. The combined troops moved up the Río Penasco fighting a number of skirmishes. The engagement described by Governor Meriwether took place on January 19.

3 Henry Whiting Stanton entered the Military Academy as a cadet at large from New York and was commissioned 2nd lieutenant of the First Dragoons on July 1, 1842, and captain on July 25, 1854. Fort Stanton was established in May, 1855, on the Río Bonito, twenty-two miles west of Lincoln, and named in his honor. Bennett, *Forts and Forays*, 59–62; and Heitman, *Historical Register, U.S.A.*, II, 916.

him, and she was very much distressed at the loss of her gallant husband. On her departure to return to her relatives—I think in Michigan—she begged me to try to recover her husband's sword, pistols, and watch, when the Indians should sue for peace.

On receiving the letter of the agent of these Indians, Dr. Steck informing me that he had arranged for them to meet me at Fort Thorn[4] at a certain time, I hastily prepared for the journey. I proceeded to a military post at Los Lunas (the Moon), where I got Captain Ewell once more to escort me down to Fort Thorn. On this trip we encountered a very large number of rattlesnakes, and encamping one evening on the banks of the Río Grande, we killed eleven of these reptiles on not more than an acre of land around our encampment. The next morning we proceeded across the neck of a bend in the river, when we actually had to stop two or three times to let these reptiles get out of the road, for fear of having some of our horses or mules bitten. About ten o'clock that day the wind sprang up and blew directly to the river from the road, and as the dry grass and weeds covered the ground in this bend, I lighted a match and set fire to the grass in several places, which, it is hoped, destroyed many.

On coming to within ten or fifteen miles of Fort Thorn, I met a soldier with a letter to me from Colonel Eaton,[5] who commanded the post, telling me to drive directly into the Fort, as he had a room prepared for my reception, and he would expect me to take my meals at his family table as long as I remained.

[4] Fort Thorn was established in December of 1853 in the upper Mesilla Valley, on the west side of the Río Grande near the village of Santa Barbara, being about fifty miles north of Fort Fillmore and eighty-five miles south of Fort Craig. It was named in honor of Captain Herman Thorn, who met his death by drowning on October 16, 1849. Keleher, *Turmoil in New Mexico,* 271n.; and Heitman, *ibid.,* II, 958.

[5] Joseph Horace Eaton entered West Point from Massachusetts, graduating on July 1, 1835, and was commissioned 2nd lieutenant, Third Infantry. He was breveted lieutenant colonel on February 23, 1847, for gallantry at Monterey and Buena Vista, Mexico. He died on January 20, 1865. Heitman, *ibid.,* II, 395.

This invitation I thankfully received. On my arrival I found many Indians encamped near the post, but the head chief of the White Mountain Apaches was not there. The other Indians said he would arrive the next day; but, he did not come as expected. I determined to return to Santa Fe again, when a young Indian rode up to me and said, through his interpreter, that if I would wait one day longer, he would bring in the absent chief. On leaving, this young Indian made some remark in his own language, as he rode off, and I asked the interpreter what he had said. I was informed that he said, "The absent chief has not felt the sting of the white man's bullets as he had, or he would be now more anxious to make peace, and would have been there." On inquiring I found that this young Indian was one of the party who had escaped from Lieutenant Sturgis, and was shot in the hip after he had mounted his horse and was riding off.

Next morning, this Indian, whose name was Cuchillo, returned bringing the absent chief with him, and the council commenced. The weather was exceedingly hot at this place, and the surgeon of the post informed me that the thermometer stood above a hundred degrees every day during the week that I remained there, and one day it was actually one hundred and six degrees. The day after the arrival of the chief, we were assembled in a room at the agency about twenty-five or thirty feet long and fifteen or eighteen wide, and the ceiling not more than eight feet above the floor. There was one door and two windows in this room, which were blocked by the idle and curious Indians who wanted to see what was going on inside, and I had about twenty of the principal Indians in the room, with four or five officers of the Army, myself, and two interpreters, all confined therein. This made the heat so intense that I had to get Captain Ewell to order a guard to patrol around the house and keep the outside Indians away from the doors and windows.

Our proceedings were very slow on this occasion, for I had

first to utter a sentence in English, then a Spanish interpreter would repeat it in that language to an Indian interpreter, who would again repeat it in the Indian language. I first charged the Indians with having attacked the little settlement of Galisteo and running off the Mexicans' stock, to which they replied that I ought to be satisfied, inasmuch as our soldiers had killed all but two Indians and recovered all the stock. But I told them that in the capture of the stock, we had lost one man killed and two or three wounded, and that they were the cause of the loss on both sides. I then charged them with having killed one of our officers and several men at the battle of White Mountain, to which they replied that they had lost a great many more than we in the same battle. But after a long harangue on both sides, peace was made, and they agreed not to molest the Mexicans any more.[6]

That night while at supper with Colonel Eaton and his family, he told me that the hot weather was killing his wife and children, and asked me if I would take charge of them and carry them up to Santa Fe, where the climate was always cool and pleasant, to which I readily assented. Then he informed me that he had two good mules, a carriage, and a trusty driver, and his family would hence be but little trouble on the march. All he wanted was the protection of my escort on the road, and it was agreed that we would depart next morning. But, before breakfast next morning, an express arrived from Santa Fe with an order to the Colonel to proceed there at once himself, as he had been appointed president of a court-martial which would sit there the next week. Then Colonel Eaton asked me to remain a day longer, as he had to take an inventory of the public property at the post

[6] A treaty was concluded on June 14, 1855. The original is in the Meriwether Papers. It consists of four pages in ink, apparently in the hand of David Meriwether, secured by a ribbon at the top. There are no signatures attached, probably these were on a separate sheet of paper, which was lost or possibly never attached to the original. This and other treaties made by Meriwether were never confirmed by the Senate. David Meriwether, Treaty with the Mescaleros, June 14, 1855, Meriwether Papers.

and turn it over to the next in command before he could leave, and this I also consented to do.

After the council with the Indians, I got Cuchillo in a room by ourselves and asked him if he was in the battle of White Mountain. To this he replied, "Yes." I then asked him if he knew anything of one of our officers that was killed there. To this he again responded, "Yes, I reckon I killed him. He was a brave man, for, when his men all ran away, he stayed behind to kill an Indian, and thus lost his life." I asked him what became of his sword, [and] he replied, "I know nothing about it." I then pulled out my watch and, showing it to him, asked him if the dead man had such a thing as this, when he said, "Yes." I asked him what had become of it, and he replied, "It kept talking all night, saying 'tick—tick—tick' and next day it died and I buried it." I asked him if he could find it and bring it to me if I would pay him well. He replied, "Yes, if you promise not to let my people know, you will have it by tomorrow morning." On his return, handing it to me, he said, "It is still dead." On examining it, I found nothing the matter with it, except the crystal was broken. I then told the Indian that I thought I could bring it to life again, and he said, "Can't be done as it has been dead and buried for two or three moons." I then turned my back on him, and, winding it with my watch key, without him seeing me do so, started it running and told him I had brought it back to life again. Then placing it to his ear and hearing it tick again, he said that I must be a Brujo (witch) to bring a thing to life that had been dead so long. He then asked me what it was saying, and I told him it was telling me how high the sun was, which it could do when the whole heavens were covered with clouds. I then pointed to a figure on the face of the watch and told him that when the sun got up in the morning, it would point at that figure, and when the sun was directly overhead, it would point at that figure, and when the sun went to sleep at night (as they think it does) it will point to another figure; all which appeared to astonish him very much.

This watch I carried with me the next time I went to Washington, and delivered it to a relative of Mrs. Stanton—I think, a brother-in-law—who was then employed in the Adjutant General's office, and requested that he forward it to her.

On our return trip up the valley of the Río Grande, we camped again at what we called rattlesnake camp, but we did not see a single reptile there; neither did we see one during the whole journey.

One day during this trip, we had to pass over a very sandy road, with the sun beating down upon us with great heat, and the hot sand beneath us, making us very uncomfortable. That night we camped on the bank of the river again, and on examining my carriage wheels, I found the tires and irons loose. I directed Raymond to tie ropes to the wheels and throw them in the river. I then went to the campfire of the Colonel and his family, which was thirty or forty yards distant, and on examining his carriage wheels, found them in a worse condition than my own. I called the Colonel's attention to it, when he exclaimed, "My God, what am I to do! Here I am with my family and a broken-down carriage and a hundred miles at least from a blacksmith shop." I then suggested to him that I had thrown my wheels into the river and he had better do so too. He asked what good that would do. To this I replied, "The hot sun and sand has expanded the iron and contracted the wood, and by throwing the wheels into the river, the iron will contract again and the wood expand, which will make them all tight once more." He gave orders to try the experiment. The next morning I again went to his camp, and he had his wheels removed from the river and had found them all snug and tight again. He then asked me where I had learned this, and I told him that every old farmer in Kentucky understood it. He replied that he had learned a lesson that he would not take one hundred dollars for.

We proceeded on our journey to Los Lunas, where we shook hands with and left our pleasant traveling companions, Captain Ewell and his escort, as we were then within the settlements and required their presence no longer. In due time we reached Santa Fe without further incident. I had carried Colonel Eaton's oldest boy, a bright little fellow of eight or ten years, in my carriage, so as to lighten the weight of the carriage of Colonel Eaton, which contained his wife, driver, and children.

At my late conference with the Mescalero Apaches, an old woman, probably seventy or seventy-five years of age—I think named Monica—acted as my interpreter, and I think she was the best I ever had. Being one of these Indians, of course she spoke their language well, and she also spoke the Spanish language with great fluency. After the conference with the Indians was over, I asked her how she came to speak the Spanish language so well, and she replied. "When I was a little girl, about half grown, my mother gave me to some Catholic sisters, who had taught me to read in a book, and sing and pray. But after my mothers' death, my father took me away from the sisters and carried me back to the tribe, at which time I was fully grown." I then asked her if she had ever read in a book or sang or prayed now. To which she responded, "No, I have forgotten all about books and singing and praying, and still live with my tribe, acting as interpreter for the Mexican traders, who come to trade with my people."

The Mescalero[7] Apaches derive their name from a species of plant that grows wild in their country, called the mescal plant,

[7] "There were Mescalero bands in the Sierra Blanca, the Guadalupes, and the Davis Mountains. They were people of the mountains, but they were equally at home in the parched desert wastes by which they were surrounded."—C. L. Sonnichsen, *The Mescalero Apaches*, 4.

the botanical name of which, I think, is Agave americana. This is a species of cactus which grows to a height of from three to five feet, at the top of which there forms a head, resembling that of a cabbage, the leaves of which are thick and thorny, like the prickly pear. In the spring of the year, when the head is fully formed, the Mexicans and Indians cut out the bud which forms a cup into which escapes the strong saccharine liquor, great quantities of which are drunk by them, and which is called pulque. It makes a very pleasant drink, but, being strongly saccharine, soon ferments and becomes acid, at which time the Mexicans distill from it a fiery brandy called aquadiente, or strong water. The leaves of this plant are often an inch thick or more, and equally as sweet as the sugar cane of Louisiana, and the Indians eat large quantities of these leaves after roasting them in the fire. If the bud is not taken out, during the summer it bursts open, and a sprout shoots to the height of eight or ten feet, upon the top of which there soon forms a large cluster of flowers. The Indian frequently make handles for their spears and lances of this sprout, which is often more than an inch thick and is light and strong.

I think it was during the fall of 1853 that a Pueblo Indian from the southern part of the territory came to Santa Fe and informed me that the Indians had a white woman at their village, and did not know what to do with her.[8] On inquiring, he informed me that they had found her sick in a hollow stump near the borders of the Staked Plain (Llano Estacado; this plain derives its name from the Mexicans' having driven stakes at certain intervals to prevent persons from getting lost upon it). The Indian said that she could speak a little Spanish, and, from what they

[8] Meriwether's memory of the date is confirmed by his report of the incident to the commissioner of Indian Affairs. See Letter, Meriwether to G. W. Manypenny, Santa Fe, December 13, 1853, National Archives, New Mexico Superintendency, 1849–80, Microfilm 234, roll 547; see also Davis, *El Gringo*, 248–49, here the woman's name is given as Jane Wilson, aged seventeen.

The Old Meriwether Plantation Home, Built More Than a Century Ago, Photographed by David Meriwether's Great-Granddaughter, Mrs. Betsy Graves O'Neill, in 1949.

Courtesy Mrs. Betsy Graves O'Neill

Mescalero Apache Camp in Tularoso Canyon, New Mexico,
Probably in the Late 1860's.

Courtesy New Mexico Magazine

could learn from her, she had made her escape from the Comanche Indians some time before, and his party had brought her to their village, and he had been sent to inform me of this fact.

I told Raymond to have his horse saddled and borrow a side saddle from some lady in Santa Fe and take a mule and go after her. I then gave the Indian fifty dollars as a reward for his humane treatment of the white woman. When Raymond returned, he brought with him a most pitiful looking object. She was dirty, ragged, with her hair hanging all over her shoulders, and she gave me the following account of herself and her sufferings.

She said she was born and raised to womanhood in the state of Missouri, that her maiden name was Howard, and that her father had removed to Texas some years before, where she had married a man by the name of Wilson. Four or five months after her marriage, her husband and his father with her husband's two little brothers had joined a large train who were emigrating to California from Texas, and, on ascending a steep hill in Texas, called Phantom Hill,[9] some of the harness of their wagons broke, and while repairing it, the remainder of the train passed over the hill. As soon as they were out of sight, a party of Comanche Indians fell upon them, killed her husband and his father, and took her and her two little brothers-in-law prisoners. They then rifled the wagon of everything they wanted, unhitched the mules, and departed. She further stated that they had made a slave of her and treated her in a more inhumane manner than Negroes were treated either in Missouri or Texas, that she had to get wood, make the fires, and cook all the victuals, while the two little boys had to herd the animals. She did not recollect how long she had remained with them, but they were captured in

[9] A settlement near old Fort Phantom Hill on the Clear Fork of the Brazos River, in what is now Jones County, Texas. See Edgar Rye, *The Quirt and the Spur—Vanishing Shadows of the Texas Frontier.*

the latter part of the proceeding spring, or early in the summer. She said also, that the Indians were continually roaming about the country, driving her before them; and, when her shoes wore out and her feet became sore, they would ride up behind her and apply their whips vigorously to her back and shoulders. This continued until it began to get cool, some time in the fall. One evening they camped at a spring, and one of the Indians having killed an antelope, they told her to get wood and make a fire and cook the whole of the animal, for they had a long march to make the next day or two, without any wood with which to cook. In gathering wood for the fire, she discovered a hollow cottonwood stump as high as she could reach with her hands, and, on pulling off some bark for fuel, it looked dry and comfortable inside; and, as she was often sent ahead, she determined to try and make her escape. When the meat was cooked and the Indians had eaten their supper, they told her to pack up some of the meat and start on the trail which they had been following, and, as they would be mounted, would soon overtake her.

She at once packed up as much meat as she dared, without exciting the suspicions of the Indians, wrapped it in an old ragged apron, which she had, in such a manner as to enable her to carry it, and by tying the string around her neck, the bundle rested on her back, like a knapsack. She didn't go to sleep that night, but continued watching for the moon to rise, when she adjusted her provisions on her back and started along the trail, which was quite dusty. In about a mile from camp, she came to the dry bed of the river branch, and, leaving the trail, walked up the branch some distance, until the gravel and stones had made her feet so sore that she could stand it no longer. She then left the branch and, making a circle around camp, found her way to the hollow stump before spoken of, and throwing her bundle of meat into it, she reached her hands to the top, climbed and lowered herself down.

Here she remained the rest of the night, watching the preparations of the Indians through a knothole. About daylight, the Indians arose, ate their breakfast, mounted their horses and mules, and departed, but a few hours afterwards, a party of three of them returned. She supposed they were in search of her, but not finding her place of concealment they soon started in the direction their companions had taken. She did not recollect how long she remained concealed in this stump but thought it about three weeks. She ate very sparingly of her food, as she did not know how long she might remain. Every morning before day, she would go to the spring and get a drink of water, and after night she would do the same, remaining in the stump all day watching to see if any traveler might pass along, or camp at the spring. Her provisions soon gave out, and then she employed the nights hunting for something to eat. She found a few terrapins in the spring branch, and would break the shell of these with rocks and eat the meat raw, for she had no means of starting a fire. She caught a few frogs and ate them raw, and finally she killed a large snake which she also ate raw. At last she became so weak that she could not get out of the stump, and thought she remained two or three days without either food or drink, when one morning a party of five Pueblo Indians camped at the spring. She recognized them to be Pueblos from their dress, and commenced hallooing in English and Spanish, of which language she knew a little, and also in the Comanche tongue, which she had learned while a prisoner with them. But she was so weak she could not make her voice heard. Finally one of the Indians in gathering wood, came near the stump, when placing her mouth at the knothole, she commenced hallooing in all the languages she could speak. The Indian listened for a moment or two and then broke and ran for the camp, when she commenced praying to God for deliverance. She understood from the Indians afterwards that the one who had heard her told the Indians at camp that the devil was in that stump, for he had heard him halloo, whereupon the others gathered up their arms and surrounded the stump while she was praying. The headman of these Indians chanced to discover the knothole and looking in, said to the others, "This is no devil, but a white woman who is praying, and the devil never prays."

The Indians happened to understand some Spanish, and she begged them to assist her out of the stump. An Indian then was sent to the camp for a lariat rope, while two others climbed to the top of the stump, and, each holding one end of the rope, she placed the middle of it under her arms and around her back, when, with the assistance she could render with her hands and feet, they hauled her to the top and let her down on the outside. They then assisted her to the camp and on her asking for it, gave her a gourd of water to drink. She wanted to drink more, but they would not let her, and placing a blanket before the fire, [they] made her lie down on it. They had before this placed a kettle on the fire to boil some water, and after it had boiled a while they gave her some soup in a gourd, about a tin cup full, and told her to lie down and go to sleep. She had slept some time when they awakened her and gave her some more soup and told her to go to sleep again; before day in the morning she again awakened and drank some more soup and went to sleep again. Finding that one of the number spoke the Spanish language, she begged the Indians to take her in to the settlements, and, if they would not do that, to take her with them where they were going, and told them she had escaped from the Comanche Indians. They told her they were going to trade with the Comanches, and, if they took her along, these Indians would claim her again, but, if she would remain where she had been concealed before their arrival, they would give her provisions, a blanket to sleep on, and a gourd to hold water, and on their return in a week or two, would carry her to their village. She thought they remained about three days with her, when cooking a large quantity of meat, they wrapped it in a blanket and threw it into the hollow stump, and assisting her into it, gave her a large gourd of water, and departed.

In a day or two after this she was able to go to the spring and get water for herself, and thought she remained about three weeks longer before the return of the Indians. Every night while she was in this stump, the wolves were howling around her and scratching to try to get in and eat her meat. The day after their return, the Indians furnished her with a mule to ride, but without a saddle. In four or five days, they reached their village, where she remained about a week, when a United States officer with his wife passed by, and she made her situation known to them. The officer's wife gave her a calico dress and a pair of shoes, as she was all in rags, and the officer directed the Indians who had rescued her to inform the Governor of her situation. I think she said this officer was Lieutenant Adams, and he and his wife were going in a different direction from Santa Fe. The old governor of the Pueblo dispatched the messenger to me as before stated.

I asked Mrs. Wilson how she had employed her time while living in this hollow stump, more than one hundred miles from any home. She replied, "I employed myself in singing the hymns and repeating the prayers I had learned when a girl."

All this conversation did not take place at my first interview, but was detailed at different times. Shortly after her arrival in Santa Fe, I sent for Mrs. Smith, the wife of the Baptist missionary there, and requested her to go to Mr. Messervy's store with Mrs. Wilson and purchase materials for a comfortable suit of winter clothing, of every description, and tell the merchant to present his bill, and I would pay it. As Mrs. Wilson had told me in our first interviews that she was a member of the Methodist church, I sent for Mr. Nicholson, the Methodist missionary, who came and had a long talk with her. He told me that he was boarding at a house, the lady of which belonged to the Methodist church, and this induced me to get him to make arrangements for Mrs. Wilson to board with them, Mrs. Smith had but little house room. Mrs. Spencer, the Methodist lady where Mr. Nicholson boarded, agreed to receive her as boarder at the price of one dollar per day, which was agreed upon, and she remained at this house during the ensuing winter.

The next spring before I left Santa Fe for a visit home,[10] I paid her passage on a wagon train down to her friends in Texas, the whole of which, including the amount paid the Indian, her clothing, etc., amounted to about three hundred and sixty dollars, which I had charged in my account to the contingent expenses of Indian Affairs. Some time after my return, I received a communication from the Commissioner of Indian Affairs, stating that I was not authorized to make such an expenditure without first having instructions to do so, and it could not be allowed in my account. To this I replied by letter that, on a certain date (naming it) I had sent an account against my office as to whether I should pay it or not, as it had been created by my predecessor, and to which he replied that I was too far removed from the seat of government for him to determine whether I should make payment or not, that the government had confidence in me, and I must pay such as I thought right and reject all others. But now you say I must submit such matters to you for advisement, and then I proceeded to give him a full account of Mrs. Wilson's case.

About this time a gentleman arrived in Santa Fe from Texas, who, hearing the matter spoken of, called upon me and said,

[10] This is the visit home related by Governor Meriwether in Chapter X.

"Send this account to Governor [Elisha Marshall] Pease of Texas and it will be paid, as the legislature always keeps a fund in the Governor's hands to pay for the ransom or release of its citizens. So I at once wrote a letter to the governor of Texas, and by return mail received a check on New York for the full amount. In his letter, the governor of Texas informed me that he had seen Mrs. Wilson, who spoke of the kindness of myself and son towards her, and added that if my son would make out a charge for the expenses and trouble of his trip to relieve Mrs. Wilson, he would be paid also. He likewise requested me to procure the release of the two little boys, the brothers-in-law of Mrs. Wilson, all expenses of which would be promptly paid by him.

Shortly after the receipt of the Governor's letter, I received another letter from the Commissioner of Indian Affairs at Washington, informing me that my last letter had convinced him that the expenditure was right, and therefore this item had been allowed in my accounts; so I had been doubly paid for what I had done for this lady. But I promptly returned to the Governor of Texas his draft for the money, and as Raymond would make no charges, the matter rested. Later on, the two little boys were released by the same Indians and delivered to the authorities of Texas.

I think it was during the winter of 1854 and 1855,[11] that a merchant residing in the city of Mexico came to visit his brother in New Mexico, and informed me that General Gadsden, our minister to Mexico, had negotiated a treaty with that government, by which the old boundary line claimed by the United States had been established between the Rocky Mountains and the Río Grande, but including a vast territory west of the mountains and to the head of the Gulf of California, and that his Excellency, Santa Anna, president of Mexico, had issued an order to

[11] It was the winter of 1853–54. The Gadsden Treaty was signed December 30, 1853. See Paul Neff Garber, *The Gadsden Treaty*, 74–145.

the governor of Chihuahua directing him to surrender possession of the disputed territory, as far as the boundary line had been run; but owing to some cause or other, this order had not been promulgated. This induced me to write General Gadsden, requesting him if this story be true, to send me a description of the boundary, and also a copy of this order. This letter I sent by the gentleman who gave me the information, and soon afterwards I received a letter from General Gadsden, saying that as this treaty had never been ratified, he did not feel at liberty to disclose anything it contained. By the same messenger who brought Mr. Gadsden's reply, I received a letter from the gentleman who had visited me in Santa Fe, containing a properly authenticated copy of the order of the president of Mexico, directing the surrender of the disputed territory. On receipt of this letter I addressed a communication to Governor Trias, governor of Chihuahua, requesting to know of him if, on the production of such a paper, he would feel at liberty to surrender possession of the territory in dispute. To this he responded in the affirmative, provided that I appeared with a force sufficient to protect the citizens from Indian depredations.

But before receiving his letter, a portion of the Piute [Paiute][12] tribe of Indians, who had been hostile since the pre-

[12] It is apparent that the Governor's memory tricked him into connecting the two unrelated events. He took over the disputed territory on November 16, 1854, and his conference with the Indians was held the following year. Also his reference to them as "Piutes" is in error. In a letter to Kit Carson on August 26, 1855, he said: "Several of the principal men of the Muache Utahs [Moache Utes], and Jacarilla Apaches, have recently visited me with a view of obtaining peace, and I have appointed to meet these two bands of Indians on the tenth of September next, on the Chama river above Abiquiu. The Indians have several prisoners in their possession, which they will deliver up when peace is made, and I would be glad to have those of their people which we hold in captivity, ready for delivery at the same time and place."—Letter, Governor Meriwether to Kit Carson, August 26, 1855, Bancroft Library. The Paiutes were primarily inhabitants of the Great Basin; however, they covered a wide range, venturing into southern Utah, Arizona, and southern Colorado. They are of the Shoshonean family, related linguistically to the Utes. See Hodge, *Handbook of American Indians*, II, 186–88.

ceding fall, made application to me for a conference, and I directed Kit Carson[13] (who succeeded Captain Graves as their agent in consequence of the death of Mr. Smith, and Captain Graves having been ordered to the southern agency to replace him) to assemble the Piute [Paiute] tribe at the forks of the Chama River, and to tell them, as they had taken some Mexican children prisoners and we had taken an old man and some children of their tribe prisoners, to bring all the Mexican children in their possession, and I would bring the Indian prisoners in our possession for the purpose of exchange; and I would meet at the place appointed the middle of August.

About a week before that time, I proceeded to collect the Indian prisoners for the purpose of carrying them with us, but found the old man so fat that he could neither ride nor walk, as he had been kept in the guard house at Santa Fe for nearly a year, and had been fed soldiers' rations every day without exercise. On finding the condition of the old Indian, he told me that he had two sons in the tribe I was about to meet, and for them to come in with me and take him home. I then informed him that he could walk about as he pleased, and that he would regularly find his ration at the guard house every day until my return. With this understanding, I departed for the place of meeting with the Indians.

Knowing that these Indians never had a supply of provisions on hand, and that they would expect to be fed during the conference, I, on reaching the border settlements, purchased one hundred head of sheep and put them under the charge of Raymond, to be driven to the appointed place of meeting. On reaching the designated place, I found a large concourse of Indians assembled, but Carson was not with them, though the Indians

[13] Carson reported for duty at the Ute Agency, with headquarters at Taos, January 9, 1854. This agency had supervision over the Moache Utes, the Jicarilla Apaches, and the Pueblos. See Estergreen, *Kit Carson*, 210.

informed me he would arrive within the next day or two. The Indians at once applied to me for something to eat, and, on Raymond's arriving, I directed him to give them ten or fifteen sheep, and the next morning as many more. The next day Carson arrived, accompanied by Tierra Blanca (White Earth), one of the most forbidding looking beings I ever saw in all my life.

He had but one eye, and his face was scarred with smallpox in a most terrible manner, but I soon discovered him to be a shrewd, cunning rascal. Upon the arrival of Carson, I directed Raymond to turn the remainder of the sheep over to him, with strict orders not to deliver to the Indians more than ten or fifteen each morning and evening. But that night I discovered that Carson had delivered all the sheep to the Indians, for which I lectured him in a mild manner for this disobedience of orders, whereupon he mounted a "highhorse" and said he was the agent for these Indians and intended to dispose of them and the sheep as he thought proper. But not feeling disposed to have a scene with him, I said nothing more to him. The next morning the Indians applied for more sheep, when I had to tell them that I had no more, and that there were none to be purchased near there. Then Carson came and wanted to know why I had not brought more sheep with me. I replied, "If you are the agent and have exclusive control of them, why did you not bring provisions for the Indians?" To this he answered that it was my duty to do so.

The Indians were camped on one side of the river, and I on the other with Captain Ewell commanding an escort of two companies of dragoons. I directed Kit Carson to bring over to my side of the river the chiefs and warriors of these Indians, for the purpose of a conference. This being done, the conference began, and after an hour or two spent in talking, exchange of prisoners was agreed upon. And here I was forcibly struck with the differerence between white people and Indians, for on crossing the little stream, the water of which was not over a half a leg deep, an Indian boy or girl would look among the crowd sitting on the bank, and recognizing its father or mother would go up and squat down by his side or her side, without any sign of recognition, more than this, and not even a shake of the hand. But, on returning to the Mexican children, the father or mother, recognizing it, would rush into the river and pick it up, hug it, kiss it, and bear it to the shore.

Pretty soon all the Indian men, numbering probably four or five hundred, came over to our side, when the parcel of young Indians who had charge of the Indian ponies, a mile or more above our encampment, came driving the animals in, in a great hurry, saying that the Navaho[14] Indians were coming down to attack them. And such a scene of confusion, I never witnessed in my life. Each Indian mounted his horse with his lance or other weapon, and hallooing as loud as he could yell, rode in different directions. At this time I took my interpreter and went among them saying, "I have invited you to this conference, and you shan't be molested." Seeing this, Carson came to me saying, "If you don't get under the bank of the river, these Indians will kill you." When I told him that I was not afraid of their hurting me, and directed him, as he spoke their language some, to go among them and try to quiet them. Instead of doing this, he lay under the bank of the river. At the commencement of this commotion, I requested Captain Ewell to send a detachment of troops in the direction whence the alarm had come and see if he could discover any hostile Indians coming. This detachment soon returned, saying that they could discover nothing of the kind, and that it was all a false alarm. This quieted the Indians, and they soon returned to their own side of the river, when White Earth again demanded more sheep. I had to inform him that I had none, nor could get any. Then Carson said that if he had been

[14] Meriwether at the time said the report was of an impending Kiowa attack. Letter to Kit Carson, September 20, 1856, Bancroft Library.

superintendent of Indian Affairs, as I was, these Indians should not go off hungry. To this I replied, "It is possible that if you had been superintendent of affairs, you might not have hidden under the bank of the river as you did." At this he became very abusive, and said he was not a damn fool like I was, to risk his life in the manner I did. I then informed him that he might consider himself suspended from his agency, and that he was no longer an Indian agent under me. To this he replied, "I'll let you see that you have no power to suspend me." He became so boisterous that I requested Captain Ewell to put him under guard. The Captain ordered a file of men to march him into a tent which had been pitched, and a soldier was placed over him as a guard.

Late in the evening, a little Mexican boy eight or ten years old, who had been exchanged by the Indians, came up to me with the Indian who had captured him and asked me to let him go across the river with the Indians and spend the night with his captor. This I declined doing, fearing that he might not return in the morning, for I invariably found that the boys were all willing to remain with the Indians, while the girls were anxious to leave them. But the little boy said he had left his bow and arrows on the other side, and the Indian said he would see that the boy was returned by the time the sun got up in the morning, and, liking this Indian's countenance very much, I consented that the boy might go. He returned to me early the next morning.

Having found the two sons of the fat Indian I had left in Santa Fe, they agreed to accompany me on my return. On reaching the border settlements, we camped near a cornfield, and I bought of the owner a sack of roasting ears and a sheep for our provisions. When the sheep was dressed, I gave a forequarter to the two Indians, and ten or a dozen ears of corn. They immediately covered up about half the corn with the shucks on, with ashes and sand under the fire, and proceeded to hold the leg of mutton over the blaze, and when the outside became parched and black, would pare it off with butcher knives and eat it, and again hold the meat over the fire as before. When the corn was roasted, they pulled it out of the fire and commenced eating, which they continued until I went to bed. When I awoke at day-break, I found them still eating. I asked them if they ate all night, and they replied, "No, we slept a little while, but commenced again this morning." I then asked one of the Indians what they had created such a fuss for at the forks of the river. The younger one replied, "White Earth only wanted to see if you were afraid of the Indians or not." I then asked if they had eaten all the sheep that Carson had given them on the night of his arrival. To this he answered, "No, White Earth had directed them to be driven up in a hollow between the mountains, as he thought by this means he could get more." This I had strongly suspected and was now confirmed in my suspicions.

On our arrival at Santa Fe I informed Carson that I intended to prefer charges against him and take the affidavits of the officers present at the scene between us and send them to Washington City. I told him I would furnish him with a copy of all the papers before I sent them, so that he might send his defense, if he had any to make, by the same mail.

Next morning, Judge Houghton, a great friend and admirer of Carson, came to me and said, "Carson is convinced he has done wrong and is sorry for it." To this I answered, "I am glad to hear this, but I still intend to keep him suspended until I can hear from the proper department at Washington." To this the Judge replied, "You can only suspend him for sixty days, and you cannot hear from Washington in that time." To this I replied, "I know that I can suspend him for but sixty days under the law, but when the first sixty days expire, I can suspend him for sixty more, and I will do it." This appeared to strike the Judge with a good deal of force, and he left me. I proceeded at once to draw up my charges against Kit, the first specification of which was disobedience of orders; the second, insubordination; the third, disrespectful conduct towards a superior officer; and the last was cowardice, in the presence of the Indians. I handed these charges to Captain Ewell and requested him to go before Judge Davenport and make his statement in regard to each, under oath. The next day the Captain brought the charges back, together with his affidavit, accompanied with the affidavits of several others, who were present, and which sustained every charge I had made. They concluded their affidavits by saying that what they most wondered at was the forebearance with which the Governor had treated Carson.

I had all these papers copied and sent the copies to Carson, after which Judge Houghton again called on me, bringing with him a letter signed by Carson, though written by the Judge, as Carson could not write a letter himself, but could only write his name at the bottom. This letter stated that he, Carson, was convinced that he had acted wrong, that he was very sorry for having done so, and would never be guilty of such misconduct again, and begged me to release him from suspension and let him go back home again as agent for the Indians. This I agreed to do, and I had no further difficulty with him during the remainder of my stay in New Mexico, except as to his accounts, which were always wrong. Poor Kit was a good trapper, hunter, and guide, and in the latter capacity, while employed by Colonel Frémont had acquired a reputation which spoiled him, and which in after life and in a higher position he failed to sustain.[15]

[15] There is no question but that Kit Carson was an experienced frontiersman and a capable militia and volunteer officer, serving with a certain distinction. However he was particularly fortunate in having as his chroniclers such prominent men as John C. Frémont, Edward F. Beale, Colonel Henry Inman, Colonel De Witt Peters, and others who through the medium of the press and published works have given him a wide publicity. In the summer of 1915, Al J. Noyes held a number of interviews with Bill Bent near Fort Belknap, Montana. Bill Bent was the son of William Bent of the famous Bent's Fort on the Arkansas. William's brother Charles

On my return from this Indian conference, I determined to visit Governor Trias of Chihuahua, and if possible get peaceable possession of the disputed territory. On informing General Garland of this, he said he would accompany me and take a portion of the garrison from each of the military posts in our route, so as to show to the governor of Chihuahua that we were strong enough to protect the people residing on the disputed territory from the Indians if we obtained possession of it. On arriving at Los Lunas the General ordered Captain Ewell to take a company from that post and go with us. At Fort Craig,[16] he took another company, and at Fort Thorn, he got still another com-

and Kit Carson were close friends and had married sisters; thus although Bill Bent was not exactly related to Carson by marriage, he referred to him loosely as "my uncle Kit." At the time of the interviews he was sixty-nine years old and had himself followed the career of a scout and plainsman. He commented as follows: "I remember Carson and Frémont and have eaten with them when they had been at my father's house after some of their trips that have helped to make the story of our country. In light of my own experiences I can come to but one conclusion and that is my uncle Kit was an over-rated man. These sames hair-breadth escapes, these same trials cause by hunger and cold have been gone through by many a man who has helped to make this country and not one word has been written into the story of their deeds. Kit happened to have his lines cast close to those of the Frémont, who had a way of using his pen to advantage; and getting himself into the limelight of public opinion and approval."

In the light of this estimate Chittenden's comment is significant: "It is a singular fact that so noted a character as Kit Carson should be so entirely unknown in the annals of the fur trade as he actually was. His name occurs only once in the correspondence or newspaper literature prior to 1843."—*Fur Trade,* II, 539–40.

It should be pointed out, however, that Meriwether never made any allowance for Carson's illiteracy; he reprimanded him for his chaotic records and his practice of coming to Santa Fe and running up travel expenses to bring accounts amounting to ten or fifteen dollars instead of sending them by mail. At the same time he notified Carson that any charge for the salary of an assistant would be disallowed. See A. J. Noyes, *In the Land of the Chinook; or, The Story of Blaine County* [Montana], 88; and Letter, Meriwether to Carson, August 3, 1856, Bancroft Library. See also Kent L. Steckmesser, *The Western Hero in History and Legend.*

16 Fort Craig was situated approximately 175 miles north of El Paso, on the west side of the Río Grande, nearly opposite Fray Cristobal at the north end of the Jornada del Muerto. It was established about 1853 and was merely a camping place when Garland stopped there. It was abandoned and sold in 1885. See Rex W. Strickland, ed., *Forty Years at El Paso,* 55; and for more on Jornada del Muerto, see Chapter XIII below.

pany, all of which were placed under the command of Captain Ewell.

As the roads were very heavy, we determined to spend a day at Fort Thorn for rest to ourselves and our animals. But the next morning while we were eating breakfast, an express arrived from Colonel Miles, who then commanded at Fort Webster,[17] informing the General that the governor of Chihuahua did not intend to surrender the disputed territory to us, but was placing additional troops upon it; and that he, Miles had addressed a letter to the Governor, saying that if he ventured to place additional troops there, he, Miles would order out a battery and bombard the city of El Paso [the present Juarez], across the river. On this letter being read to me, I insisted that we should start immediately for Fort Webster, when General Garland, as I thought, rather casually remarked, "There is no use in being in haste about it." But, by continuous importunity on my part, he consented to start that day after dinner.

Here we had to cross the river, as all the posts below Fort Thorn were on the eastern bank thereof. After dinner we effected our crossing, and going some ten or fifteen miles, we encamped for the night. After supper when we were chatting around the campfire, another express arrived from Colonel Miles, informing the General that Governor Trias still continued to put additional troops upon the disputed territory. Upon being made aware of [this], Miles, had addressed another letter to Governor Trias, saying that he, Miles, would bombard El Paso the next day if another soldier was added to the Mexican troops. I

[17] Fort Webster was established in 1851, as headquarters of the Boundary Commission Survey and its escort, occupying part of the fortifications of the Santa Rita Copper Mine. The first site was abandoned December 20, 1853, and a new post was erected on the Mimbres River, approximately fifteen miles south and east of the mine. Mansfield, *Western Forts*, 25–26; and Letter, Meriwether to Commissioner Manypenny, Santa Fe, November 30, 1853, National Archives, New Mexico Superintendency, 1849–80, Microfilm 234, roll 547.

Father Pierre Jean de Smet.

Courtesy Missouri Historical Society

Early View of Fort Union.

Courtesy New Mexico Magazine

at once proposed to General Garland that we should hitch up and travel all night and try to reach Fort Webster before the bombarding commenced. To this General Garland responded again, "There is no cause for hurry." I said to the General, "You may do as you please, but I intend to start immediately for Fort Webster." Then General Garland burst into a laugh and remarked to his adjutant general, Major Nichols, "The Governor don't know Miles as well as I do, Nick." "Now" said he, "there is not a word of truth in all this; Miles is only letting off a little gas." "Moreover," said he, "Fort Webster is about fifty miles above El Paso, and Fort Bliss[18] is nearly opposite that town; and, if any bombardment was intended, it would come from the latter post, not from Webster."

This explanation satisfied me, and the next day we pro-

[18] Major Jefferson Van Horne and four companies of the Fourth Infantry occupied Coons's Ranch in September, 1849, the forerunner of Fort Bliss. In 1850, Van Horne moved his headquarters to Magoffinville, while the main body of troops remained quartered at Coons's Ranch. In 1868 the post was removed to Stephenson's Concordia Ranch and became known as Camp Concordia. After two other changes of location all in the same general area a reservation was acquired five miles northeast, the present Fort Bliss. It was named in honor of Lieutenant Colonel John Bliss, who entered the army in 1812 and died November 22, 1854. John R. Bartlett described what was later the site of Fort Bliss and El Paso as follows: "On the American side there are but few houses; and these may be divided into three groups or settlements. The first is Coons's Rancho. This was the first settlement, and was the military post for about three years, under the command of Major Van Horne. Many of the buildings are now unoccupied. About half a mile below is the principal village, which was established by James W. Magoffin, Esq., a gentleman from Missouri, and one of the oldest American settlers in the country. This place is called Magoffinville, and was the headquarters of the Boundary Commission while in the country. Its enterprising proprietor has erected around a large open square some of the best buildings in the country, which are now occupied as stores and warehouses. This is an admirable situation for a town, and will, no doubt, be the centre of the American settlements at El Paso. An acequia now runs through the square, and the land around is of the finest quality. A mile further east is a large rancho belonging to Mr. Stevenson, around which is a cluster of smaller dwellings."—*Personal Narrative*, I, 192–93. See also Conkling, *The Butterfield Overland Trail*, II, 70–86; and McCrellis, *Military Reservations*, 223–25.

ceeded to the town of Doña Ana,[19] where we found Colonel Miles and several officers had gotten up a big fandango for that night in honor of our arrival. I did not feel like attending a fandango at this time, as I was much fatigued from the journey of over two hundred miles and over a rough road. But, as I had never visited this part of the Territory before, as a mark of respect to the citizens, I attended for a few hours. The next morning we were informed that the citizens would give us a public dinner that day, when I would be expected to make a speech. However, I found myself so hoarse that I was not able to do so, but met them at the dinner table, and the next day proceeded to Fort Webster. Here I found Raymond so sick as not to be able to proceed with me any further, and I had to leave him under the care of the surgeon of the post and the nursing of Mrs. Miles, the good wife of the Colonel.

The next morning we started again, and soon passed the line between the territory of New Mexico and the state of Texas, which was pointed out to me by an officer who accompanied us from Fort Webster. That night we arrived at the residence and mill of Judge Hart,[20] which was on the American side of the

[19] In 1843 the first successful and permanent settlement was founded in the Mesilla Valley, being the Doña Ana Bend Colony, organized by Don Jose Costales. A small garrison was stationed here for a time and withdrawn in 1851 when Colonel Sumner assumed command of the Ninth Military District. P. M. Baldwin, "A Short History of the Mesilla Valley," *New Mexico Historical Review*, Vol. XIII (July, 1938), 314–23.

[20] According to Strickland, Simeon Hart was born in Highland, New York, on March 28, 1816, and served in the Mexican War. In December, 1849, he married Jesusita Siquieros, of Santa Cruz de Rosales, the daughter of Don Leandro Siquieros. According to Hart's own testimony he opened his milling operations in December, 1849, although did not complete the large mill until 1854. W. W. H. Davis described his residence as romantically situated on the east bank of the Del Norte, three miles above the Mexican towns of El Paso (the present Juarez). Davis also stated as Meriwether did that Hart was a native of Kentucky. Bartlett described the milling industry in 1850: "There are now two mills at the falls near El Paso; one on the Mexican side belonging to Ponce de Leon, and one on the American side, belonging to Mr. E. Hart. The latter is a fine establishment, and now supplies the United States troops here with flour. In 1850–51 flour was selling here from

river and at its falls, where there is excellent river power. Here Major Cusenbery of the Quartermasters Department was taken so sick as to compel us to leave him. In the course of the evening, Judge Hart informed me that he was a Kentuckian from Scott County, I think, where he had been born and raised to manhood. When a young man he had emigrated to Missouri and joined Colonel Doniphan's command, then about to join General Kearny on his march to Santa Fe and the city of Chihuahua, which expedition commenced early in the Mexican War. I think he said he was elected lieutenant in one of the companies and proceeded with the command to the vicinity of El Paso. Here he was taken violently sick and had to be left at the house of a Mexican, where he remained until the close of the war, when he married either the daughter or niece, I have forgotten which, of the Mexican at whose house he had been left. By this marriage he acquired considerable funds with which he had built his present residence, and a large flour mill. Here he manufactured a fine article of flour, and had a contract with the quartermaster department to supply the western military posts in Texas and the southern posts in New Mexico.

The next morning we visited Fort Bliss and had an interview with his Excellency, Governor Trias, of Chihuahua. Having exhibited the documents which I had with me, he at once consented to deliver possession of the disputed territory to us. It was agreed that our force should cross the river above the falls at twelve o'clock the next day, and, on seeing the American flag approaching, he would pull down the Mexican flag and march his troops out of the fort, leaving the gates open for our entrance.

Many conjectures were indulged in by the younger officers present, one opinion being that this was a ruse on the part of the Governor of Chihuahua to get us under the guns of the fort,

ten to twelve and a half cents per pound."—*Personal Narrative*, I, 191. See Mills, *Forty Years at El Paso*, 182; and Davis, *El Gringo*, 376.

when fire would be opened upon us. But I indulged in no such fear, as, from the frank and manly manner of the Governor, I had no fears of the result. On reaching within a few hundred yards of the fort, I saw the Mexican flag come down, the Mexicans troops march out, and our troops march in. Then the American flag was at once hoisted to the flagstaff so recently occupied by the Mexican flag. Our flag was saluted with two pieces of artillery which we had taken across the river with us. The band played "Hail Columbia," "Yankee Doodle," and several other national airs, at the close of which I arose to make a speech to the large crowd of Mexicans who had gathered to witness the transfer. I told the Mexicans, through an interpreter, that by peaceful negotiations the disputed territory had been transferred to the United States; that I hoped they would prove themselves loyal and law-abiding citizens, but if they did not, I would feel it my duty at all hazards to see that the laws were executed; that any citizen who preferred the Mexican to the American government was at liberty to sell his possessions and move to the Mexican side of the line. But I hoped they would give the American government an opportunity of showing its advantages before doing so. I then caused a large number of proclamations which had been printed in the Spanish language before leaving Santa Fe, and which was of the same import as my speech, to be distributed among those present. The Mexicans appeared to be satisfied with what I had said to them and applauded lustily, many coming to be introduced to me, and to whom I gave a cordial shake of the hand.[21]

[21] The date was November 16, 1854, when General Garland on the order of Governor Meriwether thus took formal possession of the Mesilla Valley for the United States. Ratifications had been exchanged at Washington on June 30. See Garber, *The Gadsden Treaty*, 156–57; Report from James Gadsden to William L. Marcy, secretary of state, General Records, Dept. of State, National Archives, Record Group 59; and Letter, James Gadsden, Legation of the U.S., to Commanding Officer of the Territory of New Mexico, dated Mexico, October 8, 1853, National Archives, New Mexico Superintendency, 1849–80, Microfilm 234, roll 547.

XIII

An Attempt to Resign, Building the State House, and a Vetoed Bill

THAT NIGHT I RETURNED to Judge Hart's residence, leaving a company of United States soldiers in possession of the only military post on the disputed territory, previously held by the Mexicans. Here General Garland informed me that he would again visit Fort Bliss for the purpose of making an inspection which would detain him a day or two, and that he would have to stop a day or two for a like purpose at each of the other military posts, as he returned to Santa Fe. I was in a great hurry to return, so it was agreed that we would divide the escort. I proceeded with Captain Ewell and a part of the soldiers with as much haste as possible.

This evening I spent in social converse with Mr. and Mrs. Hart, the latter of whom understood English well, but never attempted to speak it. On asking an explanation of this, the Judge informed me that when she had first learned some of the language and attempted to speak it in company with some Americans, she had made a ludicrous mistake, at which the Americans laughed, and after this she refused to attempt to speak the English language before strangers, though she spoke English to him and her children. So I had to talk to her in English and she would reply in Spanish. I found her to be an accomplished lady in every respect. When we were about to retire for the night, she asked me at what hour we proposed leaving in the morning, and I said, "We want to get off by five o'clock." She then said, "I will see that you are called at four." At this hour we were aroused and soon after were invited into the dining room, where we found Mrs. Hart sitting at the head of the table [with] a luxurious breakfast prepared for us, after which we departed for Fort Webster.

On our arrival, I found Raymond much improved and able to travel again. Here we were informed that by leaving the Río Grande some twenty miles above, and traveling across the extensive bend in the river, we would save fifty miles of travel, but that we would have to travel between eighty or ninety miles without either wood or water. As I was in a great haste to return to Santa Fe, we determined to take the nearer route. We reached the point where the road left the river, about eleven o'clock, and finding good grass, permitted the animals to graze until three o'clock in the afternoon, when we drove them to water and let them drink as much as they would. We then entered on the dreaded Jornada de Muerto[1] or journey of death, it deriving its name from the great number of horses, mules, and oxen, together with some of their drivers, who had perished in attempting to cross it.

We found the road very good and traveled briskly along until about nine o'clock at night. We made a halt to let our animals graze again and derive whatever benefit they could from the dew that had fallen, while we boiled a cup of coffee with a little wood we had brought with us and ate some crackers. In about an hour we started and traveled on until a little before day, when we again turned out the animals to graze on the grass which was covered with dew, while we indulged in another cup of coffee and crackers. A little before sunrise we were off and traveled . . . until about eleven o'clock, when we turned out the animals to graze, but they seemed little inclined to do so and roamed

[1] The Jornada del Muerto or Journey of Death extended nearly one hundred miles south from Fray Cristobal. It was nearly level and had scant vegetation and practically no water except for water holes during the rainy season. A portion of the Jornada is now covered by the Elephant Butte Dam, near Hot Springs, New Mexico.

about as though hunting for water. Seeing they would not eat, at twelve o'clock we started again and a little before night gave them another chance for eating, which they utterly refused to do, but roamed in search of water, while we again supped on crackers and coffee. We started in less than an hour after camping and about nine o'clock came to the camp of a train going in the opposite direction. Seeing that they had a barrel of water with them, and my son's horse appearing so much exhausted as to make it doubtful if he would reach water again, I offered to buy a bucket of water from the train conductor. Although I offered him a two-and-a-half dollar gold piece for it, he refused to sell at any price. We continued our journey until a little after twelve o'clock, when we once more reached the river, where we had great difficulty in preventing the mules from running down the steep bank before we could get them unhitched from the carriage. Allowing the animals to drink their fill, they were driven up the bank to a good piece of prairie grass to feed and rest until morning. On starting across this bend in the river, the soldiers all filled their canteens and mine, which held two gallons. This had to suffice us for the journey. We continued up the valley of the river until we reached Los Lunas, where we parted with Captain Ewell and his escort, and in a few days arrived at Santa Fe.

When the September mail arrived, I received an answer from the State Department at Washington to a letter which I had written several months before, requesting that if I succeeded in getting possession of the disputed territory, my resignation should be accepted, and a successor arrive to relieve me, in time enough for me to cross the plains before winter set in.[2]

[2] Meriwether's wording gives the impression that his attempted resignation and the leave of absence that was granted him instead, occurred immediately after he took over the disputed Mesilla Valley, November 16, 1854. Perhaps he did hope for release that year; his haste in returning to Santa Fe supports that supposition. If so, he was disappointed, and as he has related in previous chapters, he was occupied with important Indian councils in the summer of 1855. His return to the East took place early the following fall, nearly a year after the boundary settlement.

The letter from the Department informed me that if I settled the question of the boundary amicably, and the Indians were all quiet, I might return home and spend the winter with my family.

About this time General Garland arrived in Santa Fe, and I applied to him for an escort, when he informed me that he had gathered up all the soldiers from the southern posts whose term of service was about to expire, and left them with Captain Ewell, with instructions to march them across the plains to Fort Leavenworth, turn in their horses, arms, and equipment, muster them out of the service, and for him (Captain Ewell) to proceed north, recruit a new company and bring them out in the spring, and these returning soldiers would afford me an ample escort.

Early in the month of September, Captain Ewell arrived with forty or fifty well-drilled men, who were to accompany me. I then made hasty preparations for my departure and hired a discharged soldier, who professed to be a good driver and cook, to drive my carriage, and as compensation he was to receive his transportation and provisions from me. Shortly after leaving Fort Union, our driver one evening said he had become violently sick and would drive no farther, so I took the reins myself and gave him my seat in the carriage. I had doubts in my mind as to whether he was not playing "old soldier" over me. This induced me to watch him, and I found him slyly eating heartily for a sick man. But as he complained very much, I continued to drive the next day. That evening I discovered some wild ducks in a small pond of water and succeeded in killing four of them. That night I asked him if he would not pick and dress the ducks, while Raymond was getting supper. He said he was too ill to do anything, so I had to give Captain Ewell two of the ducks in order to have the other two dressed for us. This man's sickness compelled Raymond to take care of the mules and do the cooking also. That night the driver refused to eat any supper, but, on my going to Captain Ewell's campfire, fifteen or twenty steps from my own, I watched our driver and saw him go to our mess chest and eat heartily of what we had left.

I returned and went to bed, after telling him that I expected to meet a government train the next day and would get this train to take him back to Fort Union, where he could get medical aid. Against this he protested, saying that he had a wife and children in the States whom he had not seen for five years, and, although he was very sick, he wanted to continue with us. To this I replied that if he died, we had no means of burying him on the plains and would dislike very much to leave his body for the wolves to eat, and he must return whenever we met the train. This medicine worked very well, for the next morning he assisted Raymond in all he had to do, and when we started, he took the reins and drove off as usual.

Nothing else occurred worthy of note until after we had left the Arkansas River. Then one morning, I discovered a carriage at a water hole about a hundred yards from the road, from which two gentlemen approached the road and introduced themselves as the sons of British noblemen, who having heard of the sport of chasing buffalo on the plains, had crossed the Atlantic to indulge in it. On reaching Independence, they had purchased a carriage, two mules, and two horses, and had hired a guide to conduct them to the buffalo range. They said that they had two or three fine chases, but on the day before we arrived, a herd of buffalo went running by, when their horses jerked up their picket-pins and started after them, and had been gone about a day and a half. They said also that the water where they were camped was nearly exhausted, and they did not know where to go to get more. I at once told them that if they would pursue the road we had traveled ten or fifteen miles, they would come to Coon Creek,[3] where they would find plenty of water.

[3] Coon Creek empties into the Arkansas near the present Garfield, Pawnee County, Kansas.

But then the question arose as to how their guide would find them on his return, when I suggested to them that they might write a little note and tie it to some of the weeds near their water hole, informing their guide where they had gone. Then the question arose, whether the guide could read the note when he returned. To this I said, that they could make a mark in the direction they had gone, and, if no train came along the road to obliterate it, any competent guide would understand this. I then asked them if they were not aware that they were committing a breach of the laws of the United States, in going into our Indian country without permission. To this they replied in the negative, or they would not have done so. I then informed them, that I was not only the governor of New Mexico, but superintendent of Indian Affairs and was authorized to grant such permission, and, taking out a large pocketbook, with pencil I wrote them a permission, to continue their hunt for two weeks longer and handed it to them, for which they appeared thankful. One of them told me that he was the son of Lord Morpeith of England, and the other name I have forgotten. Captain Ewell coming up at this time asked these gentlemen, what was the news of the seat of war in Europe. One of the men replied that the day before they left Independence, the newspaper there announced that Sebastopol had fallen. To this Ewell responded, "I'll bet five hundred dollars it is not true." This showed the universal feeling among our officers in favor of Russia, during this war. The Catholic clergy in Mexico City also took a deep interest in the event of that war. As I had subscribed for the *New York Herald*, *Washington Union*, *Louisville Democrat* and *Journal*, whenever the mail came in they either sent or came to borrow some of these papers, particularly the *Herald*, as this contained more foreign news than the others. On one occasion when a priest came to return some papers that he had borrowed, he remarked to me. "Governor, I don't know what our great God will do for I see by the papers that the French and English clergy are offering up prayers for the success of the Allies, and at the same time, the Greek church of Russia is offering up prayers for the success of the Russian army. So each party has got him by one of his coattails, each pulling his own way, so I am afraid they will pull his coat off before they are done."

At the forks of the road, one leading to Fort Leavenworth, and the other to Independence, I once more shook hands with my old friend and traveling companion, Captain Ewell, with the understanding that if I returned to New Mexico in the spring, we would once more travel the plains together. I then proceeded again to my old friend, Mr. Mickelberg, where I again left my team, telling him that if neither myself or successor would need them in the spring, I would write him and give him authority to sell all I left and forward the proceeds to me.

We proceeded to the Missouri River and boarded a descending boat for St. Louis, where we once more took boat and arrived at home early in November, where I remained until after the assembling of Congress, on the first Monday in December. I proceeded to Washington City and reported to the President, who referred me to the Secretary of the Treasury to consult about appropriations for the territory of New Mexico, to the Secretary of the Interior to consult about Indian affairs, and to the Postmaster General, as to the necessary post routes. After this I asked the President if he would not accept my resignation, to which he replied, "We both entered upon the discharge of our duties about the same time, we have gotten along harmoniously and I prefer you to continue in office until your term expires." I also mentioned the subject of my resignation to Mr. Guthrie, secretary of the treasury, who said that Congress would doubtless make a larger appropriation for the completion of the state house in New Mexico and the erection of a penitentiary, and he wished the selection of the site for the latter building to be made by me, and he wished the money appropriated for both buildings to pass through my hands. He further remarked that this would cause a good deal of labor in addition to the discharge of the other duties as governor and superintendent of Indian Affairs. But, to lessen this labor as much as possible, I might appoint a superintendent to oversee the progress of the work, and a clerk to keep my accounts, and that I fix their salaries myself. These considerations induced me to return to the field of my labors.

I consequently wrote Captain Ewell at Carlisle Barracks,[4] Pennsylvania, informing him that I was once more to become his fellow traveler across the plains, and that I would proceed to Independence as soon as I learned that the ice on the Missouri River had broken up and navigation had been resumed. To this I received an answer, stating that he would proceed to Fort Leavenworth as soon as the Missouri River became navigable, with a company of United States troops, prepared to escort me once more.

I then returned home and engaged three mechanics to go out with me, as there were none in the territory capable of finishing such a building as the state house was intended to be. I also procured from two of the banks in Louisville some small silver change as I had heretofore found it very difficult to get any change to pay off the workmen. I had agreed to advance these mechanics sufficient money to pay the cost of their journey from Independence to Santa Fe. I would have to purchase horses for them to ride, and Kentucky money was not very current in Missouri. I also obtained from the banks in Louisville about three hundred dollars in specie to be used for that purpose. This money was all placed in my trunk and about the twenty-second of March, 1856, I once more proceeded to St. Louis.

[4] Carlisle Barracks, near the town of Carlisle, Pennsylvania, had been founded in 1794. At the time Captain Ewell was there it was primarily a recruit depot. Later it was turned over to the Interior Department and became the seat of the famous Indian School. See McCrellis, *Military Reservations*, 187.

Arriving there early one morning, I learned that a Missouri River boat would depart that evening. We at once transferred ourselves and baggage to this boat. I caused my trunk to be placed in my stateroom, and Raymond or myself remained there until dinner was announced. I bolted the inside door leading out into the guards of the boat, locked the door leading into the cabin, and put the key in my pocket. When dinner was over and I returned to the stateroom, I found that the door leading out on the guards had been opened and my trunk broken open; my clothes were all over the floor of the room and the money all gone. I immediately apprised the captain of the boat of what had happened and requested him to institute a search on board the boat, while I hastened to the office of Mr. Grover, my brother-in-law, a lawyer resident in St. Louis, and we went together to the office of the chief of police, to whom I made my loss known.[5] The latter gentleman returned with me to the boat, and we made a strict search, as to the manner in which the theft had been committed. We found that the thief had cut out a small light of glass in the door leading out on the guard, thrust his hand in at the aperture, and withdrawn the bolt. The chief of police then advised me to remain in St. Louis during the night, let my company proceed in the boat, and I get on the railroad, which had been completed from St. Louis to Jefferson City.

I would arrive at the latter city ahead of the boat the next morning. He accompanied me to a tavern, where I secured a room, and went with me to my room, saying that he wished to know where to find me in case any discovery should be made during the night. Here he got me to give him an accurate description of the money lost, and then asked me how much I was willing to give any of the watchmen if they recovered it. To this I replied I would give one-half of all recovered. He then said he was afraid that if the thief was arrested he would give the

[5] The amount was $525.00.—50 Cong., 1 sess., *House Comm. Rpt. 307*, 1–7.

watchman all the money to release him, but continued, "I will do the best I can and report to you early in the morning." This he did, informing me that no discovery had been made. I then took the cars and reached Jefferson City several hours before the boat arrived, when I boarded her again and proceeded to Independence. Here I found myself in great difficulty, as all my money was gone except a small amount of paper money that I had in my pocket, and I had three mechanics to take out with me. I called on a gentleman in Independence [from] whom I had always purchased my outfit of groceries, etc., by name, I think, McCoy. I asked him if he would loan me three hundred dollars on my note with Mr. Mickelberg as security. To this he replied, "I will let you have the money without any security." And immediately he proceeded to hand me that sum, for which I gave him my note. Previous to this I had made arrangements with Tom Allen, one of the mechanics, to drive my carriage, which avoided the necessity of purchasing a horse, saddle and bridle for him.

About this time I received a letter from Captain Ewell, who had arrived at Fort Leavenworth, informing me that he would leave that post about the third day following and would meet me at Council Grove. I purchased two horses, saddles and bridles, laid in provisions, and sent out to Mr. Mickelberg to have my team brought in. After having the animals shod for the trip, we went out to Mr. Mickelberg's for the night, and found his bill for wintering the four mules and a horse, only sixty dollars, although he had them five months. The next morning we departed and on arriving at Council Grove, found that Captain Ewell was not there. He arrived the same evening with a company of about fifty men. He informed me he had left Fort Leavenworth with fifty-eight men, but eight had deserted before he reached Council Grove. I then asked him where the arms of the men were, and he said the arms were boxed up and in the wagons, and he did not intend to issue them until he reached the Arkansas River.

On reaching Cottonwood Creek,[6] we encamped for the night, and, as there was some doubt as to whether we would find water at Turkey Creek, we determined to start at four o'clock in the morning; for if we found no water at Turkey Creek,[7] we would have to continue our journey to the Little Arkansas River, about sixty miles distant. On going to bed that night the Captain appointed a corporal and three men to keep watch over the camp and prevent our animals from straying off. On telling the corporal to wake up camp at three o'clock, the latter replied that he had no watch, when the Captain pulled out a fine gold watch and handed it to him, and we all retired to our blankets.

I happened to awake a little after three o'clock the next morning, and lighting a match and looking at my watch, called for the corporal of the guard, but received no answer. On the camp's being aroused, we found that the corporal and the three men were gone, and Ewell's watch with them, also four good government horses and one of my carriage mules. Ewell then said to me, "I have a few men here belonging to my old company, who have re-enlisted again and whom I can depend upon, so I will take three of them and go in pursuit of the deserters." He brought the sergeant to me, saying that I might depend upon him, and gave the sergeant instructions to obey me as he would him if he were present. The captain then started back toward Council Grove. I told Raymond to take off the double-trees from the end of the carriage tongue so that we could drive three mules instead of four, but about this time I heard a tremendous braying, and much to our satisfaction our lost mule came galloping into camp. We took with us a little wood, as we knew there was none

[6] This was known as the "Durham Crossing" for the Cottonwood, about one mile northeast of the present town of Durham, Marion County, Kansas.

[7] The Santa Fé Trail crossed Turkey Creek a few miles southeast of the present McPherson, McPherson County, Kansas.

at Turkey Creek, and resuming our journey we arrived there that evening. Finding a little water, I determined to camp for the night, so as to enable Captain Ewell to overtake us, which he did about midnight, bringing the corporal with him, having recovered the watch.

The Captain informed me that he overtook the deserters before daylight, when they scampered in every direction. By accident he took after the corporal, and being well mounted, soon overtook him, but all the others escaped. The next morning when about to start, the Captain ordered the corporal to hitch his horse behind one of the wagons, telling him that as punishment he would have to walk all the way to Fort Union, a distance of over a thousand miles.[8] He then said to him, "You start on, and we will overtake you." I happened to start a little before the escort, and on ascending the hill from Turkey Creek, discovered the corporal walking briskly ahead of us, probably a quarter of a mile in advance, but, on coming to a hollow, he started in full run down it. Raymond being a little ahead of me galloped after him and brought him back and delivered him to the sergeant. On Ewell's coming up to where we had stopped, he asked Raymond, "Why in hell did you catch him and bring him back?" Raymond replied that he thought the corporal was going to desert again. The Captain said, "That was precisely the reason I sent him ahead." He had no way of confining [the soldier], and in all probability he would desert again the next night and steal a horse or two, whereby the government would not only lose the corporal's services, but a good horse also. The Captain called the corporal to him and asked for his canteen, when the latter replied that he supposed he had lost it when running down the hill. To this the Captain said, "No, you have left it in the camp and you start back and get it, and, if you don't come into camp tonight before I go to bed, I'll give you hell."

[8] Fort Union was approximately 690 miles from Council Grove.

So the corporal took the back track, while we started ahead, and as we all expected, [we] never saw or heard of him again.

We camped at the Little Arkansas that night at an early hour, as Ewell and the three men who had gone in search of the deserters needed rest for themselves and horses. We proceeded on our journey without any incidents to the Arkansas River, where I pointed out the advantages of the northern route[9] to the Captain, and we determined to pursue it. So we continued up the Arkansas River about two hundred miles, when we came to the upper crossing.[10] I then explained to Ewell, as he had never traveled this route before, that we would have about forty miles to go without either wood or water. Therefore, it was determined to start at about four o'clock the next morning. Here we found that several of the soldiers had deserted during the night, but indeed this was the case almost every night.

That evening the Captain, feeling unwell, rode in the carriage with me, and before reaching Bear Creek[11] where we expected to camp that night, we had to descend a long steep hill. On reaching the foot of it, we had to turn abruptly to the right around a point of rocks, where the creek made a bend like a horseshoe, and where water and grass was to be found. On turning this point of rocks we discovered a large body of Indians encamped in this bend of the river. They immediately jumped under the bank for concealment. Of course we halted immediately. The Captain asked what was to be done. To this I said, "I don't know what Indians they are, or whether they are friendly or hostile, but we must try and water our animals if possible as it is about thirty-eight miles to the next water." About this

[9] That is, the Aubry Cutoff.

[10] What was known as the Upper Crossing of the Arkansas was located west of Dodge City, near the present town of Cimarron, Kansas.

[11] Bear Creek and Sand Creek, both tributaries of the Cimarron, join about seven miles above the Trails crossing, at Ulysses, while the Dry Cimarron joins the main stream at about the same distance below the Trail.

time the Indian who was at the head of the party came walking up to us with a Mexican boy about twelve years old, who acted as interpreter for him. He addressed a few words in Indian to the boy, and the boy said to us, "This Indian wants to know who you are and why you are doing traveling through his country and scaring off all the buffalo." To this I replied, "We are American officers, and we have the right to travel this road, for we have bought it from the Indians, with the privilege of killing as many buffalo as we want to eat. We want to water our animals and then depart." The Indian then said, "All that you have said is right; you can water your horses and mules, as there is plenty of water here. We are great friends of the Americans and never harm them." So Ewell and myself decided to water the animals, place them under guard of one-half of the soldiers, cook a little for ourselves to eat, while the stock was grazing, and then depart.

The cooks were directed to be quick as possible, while all the soldiers were told to retain their arms (which a short time before had been issued to them) on their persons. By this time a number of the Indians came up to our camp, looking with curious gaze at everything they saw. The headman of the party and the Mexican boy sat near me, while we conversed with each other. Pretty soon our cook spread a blanket in front of where we were sitting and placed some fried meat and crackers in the tin plates on it and a pot of warm coffee. I then asked the Indian to eat with me, which he agreed to do, and drawing himself upon the left side of the chair on which I sat (for I always carried a split bottom chair with me) ate with me. Ewell finished his meal before I did, and coming up to where I sat, said, "Governor, I can't get away from here for the Indians have stolen a number of my bridles." I replied, "This is bad indeed, but you go back to your men and tell them to drive all the animals up into camp, and be prepared for action if necessary, while I will try an experiment to get back your bridles."

I observed that around his neck the Indian wore a string of bear's claws strung on what seemed to be a strong buckskin string. I told Raymond to get into the carriage and get down a double-barreled shotgun and rifle that were suspended from under the top, get out two or three pair of revolvers, and lay them all on the seats ready for use. I told the Mexican boy not to move or that man in the carriage would shoot him; then with my hand, I seized the buckskin string encircling the Indian's neck, drew a revolver out of my belt, giving my hand a twist so as to choke the Indian and placing the muzzle of my pistol with my right hand to the side of his head. Twisting the string so as to stop his breathing, I held him so for a minute or two. Then giving him an opportunity to breathe, he spoke a few words to the Mexican boy in the Indian language. Then the boy said to me, "Big Bear wants to know why you squeeze his neck so for." I then told the boy to tell the Indian that his people had stolen our bridles, and if they were not brought back, I would blow his brains out. The Indian spoke a few words to the boy, who then got on top of my carriage and began to holler to the Indians, who had once more disappeared under the bank of the river. Presently I saw an Indian come with a bridle in his hand and throw it down and return to the creek again. This was done by a number of other Indians, each bringing a bridle and throwing it down. During this time our driver, who was hitching up our mules, reported one of my carriage lines gone. This fact I communicated to the boy, who again commenced calling to the Indians, but pretty soon he told me that the Indian who had my carriage line had gone off and could not be found. So Raymond got a small rope from the carriage box, with which we made a substitute for the line.

I then upbraided the Indian for his treachery, put my pistol close to his head, and told him I had a good notion to blow his brains out anyway, but soon released him. I then stepped into the carriage, and we drove off. But, as I had gone in past the point of rocks ahead of the other teams, I necessarily was the last to come out. I held my double-barreled shotgun in my hands and kept a close watch in the direction of the Indians. We had traveled about a quarter of a mile when I heard a hallooing behind us; looking back I discovered the Mexican boy galloping after us. Supposing that he wanted to make his escape from the Indians, I stopped the carriage. When the boy came up within twenty-five or thirty yards of us, he said, "Big Bear says he will get all your horses and mules tonight." To this I replied, "Tell Big Bear that if he or any of his men come about our camp tonight, I will riddle their hides with bullets so they won't hold corn-shucks." We traveled on that night eight or ten miles, when coming to a level piece of prairie ground, where we could see any Indian that might approach our camp at a considerable distance, we camped without wood or water.

It was agreed that the Captain should take one-half of the men and stand watch half of the night, when I and the other half of the men were to be awakened and watch the remainder of the night; but we found that we had only sixteen remaining, as all had deserted but these. This was a beautiful moonlight night, and I witnessed one of the most perfect and total eclipses of the moon that I have ever seen before or since in my long life. But we saw no Indians during the night, though I have no doubt that they reconnoitered our camp, and finding us prepared for them, did not molest us.

The next day we reached the Cimarron River, which at the upper crossing was a bold mountain stream.[12] At the lower or

[12] This is not a recognizable characterization of the dry arroyos of the upper Cimarron, but of the mountain-fed Canadian. The headwaters of the latter river

old crossing water was rarely found; but by digging a hole three or four feet deep in the bottom of the creek, it would soon fill with water. Nothing else occurred worthy of note during our trip.

On our arrival at Santa Fe I found a large amount of materials collected for completing the state house. My next difficulty was the selection of a site on which to erect the penitentiary,[13] as there were few sites in the vicinity of Santa Fe suitable for the purpose. After visiting several places a site not at all suitable for the purpose was offered me by a party of speculators, who wanted $3,000 for it, but had purchased it for $1,000 a short time before. On my declining to buy the site, they raised a great outcry against me, which I entirely disregarded, and purchased a site for $500, which was much more suitable. I immediately set hands to digging the foundation for the exterior walls, quarrying stone, burning lime, etc. I gave Mr. McGee, one of

were named Cimarron, probably through an early error in geography. Even today the "bold mountain stream" that tumbles down the scenic gorge on the east side of the mountains east of Taos is known as the Cimarron Canyon although it is one of the main sources of the Canadian River.

[13] Meriwether accepted this responsibility with reluctance. When the superintendent of buildings at Washington requested him to serve, he replied from Santa Fe, September 16, 1854: "In answer thereto, allow me to inform you, if a more satisfactory appointment cannot be made, rather than have the erection of the building delayed, I will accept the appointment and endeavor to discharge the duties as indicated." In May, 1853, Congress had appropriated thirty thousand dollars for the erection of the penitentiary. Dissention arose between the Governor and the building commissioners over the site selected, and Meriwether removed the commissioners and took over the supervision of the work himself. This action was upheld in Washington and in federal court. The buildings were not completed during his administration, rising only to about the first floor; then the work was abandoned, and later a federal building was erected on the site. Territorial prisoners were boarded in the Kansas penitentiary until 1884, when a building was completed some distance southeast of the original site. After several delays Congress finally made another appropriation for a capitol, and the building was completed in the late 1860's. See Meriwether Letters, University of New Mexico Library; Interview, Miguel A. Otero, former governor of New Mexico at Santa Fe, August 10, 1931; and Interview, Tom Gable, the first warden of the New Mexico penitentiary, at Santa Fe, July 12, 1935.

the carpenters I took out with me charge of the work on the state house, and everything proceeded briskly.

One day while dining at the hotel, at which the speculators before alluded to boarded, they commenced denouncing my conduct in not purchasing their property, in quite rough language, to which I paid no attention. Judge Davenport, chief justice of the territory, who was sitting near, remarked that he didn't see how I could listen to such language in silence. To this I replied, "These men are not to blame for trying to retard work on the penitentiary, for they know very well that when the building is finished they will be convicts in it. Therefore they wish to postpone the evil day as long as possible." This retort completely silenced them, and I heard nothing more of them afterward.

In 1856 I first visited the Indians on the Mimbres,[14] about two hundred miles west of the Río Grande. On my arrival at Fort Craig I found it in command of an old acquaintance, Major George Crittenden,[15] son of the Honorable John J. Crittenden, of Frankfort, Kentucky. I arrived at this post before breakfast one morning, proceeding at once to Major Crittenden's headquarters, breakfasted with him, and informed him that I desired a small escort to Fort Thorn. He at once agreed to furnish this and asked me whom I desired to command it. I replied that

[14] The source of the Mimbres River is in the Mimbres Range, flowing south to the vicinity of Deming, New Mexico, where it disappears under ground, and thence into the Lake Guzmán basin, Chihuahua, Mexico. The distance from the Río Grande is about sixty miles west. From his description of his route to the meeting place it would appear it was in the vicinity of the present Silver City. The Mimbres or Mimbrenos (Spanish, "people of the willows") are Apaches who received their name from the Mimbres Mountains. See Hodge, *Handbook of American Indians*, I, 863.

[15] Major George Bibb Crittenden, a native of Kentucky, graduated from West Point and was commissioned on July 1, 1832, 2nd lieutenant in the Fourth Infantry. He was breveted major on August 20, 1847, for gallantry in the battles of Contreras and Churubusco, Mexico. He resigned as lieutenant colonel on June 10, 1861, and served as a major general in the Confederate Army. He died on November 27, 1880.—Heitman, *Historical Register, U.S.A.*, II, 338.

any good sergeant would be sufficient, whereupon he told me that he wished I would select him as he desired to visit the Indians on the Mimbres River. He could not leave his post without permission from General Garland, who was at Santa Fe, some hundred and fifty miles distant. But he added if I would select him to command the escort, it would be sufficient excuse for his leaving without permission from General Garland. I at once agreed that he should command the escort and asked him how soon he would be ready to start, to which he replied, "Next morning." I answered that I was in a great haste and could not wait until morning, upon which he said, "I will have to turn over the public property to the next officer in command, pack my mess chest, and get my traveling equipage ready; and this will require a whole day." To obviate this, I invited him to be my guest during the trip, as I had accommodations sufficient for us both. He said, "After an early dinner we will start."

While he was arranging matters to leave, knowing that he was fond of a little dram, I went around to the sutler's store and purchased four small bottles of the native brandy of that country, which I placed in my carriage box. On camping that night, I got out a bottle and asked him to take a drink, when he responded, "Now Governor, I feel ashamed of myself, for I know you never drink anything stronger than coffee. I have no doubt you purchased this brandy on my account, after you found out that I was to be your guest, because you have often seen me drinking while you were in Frankfort, Kentucky. But I wish to inform you that I have abandoned the use of spirits entirely and haven't tasted a drop for a year and a half." This caused me to give him a cordial grasp of the hand and express my satisfaction. He then proposed with my permission to throw the bottles of brandy into the river, on the bank of which we had encamped. To this however, I objected, as rattlesnakes were abundant in that country, and some of our party might be bitten.

Alcohol is said to be a sovereign remedy for such a disaster. So I placed the bottle back in the carriage box and didn't take it out again during the trip. I remembered the passage in the Lord's prayer which my mother had taught me in my infancy, "Lead us not into temptation."

On reaching Fort Thorn I procured an additional escort under the command of Captain Claybourne. Here we left the Río Grande and proceeded across the mountains to the Mimbres River. The first night on camping Captain Claybourne produced the bottle and insisted on Major Crittenden and myself joining him in a drink, but we both declined. Captain Claybourne insisted again on the Major's joining him in a glass, but I was glad to see that the Major resisted firmly. Shortly after this I sought an opportunity to inform the Captain of the Major's reformation and requested him not to insist on his drinking again. The Captain complied with this request.

On reaching the Mimbres River, we found that it had disappeared entirely from the face of the earth, the water being entirely absorbed in a vast sand plain, and never making its appearance afterward, although near where it emerges from the mountains the Mimbres is a bold mountain stream of considerable magnitude.

We proceeded up the valley of this river for several days, and finally met the Mimbres Apaches encamped on its bank, where I concluded a treaty with them. I distributed among them a considerable quantity of presents which I had brought from Santa Fe. Among these Indians I found a man of the Quoetaro[16] tribe, who spoke the Spanish language quite well. On my asking him how he came to speak that language, he said that after

[16] This Apache probably belonged to the Chiracahua tribe, an untamed people that occupied the mountain fastnesses of southwestern New Mexico and southeastern Arizona and the Sierra Madres of Mexico. The names of their leaders—Cochise, Victorio, Juh, Geronimo, and others—were to be written large on the history of the Southwest during the seventies and eighties.

the death of his father and mother, while he was a boy, he was adopted by a Catholic priest and had been raised by him and educated to manhood, when he returned to his tribe again. His tribe occupied a country at the head of the Mimbres River. When we were about to distribute the presents, he wanted to know if he was to get any. I told him that I had presents for his tribe and for each of the other tribes that I intended to visit. These presents were boxed up separately. I told him also that he could return with me to his tribe and there receive his share of the presents. But he said that he could not return, for the balance of his tribe had gone down into Old Mexico and that I would be unable to find them if I attempted to do so.

The manner of delivering presents to the Indians is to have the chiefs and principal men seated in a circle around the gifts; then another larger circle is formed outside of this by the common men, and still a larger circle is formed by the women and children. Presents suitable for each circle are then distributed. While I was distributing the first circle, Major Crittenden was distributing to the second circle, and Captain Claybourne to the third. During this time the Quoetaro [?] Indian sat by himself, outside the circle on a rock. When we were pretty well through distributing, he exclaimed in a loud voice, "I am a Christian, and you give me nothing." This produced such an effect upon us, that we opened a box intended for his tribe and gave him a share of the presents. As the remainder of his tribe had gone down into Old Mexico, I found it necessary to seek them.

We then retraced our steps to Santa Fe, leaving Captain Claybourne and his company at Fort Thorn and Major Crittenden at Fort Craig, where he found that he had been promoted to the rank of lieutenant colonel. Major Crittenden was a gallant officer and had but one fault, and that was too great a fondness in early life for the flowing bowl. I was rejoiced at his reformation. On the breaking out of the Civil War he joined the Confederate Army and rose to the rank of a general officer. At the close of the war he returned to Frankfort, Kentucky, and was elected librarian by the legislature. I never again saw any evidence of his falling from grace. He died some years ago in the city of his birth and was generally respected by all who knew him.

On my return to Santa Fe I found the work on the public buildings progressing satisfactorily under the charge of Judge Houghton, whom I had appointed general manager, I having been authorized by the Secretary of the Treasury to appoint a superintendent and a clerk, and fix their salaries.

The remainder of the winter of 1856 I remained in Santa Fe, and during the session of the legislature which convened in December, 1856, assisted the members in drafting bills. Towards the close of the session I had rather a warm time of it. A number of Americans, mostly gamblers and discharged soldiers, procured the passage of a bill through both houses unanimously authorizing them to organize a company consisting of not less than fifty or more than one hundred men, to select their own officers and the government to commission these officers. [It also gave] this company authority to make at their discretion war against any tribe of Indians in the territory [and gave them] all the property that they could capture from the Indians, and where any tribe of Indians had taken property from the Mexicans, this company could claim half of all recovered as their compensation.

This bill I determined to veto, although I was not required to veto any bill passed by the legislature, for, without my signature it could not become a law. But, through respect to the legislature I determined to give them my reason for withholding my signature, and commenced at once reducing those reasons to writing. I did not intend that my purpose in reference to the bill should be known until my veto message was prepared, but, somehow or other it leaked out. Those who were to be the officers of this company sent me word that if I vetoed this bill or refused to sign it, they would tar and feather me, which did not deter me from proceeding with my veto message. I explained to the members of the legislature in this message that there were over twenty villages of the Pueblo Indians, who were good farmers and owned considerable amount of property, which would be seized by this company and appropriated to their own use. This would result in a general war with all the Indians of the territory, as these Pueblo Indians would combine together to defend themselves and property. I then informed the members that many of them were large stock raisers, having herds of sheep, cattle, and horses out on the prairies, some of them fifty miles from the owners' residences, and under the sole charge of a few Mexican herders. This company, [I told them], could dress a small number of their own men in Indian costume and direct these men to charge upon a herd, whereupon the herders would immediately abandon their animals and these pretended Indians would drive off the stock to an appointed place. There the residue of the company would capture them and take one-half for their compensation. I also reminded the legislature that the government of the United States had control of Indian affairs, and the legislature of the territory had no right to interfere with Indian affairs.

When this message was finished, I caused it to be translated into Spanish and printed in both the Spanish and English languages and had a copy placed upon the desk of each member of both Houses, while the members were at supper, as they intended to have a night session. I also sent a copy in each language to the man who had been elected captain and to other officers of the company, with a verbal message to get their tar and feathers ready. I would sleep with my doors open that night and give them a fair opportunity to carry their threat into execution. I then went to General Garland's quarters and told him what was going on, and requested him to place ten infantrymen in my back yard, with instructions to obey my orders. I also asked him not to let the men load their muskets, as I would prepare the ammunition for them myself. I requested him not to let this be known to anyone. About eight o'clock that night a sergeant appeared at my door and told me he was there to obey any orders I would issue to him. I then got some powder, told him to have his men load their muskets, not putting less than ten or more than fifteen buckshot in each gun, and took him into my bedroom by the back door. Here I showed him the position of my bed, the head of which was against my back window, and the foot pointing directly to a door, opposite the window, and which led to a long passageway six or eight feet wide, to the outer door.

I then told him I expected to be attacked that night, and would lie in my bed with a double-barreled shotgun, loaded with buckshot, by my side; and, whenever the crowd entered the passageway, I would rise in a sitting position in bed and fire both barrels down the passageway. I also told him that as soon as I had fired I would fall back on the bed, and for he and his men to fire a volley through the open window and directly over me as I lay in bed. This he promised to do, and I had my son Raymond and two or three friends armed in an adjoining room, prepared to assist if need be. We spent the night in this way, with all the doors open, but no person appeared. A day or two afterwards I met the man that was to have been captain of the company and asked him why he didn't come, to which he replied, "We had a meeting of the whole company and thought you were rather too willing to be tarred and feathered and concluded we had better not go."

Epilogue

AND so the venerable David Meriwether closed his Memoirs. The concluding activities of his life must be traced from other sources. He left Santa Fe in May, 1857, although his official term would not expire until October 30 of that year.

Historians agree that he had been an able and forceful administrator during a chaotic period in New Mexico's history. L. Bradford Prince, who was himself appointed as territorial governor in 1889, sums up Meriwether's administration as follows:

> He made an intelligent, practical Governor, but during his administration of four years there was incessant war with the surrounding Indian tribes. Incursions and depredations by the Navajos on the West, the Utes and Jicarillas Apaches on the north, the Mescaleros on the east, and the Gila and Mogollon Apaches on the south, were of frequent occurance, and the military was kept busy all the time in expeditions against the various tribes, including a number of battles in which the Indians were generally defeated and dispersed for the time.[1]

Upon his return to his home he again assumed the role of agriculturist, supervising his two farms in Indiana and Kentucky; and he became actively engaged in politics. In the following year (1858) he was elected to the Kentucky House of Representatives, becoming speaker when it convened in 1859. Intermittently for the next twenty-seven years he served as a legislator, the last time at the advanced age of eighty-five. Throughout his long public life before the Civil War he supported slav-

[1] Prince, *A Concise History of New Mexico,* 193.

ery; however, like many Kentuckians he was dedicated to the preservation of the Union. When the war ended, he, like his fellow agriculturists of the South with large acreages, was stripped of his slaves and field workers, many of whom were like members of the family, inherited from his parents.

Thus in a few years Meriwether was plunged from prosperity into financial difficulties, with the road back to success and security dim and remote for a man no longer young. It was about this time that he generously, but unwisely aided a relative by the endorsement of a note for a large sum of money, which was not honored by its maker, leaving him as a responsible endorser to pay the sum from his depleted finances. In his need he presented a claim against the government, which he had disregarded in more prosperous days: for the public money in his possession that had been stolen in St. Louis and repaid at his own expense; and for three thousand dollars in additional salary to which he believed himself entitled for serving as superintendent of Indian affairs and building commissioner while governor of New Mexico.[2] Apparently his claim was never allowed, but when he appeared in Washington in 1888 to present it he attracted much attention by his venerable appearance as a character from a vanished past. Newspaper writers recalled his experiences in the wilds beyond the frontier town of St. Louis, his service in the senate as the successor of Henry Clay, and his administration of far distant New Mexico.[3]

Meriwether's son-in-law, Captain Graves, died at Woodlawn, near Louisville July 16, 1889. Mrs. Graves then moved to the old plantation to care for her father, remaining until his death.[4] He celebrated his ninetieth birthday at the home of his son William in Louisville, where about thirty old friends and

[2] 50 Cong., 1 sess., *House Rpt.* 307, 3–4.

[3] Unidentified newspaper clippings in Meriwether Papers.

[4] John H. Graves, "A Brief Sketch of my Branch of the Graves Family," unpublished manuscript, 7 pp., San Jose, California, January, 1923.

relatives called to greet him. The *Courier-Journal* commented in a long article sharing front page space with world news the next morning:

> Gov. Meriwether experiences little of the infirmities of advanced age. His mind is as clear as it ever was. He delights in telling stories and in meeting his old friends, and took great pleasure in entertaining them yesterday. His eyesight is failing somewhat and he cannot see to read well, but experiences no difficulty in finding his way around. Yesterday Gov. Meriwether was in unusually good spirits and chatted merrily with his friends, telling them of his old frontier days. He said that he has enjoyed the occasion as much as any in his life and hoped to see many more such pleasant anniversaries. Early in the afternoon he left for his home on the river, about eight miles below the city.

The paper related many stirring incidents of his past life and his services to the state and went on to say that he was one of the seven surviving members of the Constitutional Convention that met in 1849 and framed the document that was still the organic law of Kentucky. "He devotes a great deal of attention to State matters, and . . . enjoys having the news read to him."[5]

During the following two years he ventured forth rarely, and then only to visit with close friends and relatives in Louisville. Wherever he went in public he attracted attention by his patriarchal appearance, with tall, spare, slightly stooped form and his full white beard. Although his eyesight had failed, he retained the sharp penetrating gaze, which had been a marked characteristic of his youth. He liked to sit on the porch of the old plantation house, facing the river, with its tree lined banks, its lights and shadows and its ever busy traffic. The waters he had known so well in his youth were now churned by huge paddle

[5] *Courier-Journal* (Louisville), October 31, 1890, p. 1.

wheels as the big steamboats with their streamers of smoke from tall stacks displaced the keelboats with their cordelle lines and their hardy vigorous crews.

There in the old home he died after a short illness at the age of ninety-two.[6] He was buried in the family plot on the plantation, but some years later his body was removed and interred in the historic old cemetery of Cave Hill at Louisville.[7]

[6] *San Jose Mercury-Herald,* April 7, 1892.

[7] Interview, Mrs. Betsy Graves O'Neill, September 28, 1963.

Bibliography

Unpublished Material

Manuscripts

All manuscripts, unless otherwise specified, are from the Meriwether Papers, O'Neill Collection.

Barclay, Alexander. Correspondence and Papers. Bancroft Library.

Davis, W. W. H. Diaries and Papers, 33 pieces. Negative photostat of original in possession of Hon. Clinton P. Anderson. Bancroft Library.

"Fort Sutter Papers." Relating to the death of Dr. B. J. Kern. Huntington Library.

"Fort Thorn Treaty." Drawn by David Meriwether with the Mescalero Apaches. Fort Thorn, Territory of New Mexico, June 14, 1855.

Graves, Captain Edmund A. "Commission of Appointment as Indian Agent, Territory of New Mexico." Signed by President Franklin Pierce and George L. Marcy, secretary of state, May 21, 1853.

Graves, John H. "Reminiscences of Gov. D. Meriwether: Unwritten History in Regard to New Mexico."

———. "A Brief Sketch of My Branch of the Graves Family." San Jose, California, January, 1923.

———. Muster Roll, U.S. Army, Company F, 16th Regt. of Infantry, Newport, Kentucky, August 5, 1848, Captain E. A. Graves Commanding.

Meriwether, D. Bill of Sale, to Catherine H. Graves, of nine Negro slaves. Louisville, January 9, 1862.

Meriwether, Captain William. Petition, Land Settlement, Bullitt, County Circuit Court. Shepardsville, Kentucky, February 17, 1816.

———. Petition to U.S. Circuit Court, Seventh Kentucky District. April 1, 1788.

Meriwether Miscellany. "Notes, Statements, Bills," 13 pieces.

Promissory Note in amount of $200. W. Meriwether, D. Meriwether, and A. G. Meriwether. Bank of the Commonwealth of Kentucky, Louisville, July 30, 1826.

Letters

Correspondence between U.S. Secretary of the Treasury and office of Supt. of Public Buildings for New Mexico, 1853–68, 42 letters signed "D. Meriwether." Zimmerman Library, University of New Mexico, Albuquerque.

James Magoffin to Hon. M. Crawford, secretary of war, Washington, April 4, 1849, Magoffin Papers, Transcript of original, New Mexico Historical Society.

James Magoffin to Hon. W. L. Marcy, secretary of war, Santa Fe, August 26, 1846, Magoffin Papers, Transcript of original, New Mexico Historical Society.

Joseph K. F. Mansfield to his cousin Edward D. Mansfield, Fort Pulaski, Georgia, September 18, 1830. Typescript of original, U.S. Military Academy, West Point, N.Y.

Col. David Meriwether to his brother Captain William Meriwether, Washington City, October 21, 1803. Relating to final vote of Congress upon "Treaty with U.S. and the French Nation." (Louisiana Purchase). Meriwether Papers, O'Neill Collection.

Col. David Meriwether to his brother Captain William Meriwether, Clark Country, Georgia, April 20, 1817. Relating to treaty negotiations between Andrew Jackson, Col. David Meriwether and Cherokee and Chickasaw Indians. Meriwether Papers, O'Neill Collection.

Gov. David Meriwether to C. Carson, Santa Fe, August 26, 1855 and August 3, September 20, 1856.

———. To Charles P. Graves. Jefferson County, Kentucky, January 5, 1867. Meriwether Papers, O'Neill Collection.

James Speed to Gen. James A. Eakin, attesting to loyalty to the Union of Captain E. A. Graves during the course of the Civil War, Louisville, December 30, 1878. Meriwether Papers, O'Neill Collection.

Interviews

Gable, Tom. Santa Fe, New Mexico, July 12, 1935.

O'Neill, Betsy Graves. Interviews at Redwood City, California, July 12, 1929; January 15, 1931; August 10, 1933; Reno, Nevada, July 22, 1934; Redwood City, October 26–27, 1963; Santa Fe, New Mexico, November 28, 1964.

Otero, Hon. Miguel A. Santa Fe, New Mexico, August 10, 1931.

Government Documents and Publications

Congressional Records

30 Cong., 1 sess., *House Exec. Doc. 31*, "Report of Lt. J. W. Abert on His Examination of New Mexico in the Years 1846–47."

30 Cong., 1 sess., *House Exec Doc. 60*, "Secretary of War Marcy to Brig. Gen. S. W. Kearny, January 11, 1847."

31 Cong., 1 sess., *House Exec. Doc. 45*, "Report of Exploration and Survey of a Route from Fort Smith, Arkansas, to Santa Fe, New Mexico, Made in 1849, by First Lieutenant James H. Simpson, Corps of Topographical Engineers."

32 Cong., 1 sess., *Sen. Exec. Doc. 121*, August, 25, 1852. Report of Secretary of War.

32 Cong., 1 sess., *Sen. Rpt. 345*, August 20, 1852. "Report from Secretary of Interior in Relation to Fixing the Initial Point in the Boundary Line between the United States and Mexico."

32 Cong., 1 sess., July, 1852. "Report of the Secretary of the Interior, Mexico and U.S. Boundary Survey."

32 Cong., 2 sess., *House Exec. Doc. 1*, September 24, 1852. Col. [Edwin Vose] Sumner to Col. Samuel Cooper (Adj. Gen.).

33 Cong., 1 sess., *House Misc. Doc. 53*, Memorial of the Legislative Council of New Mexico, Increased Facilities of Communication with the States. Santa Fe., February 25, 1854.

33 Cong., 1 sess., *House Exec. Doc. 1*, December 5, 1853. Meriwether, Gov. D. Report to George W. Manypenny, commissioner of Indian Affairs. Santa Fe, August 31, 1853.

33 Cong., 1 sess., *House Misc. Doc. 47*. Memorial of the Legislative Council of New Mexico, Asking the Reinstatement of Fort Atkinson, February 25, 1854.

33 Cong., 1 sess., *House Exec. Doc. 1*. "Instructions to Captain J. W.

Gunnison, War Department, May 20, 1853, from Jefferson Davis, Secretary of War."

33 Cong., 1 sess., *Sen. Exec. Doc. 28,* December 5, 1853. Letter, George W. Manypenny, Commissioner of Indian Affairs, to Hon. R. McClelland, Secretary of the Interior, February 2, 1854.

34 Cong., 1 sess., *House Exec. Doc. 1,* part 2, January 31, 1855. Brig. Gen. John Garland: "Report on Department of New Mexico."

34 Cong., 1 sess., *House Exec. Doc. 1,* part 1, March 16, 1855. Instructions to Indians in New Mexico from Commissioner Manypenny. Addressed to Gen. Meriwether, in regard to negotiations to be made with the Indians of New Mexico.

34 Cong., 1 sess., *House Exec. Doc. 135,* 3 parts, August 1, 1856. "Message on Mexican Boundary, President Franklin Pierce. Report of Maj. W. H. Emory, United States Commissioner on the Survey of the Boundary Between the United States and the Republic of Mexico."

50 Cong., 1 sess., February 7, 1888, *House Rpt. 307.* Concerning David Meriwether (the Committee on Claims).

Annual Report of the Commissioner of Indian Affairs, transmitted with the message of the President at the opening of the first session of the Thirty-third Congress, 1853. Washington, Robert Armstrong Printer, 1853.

Beckwith, Edward Griffin. *Report of Exploration of a Route for the Pacific Railroad, Near the 38th and 39th Parallel of Latitude from the Mouth of the Kansas to Sevier River in the Great Basin.* Washington, Government Printing Office, 1855

Biographical Dictionary of The American Congress, 1774–1961. Washton, Government Printing Office, 1961.

1st Annual Report of the Bureau of Ethnology, To the Secretary of The Smithsonian Institution, 1879–80. By J. W. Powell, Director. Washington, Government Printing Office, 1881.

Heitman, Francis B. *Historical Register of The United States Army, From its Organization, September 29, 1789, to March 2, 1903.* Washington, Government Printing Office, 1903.

Hodge, Frederick Webb, ed. *Handbook of American Indians North of*

Mexico. Bureau of American Ethnology *Bulletin No. 30.* 2 vols. Washington, 1912.

Humphreys, Brigadier General A. A. *Preliminary Report Concerning Explorations and Surveys Principally in Nevada and Arizona.* Washington, Government Printing Office, 1872.

McCrellis, James B. *Military Reservations, National Military Parks, and National Cemeteries. Title And Jurisdiction.* Washington, Government Printing Office, 1898.

Marcy, Randolph B., Assisted by George B. McClelland. *Exploration of the Red River of Louisiana in the Year 1852.* Washington, Beverly Tucker, Senate Printer, 1854.

National Archives. *Letters Received By The Office of Indian Affairs, New Mexico Superintendency 1849–1880.* Microfilm 234, Roll 547.

———. Mansfield, Joseph K. F. *Report of Inspection of the Department of New Mexico, 1853.* Records of the Office of the Adjutant General, Washington, D.C.

———. *Report From James Gadsden to William L. Marcy, Secretary of State.* General Records, Department of State, Record Group 59.

McDermott, John Francis, ed. *Journal of an Expedition to the Mauvaises Terres and the Upper Missouri in 1850. By* Thaddeus A. Culbertson. Smithsonian Institution, Bureau of American Ethnology *Bulletin 147.* Washington, Government Printing Office, 1952.

Royce, Charles C. *The Cherokee Nation of Indians: A Narrative of the Official Relations with the Colonial and Federal Government. Fifth Annual Report, 1883–84. Bureau of American Ethnology.* Washington, Government Printing Office, 1887.

Wheeler, George M. *Preliminary Reports Concerning Explorations and Surveys Principally in Nevada and Arizona.* Washington, Government Printing Office 1872.

Books

Alter, J. Cecil. *James Bridger, Trapper, Frontiersman, Scout and Guide: A Historical Narrative.* Salt Lake City, Shepard Book Co., 1925.

Appleton's *Cyclopaedia of American Biography.* Ed. by James Grant Wilson and John Fiske. New York, D. Appleton & Co., 1888.

Bancroft, Hubert Howe. *History of Arizona and New Mexico, 1530–1888*. San Francisco, The History Co., 1889.

———. *History of the North: Mexican States and Texas*. San Francisco, The History Co., 1886.

Barnes, Will C. *Arizona Place Names*. Tucson. University of Arizona, 1935.

Bartlett, John R. *Personal Narrative of Explorations and Incidents in Texas, New Mexico, California, Sonora, and Chihuahua, Connected With the United States and Mexican Boundary Commission During the Years 1850, 51, 52, and 53*. . . . 2 vols. New York, D. Appleton & Co., 1854.

Beck, Warren A. *New Mexico: A History of Four Centuries*. Norman, University of Oklahoma Press, 1962.

Bell, Captain John R. *The Journal of Captain John R. Bell: Official Journalist for the Stephen H. Long Expedition to the Rocky Mountains, 1820*. Ed. by Harlin M. Fuller and LeRoy R. Hafen (Far West and Rockies Series). Glendale, Arthur H. Clark Co., 1957.

Bennett, James A. *Forts and Forays: A Dragoon in New Mexico, 1850–1856*. Ed. by Clinton E. Brooks and Frank D. Reeve. Albuquerque, University of New Mexico Press, 1948.

Benton, Thomas Hart. *Thirty Years View*. 2 vols. New York, D. Appleton & Co., Boston, F. Parker, 1854–56.

Bieber, Ralph P., ed. *Exploring Southwestern Trails*. Glendale, Arthur H. Clark Co., 1938.

Billon, Frederic L. *Annals of St Louis in Its Early Days Under the French and Spanish Dominations*. St. Louis, 1886.

Boddie, John Bennett. *Historical Southern Families*. Redwood City, California, Pacific Coast Publishers, 1959.

Boller, Henry A. *Among the Indians: Eight Years in the Far West, 1858–1866*. Ed. by Milo Milton Quaife (Lakeside Classics). Chicago, R. R. Donnelley & Sons Co., 1959.

Bolton, Herbert Eugene. *Spanish Borderlands*. New Haven, Yale University Press, 1921.

———. *Coronado on the Turquoise Trail*. New York, Alfred A. Knopf, 1939.

Bonsal, Stephen. *Edward Fitzgerald Beale: A Pioneer in the Path of Empire 1822–1903*. New York, G. P. Putnam's Sons., 1912.

Brackenridge, Henry. *Journal of a Voyage Up the River Missouri Performed in 1811*. Vol. VI in R. G. Thwaites, *Early Western Travels*. Cleveland, Arthur H. Clark Co., 1904.

Bradbury, John. *Travels in the Interior of America in the Years 1809, 1810, and 1811; Including a Description of Upper Louisiana, Together with the States of Ohio, Kentucky, Indiana, and Tennessee, with the Illinois and Western Territory, and Containing Remarks and Observations Useful to Persons Emigrating to Those Countries*. Vol. V. in R. G. Thwaites, *Early Western Travels*. Cleveland, Arthur H. Clark Co., 1904.

Brandes, Ray. *Frontier Military Posts of Arizona*. Globe, Dale Stuart King, 1960.

Carvallo, S. N. *Incidents of Travel and Adventure in the Far West with Colonel Frémont's Last Expedition*. New York, Derby & Jackson, 1857.

Chittenden, Hiram Martin. *The American Fur Trade of the Far West*. 2 vols. New York, Barnes & Noble, 1935.

Chittenden, Hiram Martin, and Alfred Talbot Richardson. *Life, Letters and Travels of Father Pierre—Jean De Smet, S.J.* 4 vols. New York, Francis P. Harper, 1905.

Cluskey, M. W., compiler. *The Democratic Hand-Book*. Washington, R. A. Waters, 1856.

Collins, Richard H. *History of Kentucky*. 2 vols. Covington, Collins & Co., 1882.

Conard, Howard Louis. *Uncle Dick Wootton: The Pioneer Frontiersman of the Rocky Mountain Region*. Columbus, College Book Co., 1950.

Conkling, Roscoe P., and Margaret B. Conkling. *The Butterfield Overland Mail, 1857–1869*. 3 vols. Glendale, Arthur H. Clark Co., 1947.

Connelley, William E., ed. *Doniphan's Expedition and the Conquest of New Mexico and California* (Includes a reprint of the work of Col. John T. Hughes). Kansas City, Mo., Bryant & Douglas, 1907.

Cotterrill, R. S. *The Southern Indians: The Story of the Civilized Tribes Before Removal.* Norman, University of Oklahoma Press, 1954.

Coues, Elliott, ed. *The Journal of Jacob Fowler Narrating an Adventure from Arkansas through the Indian Territory, Oklahoma, Kansas, Colorado, and New Mexico, to the Sources of Rio Grande Del Norte, 1821–22.* New York, Francis P. Harper, 1898.

———. *The Journals of Lewis and Clark.* 4 vols. New York, Francis P. Harper, 1904–1905.

Cremony, John C. *Life Among the Apaches.* San Francisco, A. Roman & Co., 1868.

Croghan, Colonel George. *Army Life on the Western Frontier.* Ed. by Francis Paul Prucha. Norman, University of Oklahoma Press, 1958.

Cumming, Fortescue. *Sketches of a Tour to the Western Country Through the States of Ohio and Kentucky.* Vol. IV in R. G. Thwaites, *Early Western Travels.* Cleveland, Arthur H. Clark Co., 1904.

Dale, Edward Everett. *The Indians of the Southwest: A Century of Development under the United States.* Norman, University of Oklahoma Press, 1949.

Dale, Harrison Clifford. *The Ashley Smith Explorations and the Discovery of a Central Route to the Pacific, 1822–1829.* Cleveland, Arthur H. Clark Co., 1934.

Davis, W. W. H. *El Gringo; or, New Mexico and Her People.* New York, Harper and Brothers, 1857.

Emory, Lt. William Hensley. *Notes of a Military Reconnaissance from Fort Leavenworth, in Missouri, to San Diego, In California . . . 1846–47.* Washington, Wendell & Van Venthuysen, 1848.

———. *Report of William H. Emory, Major First Cavalry and United States Commissioner.* 2 vols. Washington, Cornelius Wendell, Printer. 1857.

Epes, Sargent. *The Life and Public Services of Henry Clay, Down to 1848,* Ed. and completed at Mr. Clay's Death by Horace Greeley. New York, Miller, Orton & Mulligan, 1856.

Estergreen, M. Morgan. *Kit Carson: A Portrait in Courage.* Norman, University of Oklahoma Press, 1962.

Ewell, General R. S. *The Making of a Soldier.* Arranged and edited by Captain Percy Gatling Hamlin. Richmond, 1935.

Eyell, John S. *The South Since 1865.* New York, Macmillan Co., 1963.

Farish, Thomas Edwin. *History of Arizona.* 6 vols. Phoenix, 1915.

Favour, Alpheus H. *Old Bill Williams, Mountain Man.* Chapel Hill, University of North Carolina Press, 1936.

Folk, Reau E. *Battle of New Orleans: Its Real Meaning.* Nashville, Cullom & Ghertner, 1935 (pamphlet, wrappers).

Forbes, Jack D. *Apache, Navaho, and Spaniard.* Norman, University of Oklahoma Press, 1934.

Foreman, Grant. *The Five Civilized Tribes.* Norman, University of Oklahoma Press, 1960.

Garber, Paul Neff. *The Gadsden Treaty.* Philadelphia, University of Pennsylvania Press, 1923.

Gilbert, E. W. *The Exploration of Western America, 1800–1850; An Historical Geography.* Cambridge, Harvard University Press, 1933.

Grant, Blanche C. *When Old Trails Were New: The Story of Taos.* New York, Press of the Pioneers, 1934.

———., ed. *Kit Carson's Own Story of His Life: As Dictated to Col. and Mrs. D. C. Peters About 1856–57, and Never Before Published.* Taos, Santa Fe *New Mexican,* 1926.

Gregg, Josiah. *Diary & Letters of Josiah Gregg.* Ed. by Maurice Garland Fulton. Norman, University of Oklahoma Press, 1944.

Grinell, George Bird. *Blackfoot Lodge Tales: The Story of a Prairie People.* New York, Charles Scribner's Sons, 1892.

———. *The Fighting Cheyennes.* New York, Charles Scribner's Sons, 1915.

———. *Pawnee Hero Stories and Folk Tales: With Notes on the Origin, Customs and Character of the Pawnee People.* New York, Charles Scribner's Sons, 1904.

Hafen, LeRoy R., and W. J. Ghent. *Broken Hand: The Life Story of Thomas Fitzpatrick.* Denver, Old West Publishing Co., 1931.

Haley, J. Evetts, *Fort Concho and the Texas Frontier.* San Angelo, San Angelo *Standard Times,* 1952.

Hamer, Philip M., ed. *A Guide to Archives and Manuscripts in the*

United States. Compiled for the National History Publications Commission. New Haven, Yale University Press, 1961.

Hammond, George P., and Agapito Rey, eds. *Don Juan Oñate, Colonizer of New Mexico, 1595–1628.* Albuquerque, University of New Mexico Press, 1953.

Harris, Malcolm H. *History of Louisa County, Virginia.* Richmond, Dietz Press, 1936.

Hart, Adolphus M. *History of the Valley of the Mississippi.* Cincinnati, Moore, Anderson, Wilstach & Keys, 1853.

Heap, Gwinn Harris. *Central Route to the Pacific.* Ed. by LeRoy R. and Ann W. Hafen, with related material on railroad explorations and Indian Affairs by Edward F. Beale, Thomas H. Benton, Kit Carson, and Col. E. A. Hitchcock, and in other documents (Far West and Rockies Series). Glendale, Arthur H. Clark Co., 1957.

Heitman, Francis B. *Historical Register of Officers of the Continental Army. During the War of the Revolution, April, 1775, to December, 1783.* Washington, D.C., W. H. Loudermilk & Co., 1893.

Hoopes, Alban W. *Indian Affairs and Their Administration, with Special Reference to the Far West, 1849–60.* Philadelphia, University of Pennsylvania Press, 1932.

Horn, Calvin. *New Mexico's Troubled Years: The Story of the Early Territorial Governors.* Albuquerque, Horn & Wallace, 1963.

Hunt, Aurora. *Major James Henry Carleton, 1814–73: Western Frontier Dragoon.* Glendale, Arthur H. Clark Co., 1958.

Inman, Colonel Henry. *The Old Santa Fe Trail.* Topeka, Crane & Co., 1899.

Irving, Washington. *Journals.* Ed. by William P. Trent and George S. Hellman. 3 vols. Boston, Bibliophile Society, 1919.

———. *The Adventures of Captain Bonneville, U.S.A., in the Rocky Mountains and the Far West.* New York, G. P. Putnam, 1868.

———. *The Western Journals of Washington Irving.* Ed. by John Francis McDermott. Norman, University of Oklahoma Press, 1944.

James Edwin. *Account of an Expedition from Pittsburgh to the Rocky Mountains: Performed in the Years 1819, 1820, By Order of the Hon. J. C. Calhoun. . . .* 4 vols. Vols. XIV–XVII in R. G. Thwaites, *Early Western Travels.* Cleveland, Arthur H. Clark Co., 1905.

Jefferson, Thomas. *Writings of Thomas Jefferson.* Ed. by H. A. Washington. 9 vols. Washington, Taylor & Maury, 1853–54.

Johnston, J. Stoddard, ed. *Memorial History of Louisville From Its First Settlement to the Year 1896.* Chicago, American Biographical Publishing Co., n.d.

Keleher, William A. *Turmoil in New Mexico.* Santa Fe, Rydal Press, 1952.

Kendall, G. Wilkins. *Narrative of the Texan Santa Fe Expedition: Comprising a Description of a Tour Through Texas.* 2 vols. Austin, Steck Book Co., 1935.

Lang, Walter B. *The First Overland Mail: The Butterfield Trail St. Louis to San Francisco 1859–1861.* Washington, 1940.

Larpenteur, Charles. *Forty Years a Fur Trader on the Upper Missouri: The Personal Narrative of Charles Larpenteur, 1833–1872.* Ed., with many critical notes by Elliott Coues. New York, F. P. Harper, 1898; Chicago, The Lakeside Press, R. R. Donnelley and Sons Co., 1933.

Leonard, Zenas. *Narrative of the Adventures of Zenas Leonard.* Ed. by Milo M. Quaife (Lakeside Classics). Chicago, R. R. Donnelly & Sons Co., 1934.

Lockwood, Frank C. *The Apache Indians.* New York, Macmillan Co., 1938.

McNitt, Frank. *The Indian Traders.* Norman, University of Oklahoma Press, 1962.

Magoffin, Susan Shelby. *Down the Santa Fe Trail and into Mexico: The Diary of Susan Shelby Magoffin, 1846–47.* Ed. by Stella M. Drumm. New Haven, Yale University Press, 1926.

Mansfield, H. *The Descendants of Richard and Gillian Mansfield Who Settled in New Haven, 1639. With Sketches of Some of the Most Distinguished. Also, of Connections of Other Names.* New Haven, Compiled and Published by H. Mansfield, 1885.

Mansfield, Colonel Joseph K. F. *Mansfield on the Condition of the Western Forts, 1853–54.* Ed. and with an introduction by Robert W. Frazer. Norman, University of Oklahoma Press, 1963.

Manypenny, George W. *Our Indian Wards.* Cincinnati, Arthur H. Clark Co., 1880.

Marshall, H. *History of Kentucky Exhibiting an Account of the Modern Discovery: Civil and Military Transactions, and the Present State of the Country*. 2 vols. Frankfort, George S. Robinson, Printer, 1824.

Maximilian, Prince of Wied-Neuwied. *Travels in the Interior of America.* Trans. by H. Evans Lloyd. 3 vols. Vols. XXII–XXIV in R. G. Thwaites, *Early Western Travels.* Cleveland, Arthur H. Clark Co., 1905.

Miller, Alfred Jacob. *The West of Alfred Jacob Miller.* Norman, University of Oklahoma Press, 1951.

Mills, W. W. *Forty Years at El Paso, 1858–1898.* Introduction and Notes by Rex W. Strickland. El Paso, Carl Hertzog, 1962.

Minor, Louisa H. A. *The Meriwethers and Their Connections: A Family Record, Giving the Genealogy of the Meriwethers in America Together with Biographical Notes and Sketches.* Albany, N.Y., Joel Munsell's Sons, Publishers, 1892.

Montana, *Contributions* to the Historical Society of. The Fort Benton *Journal* (1854–56). The Fort Sarpy *Journal* (1855–56). Vol. X. Helena, 1940.

Morgan, Dale L. *Jedidiah Smith and the Opening of the West.* Indianapolis, Bobbs Merrill Co., 1953.

Murray, Charles Augustus. *Travels in North America During the Years 1834–35, and 1836. Including a Summer Residence with the Pawnee Tribe of Indians, in the Remote Prairies of theMissouri, and on a Visit to Cuba and the Azore Islands.* 2 vols. London, Richard Bentley, 1839.

Nasatir, A.P ., ed. *Before Lewis and Clark: Documents Illustrating the History of the Missouri, 1785–1804.* 2 vols. St. Louis, St. Louis Historical Documents Foundation, 1952.

National Cyclopaedia of American Biography, Being the History of the United States. Vol. XII. New York, Jas. T. White & Co., 1904.

Nebraska, *Collections* of the Nebraska State Historical Society, Vol. XVI. Lincoln, 1911.

———, *Publications* of the Nebraska State Historical Society. Vol. XX. Lincoln, 1922.

Nevins, Allan. *Frémont the West's Greatest Adventurer.* New York, Harper and Brothers, 1928.

Nichols, Roy Franklin. *The Democratic Machine, 1850–54*. New York, Columbia University, 1923.

Nidever, George. *The Life and Adventures of George Nidever*. Ed. by William Henry Ellison. Berkeley, University of California Press, 1937.

Noyes, A. J. *In the Land of the Chinook; or, The Story of Blaine County* [Montana]. Helena, State Publishing Co., 1917.

Nunis, Doyce Blackman. *Andrew Sublette, Rocky Mountain Prince*. Los Angeles, Dawson's Bookshop, 1960.

Nye, Wilbur S. *Carbine and Lance: The Story of Old Fort Sill*. Norman, University of Oklahoma Press, 1937.

Oglesby, Richard Edward. *Manuel Lisa and the Opening of the Missouri Fur Trade*. Norman, University of Oklahoma Press, 1963.

Pattie, James Ohio. *The Personal Narrative of James Ohio Pattie*. Cincinnati, John H. Wood, 1831.

Pike, Zebulon. *Account of an Expedition to the Sources of the Mississippi and Through the Western Parts of Louisiana . . . and a Tour through the Interior Parts of New Spain*. Ed. by Elliott Coues. 3 vols. New York, Francis P. Harper, 1895.

Phillips, Paul Chrisler. *The Fur Trade*. With concluding chapters by J. W. Smurr. 2 vols. Norman, University of Oklahoma Press, 1961.

Preuss, Charles. *Exploring with Frémont: The Private Diaries of Charles Preuss*. Ed. and translated by Erwin G. and Elizabeth K. Gudde. Norman, University of Oklahoma Press, 1958.

Pride, Captain W. F. *The History of Fort Riley*. Fort Riley, Kan., 1926.

Prince, L. Bradford. *Historical Sketches of New Mexico from the Earliest Records to the American Occupation*, Kansas City, Ramsey, Millet & Hudson, 1883.

———. *A Concise History of New Mexico*. Cedar Rapids, Torch Press, 1914.

Riddle, Kenyon. *Records and Maps of the Old Santa Fe Trail*. Raton, New Mexico, Raton *Daily Range*, 1949.

Robertson, George. *Scrap Book on Law and Politics, Men and Times*. Lexington, Ky., A. W. Elder, 1855.

Rye, Edgar. *The Quirt and the Spur: Vanishing Shadows of the Texas Frontier*. Chicago, W. B. Conkey Co., 1909.

Sabin, Edwin L. *Kit Carson Days, 1809–1868 . . . Adventures in the Path of Empire.* Rev. ed., 2 vols. New York, Press of the Pioneers, 1935.

Scharf, J. Thomas. *History of St. Louis, City and County.* 2 vols. Philadelphia, Evarts, 1883.

Simpson, James H. *Navaho Expedition: Journal of a Military Reconnaissance from Santa Fe, New Mexico, to the Navaho Country, Made in 1849.* Ed. by Frank McNitt. Norman, University of Oklahoma Press, 1964.

Sonnichsen, C. L. *The Mescalero Apaches.* Norman, University of Oklahoma Press, 1958.

South Dakota Historical *Collections.* Compiled by State Historical Society. Vols. XIX and XX. Pierre, S.D., 1938 and 1940.

Stansbury, Howard. *Exploration and Survey of the Valley of the Great Salt Lake of Utah . . .* Philadelphia, Lippincott, Grambo and Co., 1852.

Steckmesser, Kent L. *The Western Hero in History and Legend.* Norman, University of Oklahoma Press, 1965.

Stuart, Robert. *The Discovery of the Oregon Trail: Robert Stuart's Narratives of His Overland Trip Eastward from Astoria in 1812–13.* From the Original Manuscripts in the Collection of William Robertson Coe, Esq. Ed. by Phillip Ashton Rollins. New York, Edward Eberstadt and Sons, 1935.

Sullivan, Charles J. *Army Posts and Towns: The Baedeker of the Army* Burlington, Free Press Printing Co., 1926.

Sullivan, Maurice. *Jedediah Smith, Trader and Trail Breaker.* Santa Anna, Calif., Fine Arts Press, 1934.

Tabeau, Pierre-Antoine. *Tabeau's Narrative of Loisel's Expedition to the Upper Missouri.* Ed. and translated by Annie Heloise Abel. Norman, University of Oklahoma Press, 1939.

Talbot, Theodore. *The Journals of Theodore Talbot, 1843 and 1849–52.* Ed. by Charles H. Carey. Portland, Ore., Metropolitan Press, 1931.

Thomas, Alfred B. *After Coronado.* Norman, University of Oklahoma Press, 1935.

Thompson, David. *David Thompson's Narrative of Exploration in West-*

ern America, 1783–1812. Ed. by Joseph Burr Tyrell. Toronto, University of Toronto Press, 1916.

Townsend, John K. *Narrative of a Journey Across the Rocky Mountains to the Columbia River.* Vol. XXI in R. G. Thwaites, *Early Western Travels.* Cleveland, Arthur H. Clark Co., 1905.

Twitchell, Ralph Emerson. *The History of the Military Occupation of the Territory of New Mexico from 1846 to 1851 by the Government of the United States.* Denver, Smith-Brooks Co., 1909.

———. *The Leading Facts of New Mexican History,* 2 vols. Cedar Rapids, Torch Press, 1912.

———, compiler. *The Spanish Archives of New Mexico.* Cedar Rapids, Torch Press, 1914.

Victor, Francis Fuller. *The River of the West.* San Francisco, R. J. Trumbull and Co., 1870.

Wallace, William Swilling. *Antoine Robidoux, 1794–1860: A Biography of a Western Venturer.* Los Angeles, Glenn Dawson, 1953.

Watson, Douglas Sloane. *West Wind: The Life Story of Joseph Reddeford Walker, Knight of the Golden Horseshoe.* Los Angeles, privately printed for friends of P. H. Booth, 1934.

Wheat, Carl I. *Mapping the American West, 1540–1857, a Preliminary Study.* Worchester, Mass., American Antiquarian Society, 1954.

———. *Mapping the Trans-Mississippi West, 1540–1861.* 3 vols. San Francisco, Institute of Historical Cartography, 1957–58.

Wheeler, Olin D. *The Trail of Lewis and Clark 1804–1904.* 2 vols. New York, G. P. Putnam's Sons, 1904.

Whitley, Edna Talbot. *Kentucky . . . Ante-Bellum Portrature.* Richmond, 1956.

Winther, Oscar Osborn. *Via Western Express and Stagecoach.* Stanford, Stanford University Press, 1945.

Wissler, Clark. *Indians of the United States: Four Centuries of Their History and Culture.* New York, Doubleday, Doran and Co., 1941.

Wright, Muriel H. *A Guide to the Indian Tribes of Oklahoma.* Norman, University of Oklahoma Press, 1951.

Young, Otis E. *The West of Phillip St. George Cooke, 1809–1895.* Glendale, Arthur H. Clark Co., 1955.

PERIODICALS

Abel, Anna Heloise, ed. "Indian Affairs in New Mexico Under the Administration of William Carr Lane," from the "Journal" of John Ward, *New Mexico Historical Review,* Vol. XVI (April, 1941).

Baldwin, Percy M. "A Short History of the Mesilla Valley," *New Mexico Historical Review,* Vol. XIII (July, 1938).

Bender, Averam B. "Frontier Defence in New Mexico, 1846–1853," *New Mexico Historical Review,* Vol. IX (July, 1934).

———. "Frontier Defence in New Mexico, 1853–61," *New Mexico Historical Review,* Vol. IX (October, 1934).

Bloom, Lansing B., ed. "Albuquerque and Galisteo, Certificate of Their Founding, 1706," *New Mexico Historical Review,* Vol. X (January, 1935).

Bolton, Herbert Eugene. "New Light on Manuel Lisa and the Spanish Fur Trade," *Texas Historical Quarterly,* Vol. XVIII (January, 1937).

———. "Escalante in Dixie and the Arizona Strip," *New Mexico Historical Review,* Vol. III (January, 1928).

Drumm, Stella M. "More About Astorians," *Oregon Historical Quarterly,* Vol. XXIV (December, 1923).

Hafen, LeRoy R. "Armijo's Journal," *Huntington Library Quarterly,* Vol. XI (January, 1947).

———. "Armijo's Journal of 1928–30: The Beginning of Trade Between New Mexico and California," *Colorado Magazine,* Vol. XXVII (April, 1950).

Hill, Joseph J. "Ewing Young in the Fur Trade of the Southwest, 1822–1834," *Oregon Historical Quarterly,* Vol. XXIV March, 1923).

———. "Free Trapper: The Story of Old Bill Williams," *Touring Topics,* Vol. XXII (March, 1930).

Historical Society of New Mexico, "Old Santa Fe and Vicinity." Santa Fe. (n.d.).

Hoopes, Alban W. "Letters to and from Abraham G. Mayers, 1854–1857," *New Mexico Historical Review,* Vol. IX (July, 1934).

Loyola, Sister Mary. "The American Occupation of New Mexico, 1821–1852," *New Mexico Historical Review,* Vol. XIV (January, 1939).

Moody, Marshall D. "Kit Carson, Agent to the Indians in New Mexico, 1853–1861," *New Mexico Historical Review,* Vol. XXVIII (January, 1953).

Nute, Grace Lee. "The Paper of the American Fur Company: A Brief Estimate of their Significance," *American Historical Review,* Vol. XXXII (October, 1926, to July, 1927).

Ogle, Ralph Hedrick. "Federal Control of the Western Apaches, 1848–86," New Mexico Historical Society *Publications in History,* Vol. IX (July, 1940).

Perrine, Fred S. "Military Escorts on the Santa Fe Trail," *New Mexico Historical Review,* Vol. II (April–July, 1927).

Reeve, Frank D. "The Government and the Navajo, 1846–1858," *New Mexico Historical Review,* Vol. XIV (January, 1939).

Sauer, Carl O. "The Discovery of New Mexico Reconsidered," *New Mexico Historical Review,* Vol. XII (July, 1937).

Trudeau, Jean Baptiste, "Trudeau's Description of the Upper Missouri," Ed. by Annie Heloise Abel, *Mississippi Historical Review,* Vol. VIII (June–September, 1921).

Twitchell, Ralph Emerson. "The Story of the Conquest of Santa Fe, New Mexico, and the Building of Old Fort March, A.D. 1846," Historical Society of New Mexico *Bulletin No. 24* (n.d.)

Tyler, S. Lyman, "The Spaniard and the Ute," *Utah Historical Quarterly,* Vol. XXII (October, 1954).

Utley, Robert M. "Fort Union and the Santa Fe Trail," *New Mexico Historical Review,* Vol. XXXVI (January, 1961).

Wagner, Henry R. "Fr. Marcos de Niza," *New Mexico Historical Review,* Vol. IX (April, 1934).

Wyman, Walker D. "F. X. Aubry: Santa Fe Freighter, Pathfinder and Explorer," *New Mexico Historical Review,* Vol. VII (January, 1932).

Newspapers

The Courier Journal (Louisville). "Ninety Honored Years," October 31, 1890. Clipping in Meriwether Papers, O'Neill Collection.

The Daily Democrat (Doylestown, Pa.). "Ex-Governor David Meriwether," December 3, 1890. Clipping in Meriwether Papers, O'Neill Collection.

Mercury Herald (San Jose, Calif.). "Remarkable Career of David Meriwether," April 7, 1893. Clipping in Meriwether Papers, O'Neill Collection.

Niles Weekly Register. September, 1819, to March, 1820. Vol. V and XVII.

Unidentified clipping. "News and Comments Section": "Gov. David Meriwether in Washington on settlement of $3,000 claim" (unidentified, n.d., presumably *Louisville Democrat*, January, 1888). Meriwether Papers, O'Neill Collection.

———. "Gov. Meriwether at Washington, on Floor of the House" (dated Washington, D.C., January 30 [1887]), Meriwether Papers, O'Neill Collection.

Index

My Life in the Mountains and on the Plains has been set on the Linotype in twelve-point Caslon Old Face with two points of spacing between the lines. The type itself is a faithful rendering of the originals of William Caslon, the eminent English type founder of the eighteenth century.

The book has been printed on paper designed for an effective life of at least three hundred years bearing the watermark of the University of Oklahoma Press.

UNIVERSITY OF OKLAHOMA PRESS
NORMAN